Druid
Theatre
Fifty Years

Druid Theatre
Fifty Years

Patrick Lonergan

Foreword by
Fintan O'Toole

THE LILLIPUT PRESS

First published 2025 by
THE LILLIPUT PRESS
62–63 Arbour Hill
Dublin 7, Ireland
www.lilliputpress.ie

Text Copyright © Patrick Lonergan & Druid Theatre, 2025
Foreword Copyright © Fintan O'Toole, 2025

All rights reserved. No part of this publication may be reproduced in any form or by any means without prior permission of the publisher.

A CIP record for this publication is available from The British Library.

10 9 8 7 6 5 4 3 2 1

ISBN 978-1-84351-958-4

The Lilliput Press gratefully acknowledges the financial support of the Arts Council /An Chomhairle Ealaíon.

Set in 11pt on 17pt Sabon LT Pro by Niall McCormack.
Printed in Scotland by Bell & Bain.

vii   Foreword by Fintan O'Toole
xiii   Introduction

1   Chapter 1:   Opening Night, 1975
21   Chapter 2:   Die or Go All the Way, 1976–1978
53   Chapter 3:   Building a Theatre, 1979–1981
81   Chapter 4:   Unusual Rural Tours, 1982–1984
111   Chapter 5:   Tom Murphy, a Writer-in-Association, 1984–1987
145   Chapter 6:   A Transforming Galway, 1987–1990
169   Chapter 7:   A New Artistic Director, 1991–1995
197   Chapter 8:   *The Leenane Trilogy*, 1996–2001
229   Chapter 9:   Druid Debuts, 2000–2007
263   Chapter 10:   John Millington Synge, House Playwright, 2004–2010
293   Chapter 11:   Cycles, 2010–2015
331   Chapter 12:   On the Outside/On the Inside, 2016–2024
365   Post-Script: Opening Night, 2025

371   Druid Productions 1975–2025
379   Druid Timeline
385   Sources
389   Acknowledgments
395   Picture Credits
397   Index

Foreword
Fintan O'Toole

IN THE EARLY 1980S, Dublin-based theatre critics didn't bother going to Galway. I suppose I had the additional excuse that *In Dublin*, the fortnightly listings magazine I wrote for, was explicitly centred on the capital. It still feels in retrospect rather shameful that I first encountered Druid out of their native habitat in the Peacock theatre in Dublin in June 1981. The production was *Island Protected by a Bridge of Glass* and it had opened at Druid Lane in May of the previous year.

Apart from Mick Lally, this was pretty much the core of the original Druid repertory company featuring bold and fluent actors I had never seen before: Ray McBride, Maelíosa Stafford, Sean McGinley and Marie Mullen. They had a fierce, direct, unabashed presence that seemed utterly self-confident without being self-conscious. They seemed in the best sense very sure of themselves.

The director was called Garry Hynes and, in telling the story of Gráineuáile and Elizabeth I, she was drawing with aplomb on almost every trick in the theatrical book, from modernist estrangement to the old rhythms of Irish music (played live by De Danann). She could speak in several dramatic tongues at once. It was, as I wrote in my review, 'a triumph not only for Garry

Hynes's mastery of technique and language but also for Marie Mullen's strength and depth as an actress.'

Galway people already knew this, of course. Druid, as Patrick Lonergan narrates in this wonderfully vivid history, already had a previous life of which I was largely ignorant. The craft and coherence I was experiencing for the first time had been forged over the previous six years of hard labour by a group of young people who had committed themselves completely to their art and made what then seemed highly improbable – a professional theatre company in Galway – not merely possible but imperative.

Yet ignorant as I was of the company's past, I did have inklings of the future. In my review I wrote that 'Hynes has achieved a dramatic language which encompasses fully the poetry of speech, the rhythm of movement and the direct visual impact of physical objects. She has done so in such an original and essentially native way as to suggest that if there is to be a revitalization of Irish theatre it is most likely to be inspired by Druid.'

In retrospect revitalization was not a fortunate choice of word. For if the sheer accomplishment of this young company was the first surprise, the second was that Druid was also profoundly and authentically traditional. Hynes was committed, among other things, to a revival of the Irish Revival, a contemporary reconnection with the wild and ferocious energies of the early years of the Abbey.

W.B. Yeats and John Synge and Augusta Gregory had the radicalism of artists who are having to start from scratch. Galway, though by no means a theatrical tabula rasa, had for Druid something of that same frontier freedom. But it was also part of a real, disillusioned, unmagical West of Ireland. The poetry of the tradition had to find its voice in a place and a time where many of the promises of Irish modernity were proving, in the grim 1980s, to be hollow.

The crossing of these currents had its immediate electrifying effect in Druid's landmark 1982 production of Synge's *The Playboy of the Western World*. I had seen the play before. It was overripe – it had gone soft. The tension between the beauty of Synge's lyrical language and the violent ugliness of the action had slackened into a colourful romanticism. Druid's staging was like being jolted back into 1907 when this play was so shocking, so mind-blowing in its dizzying shifts between farce and tragedy, that it provoked riots. This production was itself riotous. It smashed through all the layers of over-familiarity that had become encrusted, not just on *The Playboy* but on the whole Revival repertoire.

That *Playboy* was a moment of revelation but also of liberation. It freed up the great legacy of early twentieth-century Irish theatre by cracking open its apparent realism to release its inherent surrealism. It opened the way to the company's astonishing later engagements with that legacy in *DruidSynge*, *DruidGregory* and *DruidO'Casey* and. It also, oddly enough, made possible a thrillingly distinctive approach to the English Renaissance tradition that flowered in productions like Hynes's great staging of John Ford's *'Tis Pity She's a Whore*, the *DruidShakespeare* history cycle and the staggering fiftieth anniversary staging of *Macbeth*.

There was a false opposition between tradition and modernity that was playing out at many levels of Irish culture and society – we must either accept the given forms of religion and politics or walk away from history (often, in the 1980s, by literally moving away from the island). Druid refused to be bound by that binary: it found the avant garde within the old guard. It grabbed history and translated into the only kind of time that matters in the theatre – the eternal present tense of *now*.

It struck me, when I was reviewing *The Leenane Trilogy* in 1997 that 'the company's veterans – Marie Mullen, Maelíosa Stafford, Mick Lally – have often been at their very best when exploding naturalism from within, starting with the apparently familiar and making it very strange'. Successive clusters of great actors have stayed true to that Druid aesthetic of building performance from the ground up. The ground (as in Druid's Shakespeare productions) is often the dirt and at least one foot is always on it even if the rest of the body is reaching for mythic heights.

Thus, Druid's distinctive magnetism is a reversal of polarities – the ordinary made mysterious, the outlandish given a local habitation and a name. If a cliché is language worn down into hollowness, Druid's existence can be seen as a half-century war on cliché in which the cutting edge of language (verbal, physical and emotional) is hammered back into razor-edge sharpness.

If, then, Druid has functioned in one dimension as a great reviver of Irish tradition (including half-forgotten plays like M.J. Molloy's *The Wood of the Whispering*, Seamus Byrne's *Little City* and George Fitzmaurice's *The Ointment Blue*) it has also forged new classics. It made complete sense that Druid recognized Tom Murphy for what he is: a master among the great playwrights. Murphy's ability to pitch a drama between the earthy and the operatic – so breathtakingly realized in 1985 in Siobhán McKenna's astounding performance as Mommo in *Bailegangaire* – dovetailed perfectly with Hynes's own style.

And that collaboration in turn created the template for fruitful relationships with John B. Keane, Martin McDonagh, Marina Carr, Enda Walsh, Sonya Kelly, Mark O'Rowe and others. Druid has kept faith with the idea of the literary play as a unique artform that can hold its nerve amidst the waves of great cultural change. The space where words become acts is still its sacred ground.

This living tradition has been one of the great arenas in which the whole idea of Ireland has been tested, weighed, taken apart, remade, exposed and confirmed over half a century. The founders of the Abbey believed that a theatre was as important to a nation's consciousness as a parliament and there have been times in Druid's life when it has seemed considerably more so. Much of the public world over the last fifty years has been characterized by violence, betrayal, evasion and dishonesty. Druid has enacted all of those things on stage while standing out against them all.

'Mad Ireland', wrote W.H. Auden of W.B. Yeats, 'hurt you into poetry' – and this might have been written over the door of the Mick Lally Theatre. Druid is where we have gone, sometimes to laugh and forget, but mostly to be hurt into poetry, to pass through pain into transcendence.

There is a line in one of Murphy's great plays *The Gigli Concert*, spoken by a man who can scarcely believe of his lover that 'you and I are alive in time at the same time'. All through its first half century, Druid has been alive in our time, a constant, pulsing counterpoint to the tumults of a transforming society. In dark periods, that pulse told us that we were not dead yet. In more euphoric interludes, it throbbed with the energy of contest and challenge. It has been a wonder to be alive in Ireland at the same time as Druid. Patrick Lonergan's feat in this gloriously vibrant history is to reanimate those marvels and leave us hungering for the ones to come.

The Foyer of the Mick Lally Theatre.

Introduction

THERE'S A TINY side street in Galway that has had many names during the last thousand years. It used to be called Red Earl's Lane, taking its name from an Anglo-Norman earl called Richard de Burgo. He had built a hall there sometime during the 1200s, using it as a courthouse and tax collection office, but also occasionally hosting banquets there.

The street fell into ruin during the 1400s, when the De Burgos were forced out of the city after the Tribes of Galway seized power. But its name stayed in place for hundreds of years, both in English and in its Irish form, Bóthar an Iarla. By the nineteenth century, it was going by two new names – sometimes called Courthouse Lane, and sometimes Chapel Lane. And then, finally, in 1996 Galway City Council decided to rechristen it yet again – as Druid Lane.

This change was made to celebrate the twenty-first birthday of Druid Theatre – the company that had been founded in the city in 1975, with the initially modest aim of bringing professional theatre to the west of Ireland. That company had gained so much international acclaim by 1996 that, it was often said, it had 'put Galway on the map' as a centre for Irish culture. By renaming the lane in their honour, the Council were returning the compliment by literally putting Druid on a map, writing them into the city's history – and into its geography too.

That lane is now home to the Mick Lally Theatre, Druid's home venue. If you walk into that building, you'll see several traces of the company's history.

On the wall just inside the front door is a shelf that holds many different chairs – one that's made of wood, another made of clear plastic, another of chrome – and each of them originally created as a set piece for a Druid production.

There are also posters on the walls – including one of *The Threepenny Opera*, the Brecht play that Druid chose when they opened the venue in 1979, having spent the previous six months building it.

And there are often photos hanging on the wall, from some of Druid's most iconic productions. You might see Siobhán McKenna in the role of Mommo in Tom Murphy's 1985 play *Bailegangaire*, which had premiered in that very building. Or you might catch sight of a picture of Anna Manahan from Martin McDonagh's *The Beauty Queen of Leenane* – the show that brought Druid to international acclaim when it won four Tony Awards on Broadway in 1998. And often you'll see photos of the company's three co-founders: Garry Hynes, Marie Mullen and Mick Lally.

But you might also get into a conversation with someone who has a story to tell about Druid's past. Some of those people have been there from the beginning. They can tell you that they saw Marie Mullen in a Drama Society play directed by Garry Hynes when both were students at the University of Galway; or maybe they remember Mick Lally acting in amateur productions at the nearby Taibhdhearc theatre when he was still working as a teacher in Tuam in the early 1970s.

Or maybe you'll meet someone who first encountered the company in the early 1990s, when its second Artistic Director,

Maelíosa Stafford, had brought in new audiences by staging innovative productions such as *The Midnight Court*, which was more like a late-night traditional music session than a play.

Or they might tell you stories about how Garry Hynes's return to Druid in 1995 gave rise to memorable events such as *The Leenane Trilogy* in 1997 or the 2005 *DruidSynge* project that saw all of J.M. Synge's plays being performed in a single day.

Or perhaps they've never seen a Druid show before; perhaps they are looking forward to seeing what the company is going to do next.

A theatre history can be forged in many ways – in the naming of a street, through exhibitions in a building's foyer, and through the memories of audience members young and old.

This book is one such attempt to tell the story of Druid, from its foundation in 1975 to its fiftieth birthday celebration in July 2025. The stories that it gathers are drawn primarily from the Druid archive at the University of Galway. That resource includes press cuttings, production files, videos and photos – and also features an invaluable Oral History, carried out by Thomas Conway and Ciara O'Dowd in 2015 and 2016, which includes extensive interviews with almost thirty people who worked with the company.

To listen to those recordings makes clear that there is not one single 'history' of Druid Theatre. Partly that's because of the simple fact that people everywhere remember the same events in different ways. But it's also because the life of a theatre has so many different strands that it might be possible to write a Druid history that focuses exclusively on the experiences of actors, or designers, or audiences.

In writing this book, I've tried to create space for those different Druid memories to be recorded, letting the voices speak for themselves as much as possible. I've also drawn sometimes on my own memories of Druid productions. I first saw their work at the Town Hall Theatre in 1997 when I travelled to Galway to see *The Leenane Trilogy* – and having moved to the city soon after that I've been to almost all of their productions since then. I've also been helped by written records of the company's life, with David Burke's essay in *Druid Theatre: The First Ten Years* being particularly important as a record of the company's origins.

But a written history is like a theatre's repertoire – it's a work that is endlessly in progress. Countless stories remain to be told, not just from the archives, but also about Druid's ongoing life as one of Ireland's – one of the world's – most vital theatre companies.

Chapter 1
Opening Night, 1975

IT WAS THE third of July 1975, shortly after eight o'clock in the evening, and Marie Mullen was standing alone on a stage in the Jesuit Hall in Galway, waiting for a play to begin.

Marie had turned twenty-two just a couple of days earlier, and had also recently graduated from University College Galway (UCG), where – like many an aspiring actor before her – she had discovered her passion for theatre not in the classroom but in the student Drama Society. But this moment was unlike any she'd experienced before now: she was about to perform in her first professional role, in a company that she'd just co-founded with the aim of bringing professional theatre to the west of Ireland.

In those minutes of anticipation, she wouldn't have been able to see the audience clearly, but she would have heard them talking as they filed in for what (to everyone's relief) was a well-attended opening night for their first production – *The Playboy of the Western World,* the classic Irish play by John Millington Synge that had famously caused riots on its own opening night, in Dublin in 1907.

The set that she was standing on was faithful to Synge's stage directions. Behind her, there was a counter with bottles and jugs; nearby, there were some barrels and benches; over

Marie Mullen as Pegeen Mike, *Playboy of the Western World*, 1975.

there, a fireplace, and beside it some tools – all authentically representing the Mayo shebeen where the action happens. Marie was playing the part of Pegeen Mike (one of the great roles in Irish theatre), and she'd also designed all the costumes – including her own, which, as Synge writes, imagines Pegeen as a 'wild-looking but fine girl, of about twenty … in the usual peasant dress'.

The audience gradually hushed, a signal was given, and Marie picked up a pencil, took a deep breath, and began:

> Six yards of stuff for to make a yellow gown. A pair of lace boots with lengthy heels on them and brassy eyes. A hat is suited for a wedding-day. A fine tooth comb. To be sent with three barrels of porter in Jimmy Farrell's creel cart on the evening of the coming Fair to Mister Michael James Flaherty. With the best compliments of this season. Margaret Flaherty.

Chapter 1: Opening Night, 1975

The set for *The Playboy of the Western World*, 1975.

In that opening speech, Pegeen is writing a shopping list for her own wedding – but what she doesn't realize is that all her plans are about to be upended by the arrival of a mysterious stranger.

The history of Druid thus began with a scene that now seems emblematic of its own future: it was a moment of apparent calmness that would soon give way to something excitingly and unexpectedly new.

Earlier that year, another UCG student had been winning awards at amateur drama festivals around the west of Ireland. Her name was Garry Hynes (not *Gary*, she would explain then, and many times again in the future, but *Garry* – short for Gearóidín), and she'd been noticed in part because of her bold decision to direct the Irish premiere of a new American play, *Elizabeth I* by Paul Foster. Like many Irish university students in the 1970s, Garry had been spending her summers working in New York, where in her free time she'd immersed herself in the thriving Off-Off-Broadway scene (years later, her friends would remember her, full of excitement, coming home each year with a pile of scripts by writers she'd encountered there). Her decision to stage Foster's work gave her a chance to put into practice the ideas that she'd been absorbing in America.

Elizabeth I is a sprawling, funny play. It needs a big cast – ideally as many as eleven performers – and it also has a big theme: it's about a group of travelling actors who run into trouble when their performance of the life of England's queen is seen by Elizabeth herself. Foster considers how theatre can speak truth to power, while also showing how women in positions of leadership must perform, theatrically and in other ways, in order to survive. Although those themes might seem to anticipate much that Druid would do later, this was not an obvious production for a young director to take on in mid-1970s Ireland.

Speaking to the *Connacht Sentinel* in her first ever press interview, Garry explained her motivations:

> I found this play a refreshing change and I think the audience will agree with me, considering the dearth of comedy on the theatrical scene in recent years.

The journalist was impressed by the simplicity of that response, adding that Garry's previous productions, for UCG's DramSoc, had been 'sombre and perturbing', but that she was now 'breaking new ground'.

The festival judges tended to agree: this was a director who was doing something new, they thought – someone who wanted

Chapter 1: Opening Night, 1975

Tiny Alice, one of Garry Hynes's productions for the UCG Drama Society.

to resist trends rather than follow them, who insisted on giving her audience a 'refreshing change' rather than more of the same old thing.

The lead actor in *Elizabeth I* was Marie Mullen (she also won a number of awards for that production, including at the All-Ireland finals in Athlone). By working together on this production, Garry and Marie were deepening a partnership – and a friendship – that had begun two years earlier at UCG. Garry would later recall how they'd met:

When I originally came into DramSoc, we first-year directors were given a one-act play to direct and I was given *The Browning Version* by Terence Rattigan. I didn't know any of Rattigan's language at the time, and I didn't know how I was going to cast this play set in an English public school. So I went over to the university library and found *The Loves of Cass McGuire* by Brian Friel, and I thought 'that sounds interesting' – and then I did auditions. We were down to two people for the role of Cass, Marie and somebody else, and although that somebody else could do a better American accent, some instinct said 'Marie'.

They went on to work together many times at university and, by the time *Elizabeth I* had finished its run, it was apparent to both that they had an important choice to consider: find a way to continue making theatre together, or go their separate ways. The idea of setting up a professional company began to form.

While Garry and Marie were working on *Elizabeth I*, Mick Lally was going to work every day at the Vocational School in Tuam, in east County Galway. He'd been employed there since graduating from UCG in 1969 – and although he enjoyed teaching, he seemed to find much more satisfaction from acting with An Taibhdhearc, the national Irish-language theatre.

The Taibhdhearc had been established in Galway in 1928, with the remit of producing and promoting the Irish language, a key priority of the newly independent state. Although most of its productions were performed by amateur actors, it had launched some important careers – notably that of the actor Siobhán McKenna, who had played the lead in an Irish-language version of George Bernard Shaw's *Saint Joan* (translated by

Chapter 1: Opening Night, 1975

McKenna herself) at the Taibhdhearc in 1950. She went on to gain international acclaim when she performed the same role (in English) on Broadway just seven years later. Mick might not have imagined that he would follow McKenna's pathway into professional acting – not at first, anyway – but he certainly threw himself into the life of the Taibhdhearc, sometimes appearing in as many as eight productions a year there. He quickly became well known in Galway as a talented and distinctive actor.

In later years, local theatregoers would recall their first impressions of Mick: that he was surprisingly tall but also surprisingly nimble; that he had a voice that could move imperceptibly from gruffness to a melodic soulfulness; and that he had a firm but open gaze that seemed to imply an easy empathy with the people around him. It's possible that some of those memories were recalled under the influence of Mick's subsequent fame in Ireland but, even so, reviews in the local newspapers from the early 1970s make clear that there was no one quite like him on the Galway stage at that time.

As he looked forward to his school's summer holidays in 1975, Mick had been thinking about travelling to London to work on the building sites there (but also – although he wasn't saying it to many people – there was a question about whether he might be able to find acting work in England). He was in the Cellar Bar in Galway City on an evening in May, towards the end of the school year, when Garry and Marie approached him.

That was not necessarily an easy thing for them to do. Marie had been in school with Mick's sister but they didn't know him well: he was a few years older than they were, and he was also much more experienced on the stage. He could easily have laughed them off and continued making his plans to go to London. But they explained that they were going to stage *The Playboy of the Western World*, that they'd secured a venue and some funding to do so, and that they wanted him to play the lead male role of

Christy Mahon, the stranger who shows up in Pegeen's shebeen, claiming to have murdered his father with the blow of a loy.

Mick said he'd think about it.

By early June, Mick had joined the company. The trio now had a plan (to stage a summer season in Galway), and they had a venue: the Jesuit Hall on Sea Road, where some of Garry and Marie's earlier DramSoc productions had been staged. They also knew what plays they were going to put on, three of them altogether: first would be *The Playboy*, then a contemporary English drama called *It's a Two Foot Six Inches Above the Ground World* by Kevin Laffan, and then a revival of Garry and Marie's DramSoc production of *Cass McGuire*. Mick and Marie would be in all three, Garry would direct them all, and they would be premiered on three successive days. They filled out the company by drawing on their contacts from DramSoc and the Taibhdhearc – and began an intense schedule of rehearsals that involved tackling one play in the morning, another in the afternoon and the third at night.

Their last major task was to choose a name for themselves. Many options were considered until someone caught sight of a cartoon of *Asterix*, a long-running French comic strip which, in those years, was serialized in *The Irish Times*. Describing the adventures of the eponymous hero and his sidekick Obelix, *Asterix* is about a village in Gaul that successfully resists occupation by the Roman Empire by using a strength-inducing magic potion that is made by a man called 'Getafix', the local druid. Despite being found in a non-Irish source, the word 'Druid' seemed like it might be a good fit for this new Irish company: it provided a link with the country's heritage but also seemed appropriately professional. And if they thought of something better later – well, they could just change the name.

Chapter 1: Opening Night, 1975

Mick and Marie, rehearsing The Playboy.

As rehearsals continued, a genuine sense of expectation began to set in, with enthusiastic anticipatory press coverage appearing both locally and nationally; Druid even appeared in *The Irish Times*' popular 'Irishman's Diary' column on 17 June, which was an unusual achievement for a company that at that time had done nothing other than announcing its plans for the future. What seems to have captured the imagination of local and national reporters alike was not just that Druid were staging three plays that summer, but that this 'experiment' (as Garry had carefully described the season in press releases) might lead to the establishment of a full-time company in Galway, provided that local audiences supported the productions in sufficient numbers.

From the outset, then, Druid were not just presenting Galway theatregoers with the promise of a single evening's entertainment. Instead, they were offering a long-term, two-way relationship – one that would allow the company and its audiences to grow together.

The first Druid show programme.

If an audience member at that first performance of *The Playboy* had glanced through the show programme while they were waiting for the play to begin, they would almost certainly have been impressed by its size and substance. On its cover was an image of a Galway hooker (a kind of sailing boat that had been built on the west coast of Ireland since the late eighteenth century), and along the top of the page are the words 'Druid: the Repertory Theatre of Galway'.

In a sign of the young company's multitasking ethos, that illustration had been provided by Mairead Noone, another recent UCG graduate, who was also playing the Widow Quin in *The Playboy*. Mairead would later become better known by the Irish version of her surname, Ní Nuadháin – and would go on to occupy

Chapter 1: Opening Night, 1975

an influential role in the development of Irish-language media, her career exemplifying how the cultural vibrancy of Galway in the 1970s reverberated for decades – and not just in the theatre but in many other art forms too. Mairead's image of the hooker did much to capture the attention of those first audiences, and Druid would continue to use the logo she had designed well into the 1980s.

The written description of the company on the programme's cover would also have struck a chord with many of those first Galway audiences. There had been a previous Galway Repertory Company, which had performed a season of plays in the summer of 1969 before folding; and in 1971 a director called Frank Bailey had established a 'Celtic Arts Theatre' in the city which, despite the best efforts of its founder, closed less than a month after it began (Bailey himself tragically died in a car accident soon afterwards). Druid's description of itself as *the* repertory theatre of Galway was a confident assertion of its own ambition – but that phrasing must also have reminded their audiences that Druid were trying to do something that had failed twice already in the previous six years.

That might explain why, in her opening programme note, Garry addressed that recent history:

> There has always been a strong theatre consciousness in Galway. An Taibhdhearc can claim a great deal of the credit for this. English-language production by local and professional groups alike have always been well-attended. However, in the last few years, this interest has grown to such a degree that the need for a theatre on a more permanent basis was clearly seen.
>
> Thus, in May of this year, DRUID, with much enthusiasm and a little trepidation, was established.

Taking a moment to thank the company's first funders – the Irish tourist board and the local Junior Chamber of Commerce – Garry went on to explain what Druid would do in and for Galway, while implicitly making clear what would be different about their approach:

> Theatre has for long been regarded as a night-time fancy of the elite. I feel it must be a means of expression for the community in which it is rooted, serving its educational, recreational and creative needs.
>
> If it fails in this it will not survive. Thus, we hope to be continually aware of, and respond to, our social environment.

And she concluded with a quotation – not from Friel or Synge or any other Irish writer, but from the American dramatist Tennessee Williams:

> Make voyages. Attempt them. There is nothing else.

A picture of a Galway hooker, a quotation from Tennessee Williams and a season of productions that balanced the old and the new, the Irish and the international: while it would be some years before Druid's core identity would come into focus, it's remarkable how that first season anticipated so much of what would follow.

In *The Loves of Cass McGuire* by Brian Friel, Druid were staging a relatively new Irish play. It had received its world premiere in New York just nine years earlier, in 1966, where it had been an unexpected flop – though it fared much better when it opened at the Abbey Theatre in Dublin the following year,

Chapter 1: Opening Night, 1975

The Loves of Cass Maguire, 1975.

with Siobhán McKenna playing the lead role. Like most of Friel's plays from that time, it soon became a popular fixture on the Irish amateur and student production circuits – but in choosing to stage Friel's work, Druid were signalling a commitment to professional Irish playwriting that would continue during the years ahead.

In the play, Cass is a woman in her seventies who has returned to Ireland after spending most of her life working in the United States. Scorned for her Irishness in America, she is also rejected by her family when she returns home, because they find her American accent and mannerisms to be alienating and embarrassing. As well as dramatizing the interplay of Irish and American cultures that was already a strong element of Garry's theatrical imagination, the play explores an idea that would soon become one of Druid's key themes: that the tragedy of the emigrant is that, wherever they go, they cannot escape from themselves – which means that a sense of 'home' is paradoxically always present yet always elusive.

Laffan's *It's a Two Foot Six Inches Above the Ground World* also allowed audiences to think about Ireland and Irishness, but at a safe remove. It's about a Catholic mother whose determination to use the contraceptive pill is resisted by her husband and local priest. The play is set in England in 1969, and is presented in the form of a comedy – but its seriousness and relevance in Ireland in 1975 would have been unavoidably evident. The sale of contraceptives in Ireland had been banned in 1935 but, from the early 1970s onwards, Irish women had been campaigning vigorously for a change to that law. A government bill to reverse it was defeated in 1974 (with the then-Taoiseach Liam Cosgrave one of several members of the government who voted against the proposal), leaving the problem unresolved for many years thereafter. The mother's dilemma in this play was not theoretical for Druid's audience: it was a part of the everyday life of everyone in the country, an ongoing injustice that reinforced the sense that Irish women would never be treated equally by the Irish state.

The play had been staged by Frank Bailey in Dublin in 1970 without much protest, and Laffan's reputation as the originator of the popular English soap opera *Emmerdale Farm* might also have softened reactions to his work. Nevertheless, Druid's decision to stage this kind of drama – and to do so in a hall owned by the local congregation of Jesuits – offered one indicator of what Garry might have meant when she wrote that Druid would be aware of and responsive to their 'social environment'.

And then there was Synge's *Playboy*. In later years, Garry, Marie and Mick would all recognize that they had underrated this play when they started rehearsing it. It had been chosen for the season, they admitted, because as an Irish classic it seemed like the kind of work that might attract the audience of tourists who were expected to the city that summer, Americans mostly. It was a museum piece, they thought – hokey, old-fashioned, harmless. But, as they quickly recognized, *The Playboy* could be dangerous if played as written. Upon its premiere in 1907, it had been greeted with a week of riots by Irish nationalists, who were offended by its presentation of the country's western people. The Abbey also brought it in 1911 to America, where it again drew protests in New York, while in Philadelphia the actors were arrested for obscenity (though the charges were later dropped).

It quickly lost its power to shock, however. Somewhat ironically, the Abbey founders' determination to resist all attempts to censor and suppress the play meant that it was instead very quickly canonized, especially after Synge's untimely death in 1909, at the age of only thirty-seven. That canonical status meant that its provocative elements were quickly set aside, ignored and eventually forgotten – until the play became a caricature of itself, mostly revived at the Abbey in productions that were intended for tourists who, it was assumed, wanted to have their ideas about Ireland confirmed rather than challenged.

Synge's plays had been presented in Galway many times before – most recently in Frank Bailey's Celtic Arts Theatre season, which had included Synge's 1904 masterpiece *Riders to the Sea*. But as Druid rehearsed *The Playboy* in June 1975, they discerned that something different was happening this time. The original Abbey production of *The Playboy* had been written by an Anglo-Irish playwright who had travelled to the west in search of stories. He was a sympathetic and respectful observer – but he was still an outsider. And when his play was first performed, it was acted mostly by Dubliners: the first Pegeen Mike, for example, was played by Synge's fiancée Molly Allgood, an actress born in inner-city Dublin; and the first Christy Mahon was played by Willie

Fay, who had been born in Rathmines, then a wealthy suburb of Dublin city. The west of Ireland setting that was presented on the stage of the Abbey in 1907 was created and watched by people who in most cases didn't know very much about that part of the island – not from direct practical experience anyway.

But as Garry, Marie and Mick rehearsed the play, they started to understand that they were coming to it as insiders rather than outsiders. Garry was originally from Ballaghaderreen in County Roscommon, Marie from Drumfin in Sligo and Mick from Tourmakeady in Mayo – which meant that the landscape described in Synge's play was the landscape that they had all grown up in, that the accents in the script were accents they knew intimately from the people around them, and that the stories in the play belonged not to the Abbey in Dublin but to their own communities in the west. A couple of years would pass before they would articulate these thoughts more clearly, but they all knew that they'd discovered something unexpectedly familiar in Synge. They resolved to return to his work as soon as possible.

From that opening night onwards, *The Playboy* would prove the most popular of the three plays, but to drum up sales for the other two, the company set up a rota to send members out to sell tickets on Shop Street, Galway's main thoroughfare – offering early evidence of their determination to go to their audiences rather than waiting to be discovered by them.

Reading the press reviews of that first season, it's apparent that the critics were impressed mostly by the excellence of the acting, with Marie and Mick both being singled out repeatedly – though there would also be praise for others who would soon become Druid regulars, such as Pat Connaughton, who played Pegeen's fiancé Shawn Keogh. But what stands out from the reports is the tone – there was no condescension, no making of allowances: Druid were being held up to high standards and had met them.

Chapter 1: Opening Night, 1975

The Playboy, 1975. Mick Lally (centre); Garry stands second to Mick's right.

The company also had to address occasional changes and challenges: Garry stepped into the role of Sara Tansey for a short time when someone else had to step out, for example. But as the weeks moved on, there was a confirmed sense that this experiment was working, and that audiences wanted to see more.

As July shifted into August, the group decided to introduce lunchtime theatre to Galway – which was presented in the form of a double bill of the Spanish dramatist Fernando Arrabal's *Orison* and Samuel Beckett's *Act Without Words II*. That initiative was also successful in drawing in an audience – but as the summer tourists began to drift away, it was time to make a decision about whether Druid could have a viable future beyond its first season.

As Garry would later explain, there were different things at stake for each of the three co-founders:

Myself and Marie just decided not to look for a job, which at that time was an easy enough decision to make. But it was different for Mick. He actually had to decide whether to leave teaching or not, and throw his lot in with Druid.

That was indeed a consequential choice. Although Ireland in 1975 was beginning to see a promising reversal in high rates of emigration from the country, it was still in a deep recession at the time, with unemployment running at close to 10 per cent. By leaving teaching, Mick was giving up a permanent job, with a pension and guaranteed salary, for the insecurity of an actor's life.

Unsurprisingly, he decided initially just to take a year's leave of absence – and thus had to make an appointment with the head of Galway's Vocational Educational Committee to ask for permission. As it happened, his boss was Oliver Hynes, Garry's father.

Mick's request to go on leave was granted.

The three co-founders were now living together in a rented house in Renmore, in the Galway suburbs. They had enough money to pay themselves a small salary – £12 each per week, roughly equivalent to about €100 each today. And they had a plan for the coming months: they were going to stage *The Glass Menagerie*, a play by Tennessee Williams.

It remained to be seen if Galway audiences would come out for theatre as the days grew shorter and darker, wetter and colder – but Druid had started something; they were on their way.

Garry Hynes, 1975.

DRUID
THEATRE COMPANY

ANNIVERSARY PROGRAMME
1975 - 1976

Fo'castle Theatre,
Dominick St., Galway

Druid's First Anniversary Show Programme, July 1976.

Chapter 2
Die or Go All the Way, 1976–1978

SHORTLY BEFORE Christmas in 1976, Garry stepped off the train at Ceannt Station in Galway, where she found Marie waiting for her on the platform, looking worried.

Garry had just spent a week at the Abbey Theatre in Dublin, completing a course for young directors that had been organized by Tomás Mac Anna. She had left Marie and Mick Lally back in Galway, where they were performing in a new production called *Mother Adam*, a 1971 play by the English dramatist Charles Dyer.

That play has mostly been forgotten now, though its plot (about an old woman who forces her adult child to care for her) would reappear in modified form in many future Druid works, probably most noticeably in Martin McDonagh's *The Beauty Queen of Leenane* in 1996. But Dyer was ahead of his time in showing a willingness to tackle topics that would have been seen as mildly controversial in the 1970s, such as the fact that the son in the play was conceived outside of marriage. No one was going to start a riot at the theatre in response to his treatment of that theme, but Irish dramatists at that time were often comparatively reluctant to tackle those kinds of issues directly – which meant that Druid's choice to take on this play was a subtle signal of intent. They had already shown, when they included Laffan's *It's a Two Foot Six Inches Above the Ground World* in their premiere season, that they were unafraid to stage international dramas in order to scrutinize Irish taboos. With *Mother Adam*, they were doing it again.

But their biggest challenge as they'd prepared for the production was actually about make-up – specifically about how to ensure that the 23-year-old Marie could be made to look like the old woman in Dyer's play. Years later, Garry would laughingly recall that, in her early twenties, she had often tried to straighten her hair by putting Sellotape into it before she went to bed, hoping that it would be flattened by the time she woke up. As a haircare routine, that approach wasn't particularly effective – but it did inspire an idea for Marie's performance. 'We bought Sellotape that was the same colour as Marie's skin,' explained Garry, 'and we stuck it all over her face and hair. We then got surgical gloves, and filled them with lumps to look like her hands had been withered by age'.

Viewed in retrospect, those techniques seem likeably improvisational – but they worked well in practice. Archival photos show that Marie looked both formidable and ancient in *Mother Adam*, perhaps even a little frightening. She certainly doesn't look ridiculous: audiences probably would have been more unnerved by her than anything else. Mick was playing her son Adam, and as rehearsals finished, the company's core trio were looking forward to another successful run. The production would open on 20 November and was due to finish three weeks later.

But when Garry stepped off that train, she soon learned that they were going to have to change their plans completely. Mick had been injured, Marie told her, and had been rushed to hospital with a suspected hernia. The run of *Mother Adam* could not continue but – with Mick out of the company for the next few weeks – their plans for 1977 were also suddenly in doubt. 'There was only me and Marie left,' recalled Garry. 'I thought that was the end.'

Marie and Mick in *Mother Adam*, 1976

Gradually, though, a plan started to form. As Marie often explained later, Garry's theatrical imagination had been deeply influenced by her time in New York in the early 1970s: 'She was fortunate because the American scene was so healthy at that time – and her talent was lit up by what she experienced there.' Those experiences had already inspired the two of them to bring the American drama *Elizabeth I* to the All-Ireland finals in Athlone in 1975 – one of their first shared successes. Now they were talking about staging another Paul Foster play, and it would be bigger, more ambitious and about a topic that (for Irish audiences) was much less familiar: the life of Thomas Paine, the American revolutionary. Years later, Marie would recall Garry's exact words when they finally decided to produce it:

'You know what?' Garry said, 'I'm going to make this happen. We'll give it one last spurt, and if we can pull it off... We'll either die, or go all the way.'

So Garry and Marie staged *Tom Paine* in the Spring of 1977 – and it became the first Druid show to sell out.

By the time Druid staged *Mother Adam*, they had already presented eighteen plays in Galway – most of which had been critically well received, and most of which had also been moderately well attended, bringing in just enough money to keep the company afloat. Their financial worries had been eased slightly in early 1976, when the Arts Council awarded them £1,500. That wasn't a huge amount of money to cover a year's work, but it was unprecedented, given that Druid were based outside Dublin and had been in operation for only six months. The Arts Council's Theatre Officer, David Collins, seemed to believe in the company, and he quickly became a major supporter.

But of course, Druid weren't doing it only for the money. 'We did it because we wanted to keep on doing it,' Garry explained. She, Mick and Marie quickly fell into a pattern of rehearsing from midnight until about 6 am in the Jesuit Hall, which was in use by the nearby school and was thus out of bounds to them during the daytime. After that they'd return to the shared house they were renting, sleep for a few hours, and then do another day's work, building sets, making costumes and always – *always* – trying to find new ways to drum up support for the company.

Bringing in money – that was one of Druid's earliest challenges, but they stuck at it tenaciously and inventively. In May 1976, for example, their production of Christopher Hampton's *Treats* was accompanied by a campaign to recruit a group of 'Friends of

Chapter 2: Die or Go All the Way, 1976–1978

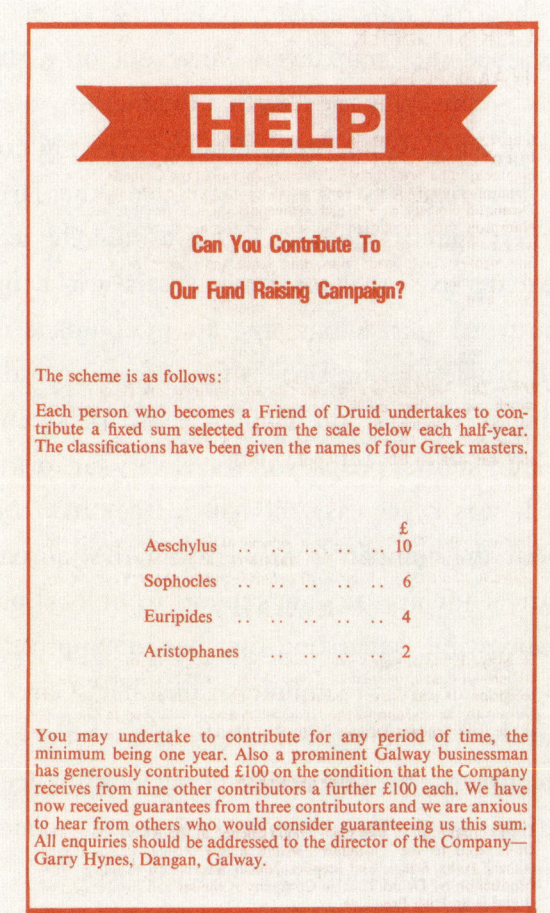

From the *Treats* show programme, 1976

Druid'. Donors would be given names based on how much money they had donated: £10 would allow you to call yourself Aeschylus, £6 would get you the name Sophocles, £4 for Euripides and £2 for Aristophanes. As part of that campaign, Druid also told their audiences that a local businessman had promised to donate £100 – provided that nine other businesses would match his pledge. No one else was doing this kind of thing in Ireland at the time.

Many of the company's early press interviews – especially in the national newspapers – focused on their need for funding, and Garry showed an exceptionally canny understanding of how media coverage could be harnessed for Druid's benefit. Speaking to the *Irish Independent* in July 1975, for example, she had described the company as 'alive but on a week-to-week basis only' – conveying the idea that their ability to produce artistically daring work with limited resources was a minor miracle.

That regularly repeated narrative – that Druid were achieving success against the odds – was absolutely accurate, but it also created a sense that something special was happening in Galway. The word 'miraculous' appears in countless newspaper articles and profiles during Druid's first decade, mostly when they were being profiled by the Dublin newspapers. And, as everyone in Ireland knows, people will travel very far to witness a miracle.

It was never easy though. In that *Irish Independent* article about the company's first season, the journalist reported that Garry's attempts to gain support from local businesses had been unsuccessful, suggesting that her 'diminutive size and youthful appearance seem to militate against her'. Garry told the journalist that she was finding that tough: 'It is a bit annoying when people tend to write me off because of my looks or age.' It probably goes without saying that, within a few years, no one in Galway would write Garry off under any circumstances.

Druid proved similarly adept at devising ways to build an audience for English-language theatre in the west of Ireland. Lunchtime theatre, they discovered, could be an effective vehicle for tempting in would-be theatregoers. Galwegians might baulk at the idea of going to see a full-length play in the evening, Druid knew – but perhaps they could be persuaded to pay 50p for a short performance during their lunch break? After all, even if the play wasn't good, it would be short – and the price of entry included a sandwich anyway.

Those lunchtime performances didn't always work out as planned, however. In October 1976, Druid had decided to stage Samuel Beckett's *Happy Days*, which would have been an unusual choice for lunchtime theatre anywhere, given that the script is

Chapter 2: Die or Go All the Way, 1976–1978

Mick and Marie in *Happy Days*.

so dense and its mood so bleak. But, to make things even more challenging, Garry, Mick and Marie realized only when they were halfway through rehearsals that the play was much too long, running for at least two hours when performed in its entirety.

Press reports show that Marie's performance as Winnie – for which she was buried up to her waist in the first act and then up to her neck in the second – was admired, but she found the experience much too stressful. 'There were only eleven days of rehearsal,' she said, 'and I was *so* insecure about my performance.' Unsurprisingly, the play itself was mostly unloved, and there was some mild criticism in the local press about the decision to stage it at all.

'We were so innocent then,' Garry later recalled – though she also often pointed out that their naivete gave them a kind of freedom: it meant that they were willing to try anything, that they could be fearless. Some of their production choices were

Marie Mullen and Sabina Coyne in *Children of the Wolf*.

therefore very adventurous, and maybe even a little reckless. Early on, there is the example of their staging in November 1975 of John Peacock's *Children of the Wolf*, a strange and somewhat disturbing thriller that touches on the themes of abortion and madness. That production featured a young actress called Sabina Coyne, who was making her Druid debut. Sabina had moved to Galway when she'd married the local Labour Party senator Michael D. Higgins – later to become President of Ireland, with Sabina as First Lady.

Gai Matthews, Marie Mullen and Mick Lally in *The Glass Menagerie*, 1975.

Even Druid's seemingly safe choices were potentially risky. One of their first major critical successes came in October 1975, when they staged Tennessee Williams's *The Glass Menagerie*, with Mick and Marie being joined by Pat Connaughton and Gai Matthews. That play is now regarded as a classic – so much so that a theatre producing it today might be accused of conservative or even boring programming. But in 1975 in Ireland, Williams remained a somewhat dangerous figure. The printed editions of many of his plays had been banned upon publication, and at least nine different film adaptations of his work had also been banned or severely cut by the Irish censors. And as the Druid co-founders also knew, it was the production of a Tennessee Williams play – *The Rose Tattoo* – that had infamously brought about the closure of another small Irish theatre, the Pike, in 1957.

Similarly, Druid's production of Edward Albee's *Who's Afraid of Virginia Woolf?* in the spring of 1976 was critically quite well received, but the company knew that they were staging a play that would have been viewed as morally suspect by at least some people in Ireland. After all, the film adaptation featuring Elizabeth Taylor and Richard Burton had been limited to audiences aged twenty-one or older upon its release in Ireland in 1966, becoming one of only four films ever to be granted so limited a classification (and even then the censor had insisted upon cuts). Unlike books and films, the Irish theatre was not subject to censorship in the 1970s, and in any case the society was gradually liberalizing. But in choosing plays like *The Glass Menagerie* and *Virginia Woolf*, Druid were not exactly playing it safe.

Nevertheless, their successes were beginning to accumulate, and they were more urgently in need of a venue of their own. Having a venue in which they could rehearse during the daytime was essential, and they also knew they were pushing their luck by staging controversial plays in a building owned by the Jesuits. They therefore made a new home for themselves at the Fo'castle, a tiny function room at the back of the Coachman Hotel on Dominick Street.

It wasn't a perfect venue. There were only about fifty seats in it (and they had to take some of those away when they were serving sandwiches); there was no changing room or backstage area, and the performances were sometimes interrupted by the sound of a toilet flushing in one of the flats above them. But Druid's occupation of their own space was an important statement of their seriousness and their status. As Garry explained:

Chapter 2: Die or Go All the Way, 1976–1978

Druid at the Fo'Castle.

Moving into our own theatre meant that we were a real professional company. We weren't doing the amateur run of staging plays only from Friday to Sunday; in our first productions at the Fo'castle, we ran for three weeks. Now we were a proper theatre company.

Tom Paine opened in April 1977. By then, Mick had recovered fully and was able to join the cast, which was one of Druid's largest up to that time. As well as Mick and Marie, it also featured Michael McMullin (who played the eponymous lead), Moya Henry, Noel McGee and Michael O'Sullivan – and between the six actors, they played more than thirty roles.

But Druid had almost been blocked from staging the play altogether. Having finally decided to put it on, Garry was shocked when Foster's agent refused to grant them the rights to perform it. But – in another example of how youthful innocence can sometimes manifest itself as fearlessness – she made the decision to contact Foster directly; she had met him by chance a couple of years earlier, and hoped that a personal appeal might make a difference. So she phoned La MaMa, his theatre company in New York, only to be told that he was on a lecture tour somewhere in South America – but no one was sure exactly where. So, naturally enough, Garry decided to call all the American embassies in that continent, drawing a blank with the first five before finally tracking him down in Brazil. She and Foster spoke; she explained the urgency of the situation – and he granted the rights. They could go ahead after all.

Promotional poster for *Tom Paine*.

That determination to produce the play no matter what was based on the fact that it had so thoroughly captured Garry's imagination: she knew exactly what she wanted to do, and she knew that it would mark a major step forward for Druid's staging style. Marie would later describe *Tom Paine* as a turning point in the company's life. 'With that production,' she recalled,

> Garry kept coming up with these amazing styles of theatre that no one in Galway had ever seen before. It was so exciting

Chapter 2: Die or Go All the Way, 1976–1978

Show programme, Off Obie.

for us. There was scaffolding all around the Fo'castle, on all levels – and it was terribly physical.

It was also one of the first Druid productions to feature live musical accompaniment, with Foster's songs being performed by Lily Cooke and Mike Arrigan on piano and drums, respectively.

The resultant sense of excitement quickly filtered out into Galway City, especially to younger audiences. For the first time, Druid were turning people away from the door each evening.

Soon after *Tom Paine*, Garry and Marie would themselves go to Dublin when they staged a Druid show there for the first time, in May 1977. The play was Leonard Melfi's *Birdbath*, a one-act American drama that they had originally presented in in a programme called *Off Obie*, which showcased Druid's ongoing indebtedness to contemporary American influences.

They performed *Birdbath* at Dublin's Project Arts Centre, then a fringe venue that was drawing in younger audiences by hosting exciting theatre, music and visual art. As usual, Garry and Marie were broke – so they slept in the Project after the performances and had breakfast in the nearby Bewley's Café.

Garry later described *Birdbath* as being the occasion of Marie's 'first great performance' – it was, she said, 'a stunning performance and I've never forgotten it'.

With the success of *Tom Paine* and the first stirrings of a national reputation, there was now no doubt about it: Druid was here to stay.

But Mick wasn't. Although he'd returned to Galway to be in *Tom Paine*, by the summer of 1977 he had reached a decision: he was going to move to Dublin and would try to make a living as an actor there. He reassured Marie and Garry that he wanted to continue acting in Druid productions – and he would keep that promise, appearing with them regularly until his untimely death in 2010. But he told them that he wouldn't be part of the day-to-day life of the company in the way that he had been.

We now know that Mick made the right decision. Within a year, he was picking up film work (appearing in Bob Quinn's *Poitín* in 1978), and soon after that he gained the role that made him famous in Ireland, playing the character of Miley Byrne in the RTÉ serials *Bracken* and *Glenroe*, the latter of which ran for eighteen seasons. He also got married in 1979, to a nurse named Peige Ní Chonghaile, who was originally from the Irish-speaking Aran Island of Inis Meáin. They settled down together in a house off the South Circular Road in Dublin and started a family, with three children, Saileog, Darach and Maghnus.

For Marie and Garry, Mick's departure was less of a shock after *Tom Paine* than it might otherwise have been. As Garry later explained, when the company began,

> Mick did kind of behave older, even though he was only six or seven years older than me and Marie. At the time he had left college and he was acting in the Taibhdhearc and was teaching in Tuam. So Mick was very much the *eminence grise* at the ripe old age of twenty-eight or twenty-nine when we started Druid together.

Chapter 2: Die or Go All the Way, 1976–1978   35

Mick in *The Playboy of the Western World*, 1975.

And certainly he was a huge influence on me. Mick was a fastidiously moral person, and if something wasn't right, then it wasn't right. I was very influenced by Mick on that, and I very much looked up to him. Obviously, as time went on we became more like equals, but in those early years he was a huge influence on myself and Marie's thinking; if

Mick thought it was a good thing to do then we probably did as well.

Mick was definitely a loss. But because they had gone through the anxiety of losing him once already during the run of *Mother Adam*, they knew not only that Druid would survive but that it could continue to evolve and grow.

———

With Mick gone, Garry in particular was starting to develop a firmer understanding of Druid's identity. 'One thing that was becoming really clear,' she said, 'was that we had an incredibly strong sense of place, and we had an incredibly strong mission – that we were going to make theatre in the west of Ireland, about the west of Ireland – and that the west of Ireland was different.'

But different from what?

Different, certainly, from the rest of Ireland. The whole country had struggled economically and culturally since achieving independence in 1922, but the west had suffered disproportionately, with its population falling from 647,000 in 1901 to 391,000 in 1971, around the time when Garry and Marie were beginning their studies in UCG. Much of that decline had been due to emigration, especially during the 1950s, as young people fled Ireland in the hope of making a better living – but also from a desire to live better, to escape the censorious atmosphere in Ireland that demanded conformity to a version of Catholicism that was rigid and intolerant.

Ireland in its entirety had been slow to industrialize, opening itself up to foreign direct investment only in the late 1950s – but the west had been almost entirely left behind by those developments. When Druid were starting out, there was a sugar factory in Tuam, some agriculture and fisheries, and a small but expanding tourism sector – but not much else. And even in agriculture, it was hard for people to make a good living. The western landscape was famously beautiful, but it was also difficult to cultivate: it could support sheep-farming but was less suited to dairy farming and tillage, because the ground was either too rocky or too mountainous and, with over 230 days of rain each year, it was also often too wet. Faced with such limited opportunities, it would have been normal for graduates like Marie and Garry to be lured towards the opportunities available in Dublin or overseas.

But not only were they staying in Galway, they were also asserting that the west of Ireland had value and importance. In doing that, they were following the example of great Irish writers and artists from the past – people like John Millington Synge, Augusta Gregory and William Butler Yeats, whose writings had been inspired by the west's natural environment, and by its language and folklore. But those artists often wrote about the west from at least one remove. Synge, for example, did so initially as an ethnographer and journalist. In newspaper articles and prose accounts like his monumental book *The Aran Islands*, he described the west of Ireland with complete respect but also with a complete lack of sentimentality, celebrating the people's imagination and culture while also calling attention to their dreadful poverty in the hope that readers elsewhere (mainly in Dublin, but also in Britain) might do something about it.

Lady Gregory also wrote about the people of Galway, where she lived, with genuine affection – and she learned Irish in order to understand them better, giving her an intimacy of perspective that was unmatched by most of her peers. But she was still in a position of power, first as the wife and then as the mother of the landlords and owners of the Coole Park estate, where the peasants who inspired her work were living. And although she was a fervent nationalist, she never dropped the title 'Lady' when publishing her books about those people.

Yeats too lived in Galway for a short time – but it says much about him that he chose for his home an old Norman tower called Thoor Ballylee, setting himself apart from the people around him. In his most famous poem, 'The Lake Isle of Inishfree', he had imagined the west as a place of beauty and authenticity, but also as a place that was mostly uninhabited: for him, the west was a scene and a symbol, but it was not a society.

The co-founders of Druid admired those writers – indeed, they would come to love Synge, and they also staged many of Yeats's and Gregory's plays over the years.

But Druid were *of* the west in a way that Yeats, Synge and even Gregory never were, and they were proud of their roots, which were in not only Galway but the west in its entirety. With Garry coming from Roscommon, Marie from Sligo and Mick from Mayo, their shared imagination included Connemara, the hinterlands of Mayo and Sligo, the border county of Leitrim, the islands off the west coast and the towns of east Galway. When they thought about those places, they understood the landscape and they were familiar with the flora and fauna. They also had a deep familiarity with the language – all of them could speak Irish (Marie had even studied it at university), and they fully understood the many versions of English that were in use across the region.

But more than that, they understood the differences between all those places, and they understood the differing codes – the elements of language that hinted at some things and obscured others, the subtle expressions that conveyed distinctions of social class, gender or other hierarchies that might have been invisible to outsiders but which could mean everything to people on the inside. They understood how the pressure to conform to pre-existing roles could sometimes lead young people to rebellion but more often led them to exile. They shared that knowledge amongst themselves, and they shared it also with their first

Chapter 2: Die or Go All the Way, 1976–1978

The Pot of Broth by W.B. Yeats, 1976.

audiences. It shaped them, rooted them and gave them something to push against when necessary.

And there was a need for a certain amount of rebellion occasionally. Garry, for example, had been raised in an Irish-speaking household, but in her late teens and early twenties had begun to resist the language, and was generally becoming frustrated with an Irish culture that she perceived to be stiflingly old-fashioned. That determination to chart a new path arose to some extent from a need to define Druid's identity in relation to what it was not – the company were *not* the Taibhdhearc (though they did of course work frequently with actors from that theatre), just as they were not an amateur group, and not the university players. They were also not their parents – so many of Druid's plays, throughout its history, would allegorize the interference of an older generation in the lives of the young; when setting themselves apart, Druid were doing so not only geographically and linguistically, but intergenerationally too.

Those impulses also came from a need to connect with the emerging theatremakers in places like New York. Those artists were breaking new ground, saying new things – and, as Garry recalled, 'they looked like me, and they sounded like me, and they were making the kind of theatre that I wanted to make'. It seemed natural for her to do what most young people want to do – reject the familiar for something new.

But now the company were finding new connections to their home place, especially by staging work like *The Playboy*. 'We discovered our sense of an Irish identity through Druid,' Garry would later say. They soon faced an important question: how could they build on the legacies of writers like Synge while also making theatre that felt new?

———

The only way to answer that question was to keep making work. And so, from 1977 onwards, Druid began to stage more Irish work – revivals mostly, but as they grew in confidence and experience, they started to make original plays too.

Sometimes that work was more about having fun than exploring their heritage. In the Christmas of 1977, for instance, they staged the company's first (and also their last) pantomime, *Aladineen O'Druideen*. As the name implies, that was a Hibernicized version of the story from the Arabian nights (the suffix *-een* is from the Irish, and usually means 'little'; in rural areas in the west of Ireland it would be fairly common to hear it being used with English words, such as in the diminutive *loveen*). Joining Marie in the cast was Paul O'Neill, one of the Druid regulars in

Chapter 2: Die or Go All the Way, 1976–1978 41

Marie Mullen and Seán McGinley, *Aladineen O'Druideen*, 1977.

their early years, and a young graduate from Donegal who had recently joined the company, Seán McGinley. Seán would later achieve fame in Ireland for his leading role in a Roddy Doyle TV serial called *Family*, in which he played Charlo, an abusive and alcoholic small-time criminal. But he also appeared in many Druid productions over the years, staying with the company until 1989 and then returning occasionally thereafter. He'd been recruited by Marie, who had seen his work in the university's DramSoc. As *Aladineen* showed, the two of them had hit it off together quickly. They eventually married each other, in 1990 – an eventuality that everyone in the company had seen coming long before Seán and Marie did.

But for the most part, Druid were looking at old Irish plays not as if they were museum pieces but as if they had something urgent to say to audiences in the present, about the present. That often resulted in them producing plays that had been forgotten or ignored for decades. In the summer of 1976, for example, they put together a production that they called *In the Glens of Rathvanna*, which was a compendium of works by Synge – most of them relatively unknown. It began with selections from Synge's writing (Mick recited a poem called 'Danny', which he had set to music). It then moved to *In the Shadow of the Glen*, a 1903 play that had caused Synge considerable trouble when it premiered, with Irish nationalists objecting to his characterization of a young Irish woman whose husband pretends to be dead in order to expose her infidelity. And it concluded with *The Tinker's Wedding* – a play that had been considered so inflammatory during Synge's lifetime that it went unstaged at the Abbey Theatre until 1971, more than sixty years after his death.

As with their production of *The Glass Menagerie*, Druid's presentation of *The Tinker's Wedding* was much riskier in 1976 than would be the case if it were being produced today, concluding with a scene in which two strong and independent women gag a priest and tie him in a sack, before declaring that 'it's little need we ever had of the like of you'. At a time when it was considered dangerous to present any kind of clergy on stage, Synge himself had been all too aware of his work's power to provoke. 'It looks mighty shocking in print,' he wrote in a letter to Molly Allgood in 1907. *The Tinker's Wedding* wasn't quite as shocking in 1976 as it would have been when Synge was alive, but it remained undeniably provocative – demonstrating Druid's evolving tendency to look to the past as a way of shaking people out of their present-day assumptions and complacencies.

In 1977, they returned to Synge again – this time going back to *The Playboy*, which they presented in the Fo'castle. Aiming

Chapter 2: Die or Go All the Way, 1976–1978

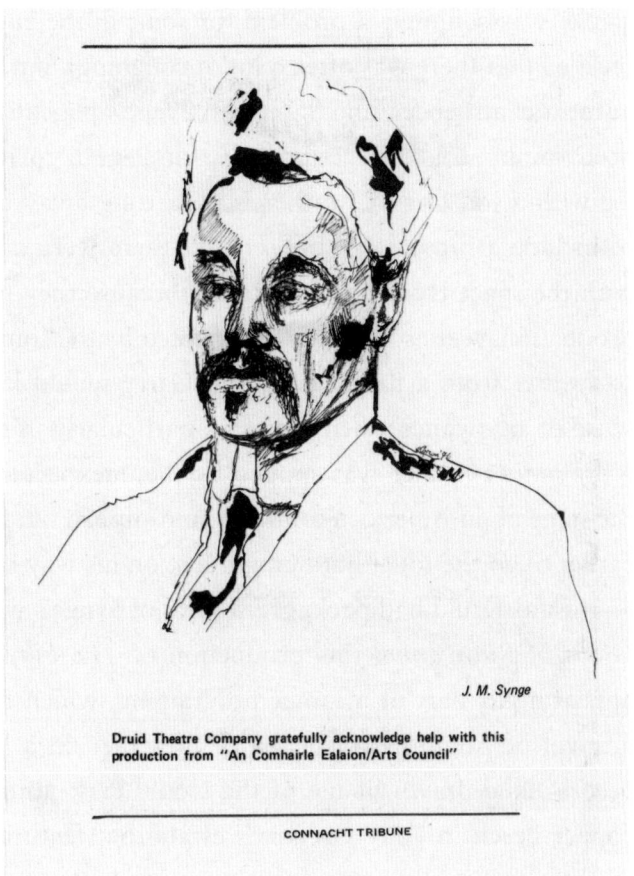

From the show programme for *In the Glens of Rathvanna*, 1976.

for realism, their set included a real fireplace with turf burning in it – but, because there was no chimney in the space, audiences often found themselves watching the play through a haze of smoke. Mick was playing the lead male role of Christy Mahon again, but Marie was now playing the Widow Quin, a powerful if cynical thirty-year-old woman who vies with Pegeen for Christy's attentions. Again it was a hit, but Garry still wasn't happy with it, feeling that there was more to explore, more to understand, about what Synge was doing. She told everyone that she wanted to come back to *The Playboy* again whenever she could.

That sense of mild unhappiness might also have owed something to the limitations of the Fo'castle space. The turf smoke was definitely a problem for some in the audience (Garry recalled that there was often a lot of coughing), but it was at least authentic: a shebeen like the one in Synge's play also would have been smoky, and the action calls for Pegeen to burn Christy's leg with a sod of turf, so there's no getting away from the need to include a fireplace in the set. But there were other problems with the space that were frustrating because they felt avoidable. Productions were sometimes interrupted by the sound of running bathwater from a flat nearby, and Garry would later recall her sense of annoyance when, during a particularly important scene, a dramatic entrance was spoiled by the unexpected arrival onto the stage of an American tourist who'd slipped out a few minutes earlier to go the toilet but had got lost on his way back.

Just as Druid had packaged several of Synge's works into *The Glens of Rathvanna*, this production of *The Playboy* was also appearing as part of a larger programme, which they called 'A Festival of Anglo-Irish Theatre' – presented in a brochure that used a hand-drawn image of the Coole Park autograph tree, a copper beech in Lady Gregory's estate that features on its bark the carved initials of most of the major Irish dramatists of the revival, including Yeats and Synge, as well as George Bernard Shaw, Seán O'Casey and many others. The appearance of Druid's logo alongside those famous names was an expression of how they were continuing a tradition – but it was also evidence of their expanding confidence that they were willing to place themselves in such esteemed company.

Alongside Synge's *Playboy*, the festival also included an almost completely unknown drama called *There Are Tragedies and Tragedies* by the Kerry playwright George Fitzmaurice. Originally published in 1948, the play had only been produced once during Fitzmaurice's lifetime (he died in 1963), and then only by an amateur group in Dublin. By including it in a festival, Druid were displaying and deploying their shrewd marketing

A Festival of Anglo-Irish Theatre.

skills, encouraging people who were keen to see their production of Synge to take a chance on something that would probably not have found an audience otherwise.

That strategy provides evidence of the beginning of a practice that would become an essential feature of Druid's work – the clustering together of seemingly different plays into a single theatrical event, one that placed those plays into dialogue with each other, and which invited audiences to engage with them over an extended period of time. And also detectable was the company's willingness to look again at Irish dramatic history: they wouldn't rely exclusively on the plays that had been canonized

> DRUID THEATRE COMPANY
> LUNCHTIME THEATRE
>
> "BAR AND GER"
> by
> GERALDINE ARON
>
> AN IRISH PREMIERE
>
> BAR .... PAUL O'NEILL
> GER .... MARIE MULLEN
>
> SET .... SEAN MCGINLEY
> LIGHTING .... DONAL HYNES
>   MAELIOSA STAFFORD
> COSTUMES .... MARIE MULLEN
>
> DIRECTION .... GARRY HYNES
>
> GERALDINE ARON, who was born in Galway, now lives in South Africa with her husband and twin daughters and BAR AND GER, which is her first play, has been extensively produced there. It has also been staged in America, Israel and it was heard on B.B.C. Radio Three last year. It was the "Play of the Month" in the U.S. theatre magazine "Dramatics" in May, 1978.

Bar and Ger flyer.

and celebrated, but would read everything, make up their own minds and encourage audiences to do the same.

Writers like Fitzmaurice had something to say, Druid showed – and it was time to listen to them. But it was also essential to understand how they'd been ignored and forgotten in the first place.

With their production of *There Are Tragedies and Tragedies*, Druid were able to do something they had never done before: to claim that they had staged an Irish premiere.

They did so again in 1978, when they produced *Bar and Ger*, a play by Geraldine Aron – a writer who had been born in Galway but had moved to Zimbabwe and then South Africa. Partially autobiographical, Aron's drama is about a brother and

Marie and Paul O'Neill in *Bar and Ger*.

sister, showing the growth of their relationship from childhood onwards. Her play had premiered in Cape Town in 1975, but Druid's production reconnected Aron's story to her own roots in a way that made it feel brand new. Galway audiences loved it. They found it funny and heart-warming; they loved the performances by Marie and Paul O'Neill – and they wanted to see more of Aron's work. Druid were now starting to think about how they could build relationships with living writers.

They were also starting to think more about creating new work themselves. They had been trying to pull together a production that would do for Oscar Wilde what they had done with Synge in *The Glens of Rathvanna*: finding a narrative that might link together different excerpts from Wilde's works. But it just wasn't working in a way that made sense – so they decided to write something new. Their show programme explained what happened next:

Seán McGinley, who 'bears not even the slightest resemblance' to Oscar Wilde.

The *Pursuit* is by no means an attempt to give insight into Oscar Wilde's life or his work but is rather a theatrical approach to that area of his life that is now part of the public imagination. The style of the piece is cabaret/revue, with an art-deco setting and fairly traditional dance routines. But the show also deals with the controversial trial and its aftermath and the mood of the piece changes rapidly from the glitter and glamour to darkness, much in the way Oscar's life did.

If *The Pursuit of Pleasure* were being produced today, it might be described as devised theatre: Garry's name is on cover of the script in the Druid Archive, but much of the action was worked out by the company in rehearsal. Seán McGinley played Wilde – a

Chapter 2: Die or Go All the Way, 1976–1978

Poster for a revival of *The Pursuit of Pleasure*, 1981.

potentially surprising choice given that, as the show programme conceded, he 'bears not even the slightest resemblance to Wilde'. But far from being something to apologize for, the dissimilarity of actor and character was deliberate: Seán was not playing the 'real' Wilde but was instead allowing the audience to imagine the Wilde who lives in the public imagination.

With this production, many of the skills and techniques that Druid had been developing up to that point came together to create something genuinely new. *The Pursuit of Pleasure* had a musicality and a freedom in its approach to stagecraft that audiences seemed to find both invigorating and exciting. It was about Ireland's past, looking again at an Anglo-Irish dramatist – but it was also about the present. As the show reminded audiences, Wilde's imprisonment had been for 'homosexual acts' – a legal prohibition that had been repealed in England in 1967 but which would remain on the Irish statute books until 1994. And perhaps most importantly it showed Druid's maturity, displaying their ability to shift registers from the 'glittering and glamour to darkness', but also from cabaret to tragedy.

The company would remain proud of *The Pursuit of Pleasure*, later describing it as 'the first work originating entirely from inside Druid'. It was also one of their most popular productions: as the show programme for one of its many revivals stated, 'it fills the theatre every time it is performed'.

Every company wants to 'fill the theatre every time' that a show is performed – but for Druid, the lack of capacity was becoming a real problem. The Fo'castle had always been a temporary solution to their need for space, and by the summer of 1978 they had definitely outgrown it – it just wasn't big enough for their audiences, and it wasn't big enough for their ambitions.

And the people of Galway were fully behind them now. Audiences were consistently turning up for their productions; even people who had no interest in the theatre wanted to help them, often by dropping bags of old clothes outside the Fo'castle in the hope that they might be useful, or even by passing bars of chocolate to the actors as they waited for their cues in the lane outside the theatre.

It was now time to make a new plan. Garry got a map of Galway City and started forming small groups from the company

– two people would head to the south of the city, another two would go east, and so on. They were looking for vacant and derelict buildings, places that might house a theatre but which they might also be able to use for free, or for as close to free as possible.

Eventually, Garry herself came across a run-down warehouse on Chapel Lane, a small backstreet off Quay Street, near the city's docks. Looking between bars on grimy windows, she saw that the building was old, had high ceilings and seemed to be empty. It might just do.

Druid poster, 1979, showing their new theatre in Chapel Lane.

Chapter 3
Building a Theatre, 1979–1981

GARRY HAD FOUND a building that might be suitable for a new theatre. The next step was to contact its owners and persuade them to hand it over – if possible, for free.

The warehouse they were interested in belonged to Thomas McDonogh and Sons, a local merchant company that had recently appointed a man called Donagh O'Donoghue as their managing director. Donagh had been a student at UCG, where he'd taken degrees in both Arts and Commerce, about ten years before Garry and Marie. They knew he had some interest in the theatre; he'd even been the President of the University Drama Society himself, in 1966; and while he was a student he'd made friends with Frank Bailey, Michael D. Higgins and others who would go on to support the development of the arts in Galway. So he just might be willing to help.

But they were also aware of his reputation in Galway as a tough businessman, as someone who wouldn't have any interest in wasting his company's money or his own time. With some trepidation, Garry made an appointment to see him.

When Marie and Garry discussed these events many years later, they had slightly different recollections about what happened next.

'Donagh was so impressed with Garry,' Marie said.

'He was not,' Garry shot back. 'He threw me out!'

'Well he was impressed with you the second time, when you went back. What happened the first time? Did he think you were rude or something?'

'No,' Garry replied. 'He thought I was an idiot. I said, "I'm from a theatre company, Druid, and we think your place looks great. Could you give it to us please, for nothing?" He asked me again how much we were willing to pay. I said "nothing" again. He said to get the hell out of his office.'

Looking back on their meeting a few days later, Garry began to wonder if Donagh had been having a bit of fun with her – and in any case the need for a new theatre hadn't gone away. So she made the decision to try to talk to him again.

Donagh's recollection of those events was similar: 'Garry came in to my office and said she wanted me to give her a building – for free,' he remembered. Although the warehouse looked empty from the outside, McDonogh's did need it: at that time, they had a wholesale grocery business, and they used the warehouse to store tea, which they would then redistribute to shops all around the west of Ireland. Giving up the space would have a definite impact on their costs, Donagh knew.

'When Garry first came in, I was sceptical. Very sceptical,' he recalled. 'But,' he added with a chuckle, 'she persisted!'

So Donagh started to think about it. He met Marie and some of the other actors with the company; years later, he would also recall talking to Mick about Druid's future, perhaps on one of his intermittent visits back to Galway. Donagh was beginning to understand what Garry and Marie were trying to do – with their company, and for Galway. He had reached a decision: 'I was always interested in drama, and I wanted to encourage them,' he said. He was coming around to their proposal.

His next step was to approach the McDonogh family to see what they thought about it. They too were sceptical at first,

Chapter 3: Building a Theatre, 1979–1981

Donagh O'Donoghue, Tom Murphy and Mick Lally, 1996.

but were eventually swayed – and with Donagh's assistance, the McDonoghs agreed that Druid would lease the space for a 'peppercorn rent' of £1 per year.

So the company now had their own building, but they had also gained a major supporter in Donagh – 'one of the greatest supporters Druid ever had,' as Marie would later describe him. When Druid reorganized as a company limited by guarantee in the mid-1980s, Donagh would become their first Chairman, and he occupied that role for almost twenty years. The acquisition of the building thus began a relationship that would prove vital for decades to come.

But for now the company had to work out how to turn a warehouse into a theatre. They made the decision to stop producing plays for six months: there wouldn't be any box office income, but they would be able to save on construction costs by doing almost all the work themselves – 'the only outside contractor we brought in was a plumber', Garry would later say, still proud of what they had achieved together. So as 1978 drew to a close, they were getting ready to make a new theatre for Galway.

By the spring of 1979, the Druid acting company had evolved again. Seán McGinley and Paul O'Neill were still with them, but they'd been joined by two other actors who would go on to have a lasting impact during the years ahead.

One was Ray McBride, who had recently returned to Galway after studying at a university in Tennessee. He had been there on an athletics scholarship, but had formed an unquenchable interest in acting when he was cast in a production of *The Playboy of the Western World* in Virginia. His mother Kathleen had met Garry and Marie several times at the Fo'castle, and had often talked to them about 'my son Raymond' who was interested in acting. 'Would Druid audition him when he got back to Ireland?' she asked them, many times.

By then, Garry was regularly being approached by people who wanted to be part of the company, so she would have been justified in not taking that request very seriously – but she did agree to meet Ray, and discovered that he was not only an excellent actor but also a gifted dancer. He had won several medals at Irish dancing *feiseanna* before going to the US, but perhaps because of his training in athletics, he had also developed a refined and specialized understanding of movement. He went on to act in several Druid productions, and he also choreographed many of them.

And then there was Maelíosa Stafford. He was a couple of years younger than Garry and Marie, but he'd been going to Druid productions since the beginning. His younger brother Conall had been in *Two Foot Six Inches* in the 1975 summer season (Conall was twelve at the time, and took the role of one of the children in the play), linking Maelíosa to the company right away – but he had been brought up with a love of the theatre anyway. His parents Seán and Máire had been involved in the Taibhdhearc for decades, and they had encouraged amateur drama throughout the city in many other ways – for example by setting up a Club na n-Óg (a youth club) for girls, which presented plays in Irish at the Áras na nGael in Dominick Street throughout the 1950s.

Maelíosa often spoke with gratitude about how his parents had brought him so often to the Taibhdhearc, where he saw (among many other productions) *Ag Fanacht le Godot*, an Irish-language version of Beckett's *Waiting for Godot*; he even appeared in some productions there as a child, mostly in Christmas pantomimes.

However, he was brought to every other form of live performance in the city as well: concerts by the Patrician Musical Society (a choral group that often presented operas and operettas), visiting productions by fit-up companies, amateur productions and so on. It was no surprise then that, when he joined UCG to take a degree in Commerce, he threw himself into the Drama Society, performing in Thornton Wilder's *Our Town* and Friel's *Philadelphia, Here I Come!*, while also appearing with the university's Irish-language drama society, An Cumann Dramaoíchta.

The story of Maelíosa's recruitment to the company is one he would tell and retell many times over the years to come. Garry and some of the actors had been buying wood from a hardware store in Shantalla, and they needed to carry it to the Fo'castle, which was about a twenty-minute walk away. Maelíosa happened to be passing by at the time and, seeing that the group needed help, he shouldered a load of timber and joined them on their way.

They got to the theatre and unloaded, and the obvious thing for them all to do at that stage was to sit down and have a cup of tea. 'What are ye up to?' Maelíosa asked, and they replied that they were thinking of staging Dion Boucicault's melodrama

Maelíosa Stafford in *The Enchanted Trousers*, 1978.

The Colleen Bawn but were having trouble getting equipment for it. Maelíosa knew someone who knew someone who had a spare reel-to-reel player, and he thought he might be able to get his hands on it. They continued chatting, and a few months later Maelíosa would get one of his first professional credits, as the sound designer on that show.

Garry then decided to cast Maelíosa in a couple of lunchtime productions: he appeared in Chekhov's *The Proposal* and then in a short play called *The Enchanted Trousers* by Oliver St John Gogarty. He had hoped that this might lead to an invitation to join the company on a more formal basis, but when that didn't happen, he decided to spend the summer months working in America before lectures at the university resumed in the autumn.

About a month before he was due back to his studies in Galway, however, he got a telegram. It was from Garry, and it

Woyzeck – Druid's farewell to the Fo'Castle.

said that they were going to do a production of Georg Büchner's *Woyzeck* – which, although Maelíosa didn't know it at that time, would be the last Druid show at the Fo'castle. Garry's telegram conveyed an exciting offer: if he came back from the US, not only would there be a place for him in the show, there would also be a place for him in the company. Maelíosa didn't have to think about it for long: 'I was on the next plane home,' he later said.

There was one other major addition to the company at around that time – but behind the scenes – and that was of Jerome Hynes, Garry's brother. He too had been watching Druid's shows since the start; together with their mother Carmel, he even had a credit in the first season's show programme, taking on front of house duties. He became ever more involved as he got older, mostly voluntarily at first – operating the lights and sound in some of the shows (he shared a credit for sound design in *The Colleen Bawn* with Maelíosa), and gradually taking on some of the administrative work in the company. He combined those responsibilities with studying for a degree at UCG, and so was quickly developing the skills that would make him so successful as the company's first General Manager, a role that he took on formally in 1981.

When people look back on Druid's early years, they often ask how such a small place could produce so many talented people in such a short period. The journey into Druid by Ray and Maelíosa suggests that this 'miracle' didn't happen *despite* Galway's size but *because* of it. Chance encounters and casual conversations were part of everyone's everyday life at that time – making it possible for Garry to hear about Ray McBride long before he returned to Ireland, or for Maelíosa to make sure he was in the right place at the right time when the company needed a hand.

But family was important too – from Kathleen McBride looking out for 'my son Raymond', to the Staffords encouraging Maelíosa to go to shows (and then not arguing too forcefully with him when he left UCG to join Druid), to Carmel and Jerome Hynes taking tickets at the door on those first nights in July 1975. If Galway could be maddening because everyone knew everyone else, it could also be nurturing – because everyone was willing to *help* everyone else too.

That willingness to help was often in evidence when the conversion of the theatre got underway during the cold early months of 1979. Seán McGinley and Garry had between them worked out a rough design for the space, and Maelíosa had just enough electrical knowledge to look after the wiring. Seán was doing a lot of the building work, and Garry and Marie were also constantly busy, pulling nails from floorboards, painting, identifying and then mending holes in the roof, and anything and everything else that needed to be done.

Chapter 3: Building a Theatre, 1979–1981

Bobby Molloy and Garry, 1979.

Friends and family would drop by whenever they could. Donal Hynes, Garry's other brother, helped from time to time – and Caoimhín Ó Maicín, a colleague of Garry's father who taught building and construction, also occasionally visited them in order to offer practical advice. Many others worked on the project, among them Páraic Breathnach (who would later become a leading figure in the Galway arts community himself), Paul O'Neill's brother Padraic, Adrian Taheny and many others.

While Paul O'Neill was busily involved with the construction work, he was also spending a lot of time on fundraising – and his campaign took off, raising more than £5,000. Roughly half that money came from local businesses, but the rest was from ordinary Galwegians, some of whom literally stopped members of the company on the street so that they could give them a few pounds. There was financial support from the Taibhdhearc too: far from being threatened by the risk of competition, they had offered to run a benefit night for Druid. There really was a powerful sense of the whole community rallying behind them.

And so on 19 May 1979, the Druid Lane Theatre opened. It was more than twice the size of the Fo'castle, with 102 seats – and at last they had dressing rooms, a backstage space and a foyer. The opening honours were performed by Bobby Molloy, a local TD and a Minister in the Fianna Fáil government. He gave his speech; Garry followed him, offering a lengthy list of thank yous, especially to her parents. And then they were ready to get underway with their opening production: Bertolt Brecht's *The Threepenny Opera*.

An audience member heading to the theatre on that opening night in May 1979 might have wondered what kind of play Druid would choose in order to christen their new space. It was a new venue for Galway – so a west of Ireland play would be an obvious choice: perhaps something by Synge? Or maybe instead another American drama, to draw on their past successes, something like *The Glass Menagerie* or *Tom Paine* – one of those shows that had become famous in part because so few people had seen them before? But maybe not: the company had been so busy during the previous few months; even in the days leading up to the opening, they'd still been adding finishing touches. It would be fair enough, really, if they kept things simple, redoing something they'd already rehearsed and produced, like *Woyzeck* or *The Colleen Bawn*. Yes: a revival – that would make sense. Wouldn't it?

Well, Garry did none of those predictable things, thus establishing a pattern that would recur in most of the big Druid nights to come – that of never doing what would have been expected. Thus, the venue's opening production was *The Threepenny Opera*, a 1928 play by Bertolt Brecht.

Chapter 3: Building a Theatre, 1979–1981   63

The Threepenny Opera, 1970.

Brecht's work had been staged intermittently in Ireland since the 1950s, with the Gate Theatre's Hilton Edwards encouraging the gradual acceptance of the German playwright in a country that initially had been a little frightened by Brecht's communism. Edwards's own approach to directing and design had been re-energized when he saw the Berliner Ensemble perform Brecht's work in London in 1956, and soon after that he cast Siobhán McKenna in Brecht's *Saint Joan of the Stockyards* for a production at the Gate in Dublin. But other than that, there hadn't been many productions of Brecht's plays. Tomás Mac Anna had done *Galileo* and *The Resistible Rise of Arturo Ui* at the Abbey in 1965 and 1974 respectively, and his work had popped up occasionally at amateur festivals or on the student circuit. But of the 100 or so people in the Druid Lane Theatre that night, most would never have seen a professional production of a Brecht play before.

What might have been more familiar, however, was the company's use of music. *The Threepenny Opera* is not actually an opera (that was typical of Brecht, a writer who himself loved subverting expectations). He described it as a 'play with music', but that wording was chosen partly because what we now call 'musical theatre' hadn't emerged as a distinctive genre in the 1920s. But as staged by Druid, this was a musical.

And Galway was a musical place. In addition to the Patrician Musical Society's concerts – which in the 1970s ranged from Gilbert and Sullivan to Verdi – there were many other opportunities to hear live music in the city. There was a strong and growing traditional and folk music scene, with regular sessions springing up at pubs and venues close to Druid's new space. Seán and Maire Stafford also frequently combined Irish-language theatre and music; in 1978, they had even produced an Irish-language version of Mozart's *Così fan tutte*. And Garry herself had been integrating music more frequently into her productions, sometimes adding popular songs (her early productions of *Cass Maguire* often featured songs by Van Morrison, for example) and, from *Tom Paine* onwards, drawing in live musicians and singers too. *The Threepenny Opera* was therefore picking up on strands that were already present in Galway's cultural life, showing audiences that Druid's imaginative roots could run in a variety of different directions.

Garry had never directed a Brecht play before, but *The Threepenny Opera* proved an ideal choice to showcase what the new venue could do. Some of the actors emerged from the wings, but others shocked audience members by popping up from trapdoors in the eating area; and Paul O'Neill would go one better by making his entrance on a motorbike. When the bows were taken at the end, there were almost twenty people on the stage. This was, in every sense, a *big* production.

Chapter 3: Building a Theatre, 1979–1981   65

The Threepenny Opera company.

And it certainly was a big cast. Maelíosa was playing Mack the Knife (the closest thing to a lead role in the play), and his parents Seán and Maire also featured, along with another Taibhdhearc actor, Colette Lardner. Maelíosa's fiancée Joyce McGreevy was in it too, as Pirate Jenny, and so was Ray McBride, who also choreographed. And of course Marie Mullen and Seán McGinley were in it as well, which meant that they'd been combining rehearsals with last-minute construction work. There were also three musicians (playing an accordion, a trumpet and drums) and two singers.

With the opening night underway, there was one last bit of good news for the company to savour. David Collins from the Arts Council was in attendance, and he had introduced Garry to

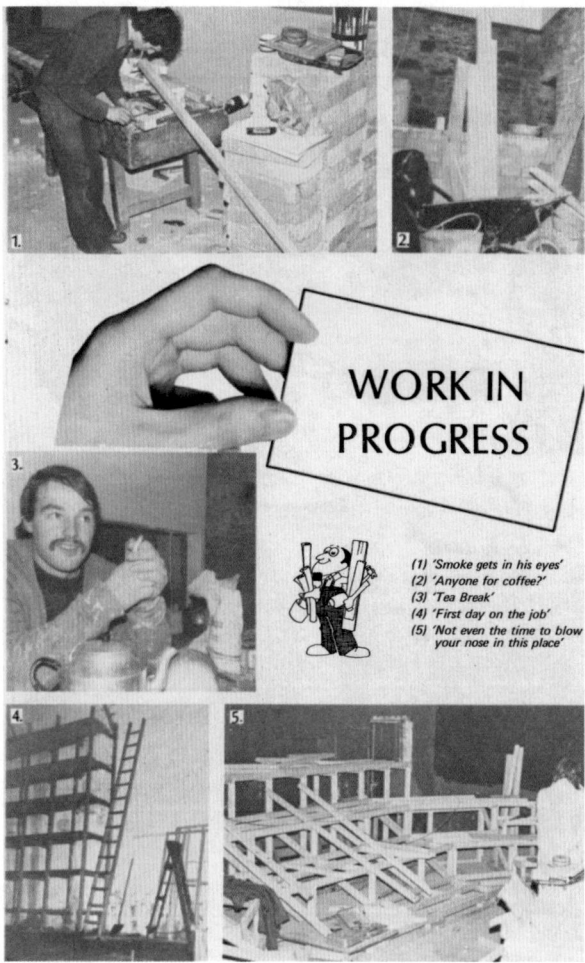

Photos from the Druid Theatre construction, *Threepenny Opera* programme.

the council's new theatre officer, Arthur Lappin. Druid's annual grant had been moving upwards since that first injection of £1,500 in January 1976, largely due to Collins's support. But the council was ready to take a major leap forward: they would now be giving them £15,000, Collins told them.

By gaining a tenfold increase in funding in less than four years, Druid had achieved something that had never been done before by an Irish theatre company.

Not a bad way to open a new venue, they must have thought.

Chapter 3: Building a Theatre, 1979–1981

As the run of *The Threepenny Opera* got into its stride, Garry could see that the production wasn't fully working, but she was mostly happy with it: it was a worthwhile experiment, she felt. The audiences kept coming in any case, and suddenly there was a buzz in a part of the city that ordinarily would have been deserted in the evenings. One local newspaper commended Druid for 'restoring a derelict building in a decaying part of the city' and expressed the hope that this 'spark' would have 'far-reaching repercussions'. There was a general sense of optimism that having a theatre in that part of the town would have a positive impact. The nearby Quays Pub had also just been refurbished (Maelíosa later remembered the two construction teams regularly having lunch together), so there was an undoubted sense that something was happening in that area.

That hope was quickly validated. With theatregoers heading to Chapel Lane in the evenings, there was suddenly more business for local restaurants and pubs. No one really spoke about the idea of 'urban regeneration' at that time, but it became clear that Druid's presence was having an unexpectedly positive impact in the streets around it.

Occupying their own space also meant that Druid could now start thinking more strategically about their future. Then as now, 'national' coverage in Ireland mostly meant being noticed in Dublin – not just by government ministers like Bobby Molloy and state agencies like the Arts Council, but also by media organizations such as *The Irish Times* and RTÉ, which, together with the two universities in the capital city, made up an informal ecosystem that had a decisive influence on who was funded, who was published, who was reviewed, whose work appeared on academic curricula – on all the things that can assure the longevity of a career in the arts, both for individuals and organizations.

The Threepenny Opera company.

One way for Druid to have gained that national attention would have been to go to Dublin more often, as they had done with *Birdbath* at the Project Arts Centre in 1977. But a recurrent lesson from Irish theatre history is that if you want to be noticed at a national level, it helps if you've been celebrated abroad first (Druid would prove the validity of that maxim many times again in the future). They therefore started to think about touring overseas for the first time, and in early 1980 Jerome Hynes made a trip to Edinburgh to explore the possibility of bringing Druid's work to that year's Fringe Festival.

Once the decision had been made to go to Scotland, Druid chose, once again, not to do the simple or predictable thing. They could have brought one production but instead brought four, and they could have presented a classic Irish play but instead travelled with work that was entirely unknown – two plays by Geraldine

Chapter 3: Building a Theatre, 1979–1981

Island Protected by a Bridge of Glass show programme and poster.

Aron, a revival of *The Pursuit of Pleasure*, and a newly devised play called *Island Protected by a Bridge of Glass*.

A revival of *Bar and Ger* was joined by another two-hander by Aron called *A Galway Girl*, a funny but intermittently biting portrait of a husband and wife's relationship from the 1950s onwards. It too had appeared first in South Africa before Druid gave it its Irish premiere, at the Druid Lane Theatre in the spring of 1980. Showing how well he was fitting in to the company, Ray McBride had been cast in one of the two roles in *A Galway Girl*, alongside a young actor called Ailbhe Garvey; the play became a long-term favourite with Druid's audiences. The two Aron plays were performed only twice each at Edinburgh, but were very well received.

Island Protected by a Bridge of Glass was a new play, drafted by Garry before being rewritten by the whole company during

Rebecca Bartlett first appeared with Druid during their Winter 1979 Season when she played Miss Prism in "The Importance of Being Earnest" and Mrs. Drudge in "The Real Inspector Hound". Born in Belfast, she played with the Marian Players while at school and since moving to Galway she has been actively involved in drama classes with a number of National schools in the city.

Peter Lawson, who comes from Cornwall, joined the company earlier this year. He had previously worked in repertory in London and in Cornwall, with the Shiva Group, as well as appearing in numerous episodes of the popular B.B.C. series "The Onedin Line". This is his first production with Druid.

Ray McBride made his Druid debut one year ago in the company's production of "The Threepenny Opera" and has appeared in many productions since, including "A Galway Girl", "The Rising of the Moon" and "Thirst". He spent a number of years studying in East Tennessee State University during which time he played Christy Mahon in "The Playboy of the Western World" and directed a production of "Fiddler on the Roof".

Sean McGinley joined Druid in 1977. A graduate of U.C.G. he acted in numerous productions with Dramsoc there. He has taken lead roles in "Woyzeck", "The Colleen Bawn", "Hyacinth Halvey" and he played the part of Oscar Wilde in the company's original show "The Pursuit of Pleasure".

Marie Mullen, a founder member of Druid was born in Sligo. During her years in U.C.G. she took lead roles in "The Loves of Cass McGuire", "Sticks and Bones" and "Elisabeth One". Her many appearances with Druid include both Pegeen Mike Quinn (1975) and the Widow Quinn (1977) in "The Playboy of the Western World", Amanda in "The Glass Menagerie", Velma Sparrow in "Birdbath" and Lady Bracknell in "The Importance of Being Earnest".

rehearsals. It explores the life of Grace O'Malley, or Gráinne Mhaol as she's better known in Ireland – a sixteenth-century pirate queen who met Queen Elizabeth I when her children were taken captive by the English governor of Connacht.

The influence of Paul Foster might have been a factor in choosing that theme (he too had adopted experimental staging techniques to reconsider the lives and reputations of well-known historical figures), but Garry had always had an interest in Irish history – History being one of her subjects at UCG – and, with ever-increasing levels of violence in Northern Ireland, it was an opportune time to consider the roots of Anglo-Irish conflict.

And there were other important contexts at play. Although the word 'feminism' does not appear in any of the archival records about the show, this was an undeniably feminist production, focusing on two powerful women and thinking carefully about how they saw themselves and were seen by others. Marie played

Production headshots for *Island Protected by a Bridge of Glass*.

Chapter 3: Building a Theatre, 1979–1981　　71

From *Island Protected by a Bridge of Glass*.

Gráinne, while Rebecca Bartlett (another actor new to Galway, having recently arrived from Belfast) took on the role of Elizabeth. They were joined by the four men in the Druid company (Seán, Maelíosa, Paul and Ray) and by two other newcomers, Mike Williams and Peter Lawson.

The theatrical style of *Island* showed many traces of the company's earlier innovations, up to and including *The Threepenny Opera*. The male actors were dressed uniformly, so their shift from character to character required the audience to use their imagination, showing them that this was not a representation of 'real life' but a deliberate act of theatricality that needed to be actively interpreted, not passively consumed. The actors sometimes made eye contact with their audiences, sometimes even speaking directly to them – not just breaking the fourth wall but blurring the boundaries between the past on stage and the present in the auditorium. And they moved with a fluidity and elegance that was sometimes like dance, and sometimes almost ritualistic (the show was jointly choreographed by Ray and Garry).

Rebecca Bartlett later remembered Ray's contributions as giving the production a 'multi-dimensionality' that allowed the audience to engage not only with the text but with the whole theatrical experience: 'It was elemental,' she said. 'There was a primal quality about it that came out of the music but also came out of Ray's dances. It gave it an energy that infused the whole performance.' That mood of strangeness was both heightened and focused by the production's inclusion of the Irish folk group Dé Dannan, who composed and performed music for it. Thus, the overall experience was more like a dream than a history play, which Druid emphasized by calling it 'a fantasy' in the publicity materials.

Audiences in Galway had been exceptionally enthusiastic about *Island* when it had opened at the Druid Lane Theatre in May 1980, but bringing it to Edinburgh was a very bold choice. Galwegians knew the story of Gráinne Mhaol, so they didn't need help with the context – but would the same be true in front of an international audience? Similarly, the music of Dé Dannan had been increasing in popularity across Ireland since they'd formed in Galway in 1975, but they were popular because they were playing folk music in new ways. Would they seem *too* innovative outside of that Irish context?

And there was a similar risk for Druid itself. One of the reasons they were so popular in Ireland was because they were making old plays seem new again, defying expectations not by ignoring the past but by remaking it. But in order to understand how Druid were breaking new ground, it was necessary to know something *about* the history that was being remade. Put simply, would *An Island Protected by a Bridge of Glass* make sense to anyone outside Galway?

Druid's Edinburgh Fringe booklet, 1980.

The answer to those questions came quickly and resoundingly. Press coverage from the British newspapers was extraordinarily positive, and by the end of the week Garry found herself accepting a Fringe First award from Dame Peggy Ashcroft, for *Island* and *The Pursuit of Pleasure*. That award led to celebrations in Galway – and to widespread national coverage too, with Druid's achievement being characterized as a win for Ireland in its entirety.

Those artistic successes can and must be explained by the excellence of the artists themselves, of course: by Garry's direction, by the skill and cohesion of the ensemble, by the strength of the writing and so on. But it's hard to imagine how Druid's first visit to

Edinburgh would have gone without the work of Jerome Hynes. He played a huge role in getting the company to Scotland, and then in making sure they were noticed once they had arrived. He'd been centrally involved in raising money before the tour – there was a grant from the Department of Foreign Affairs and sponsorship from Sealink, the operator of a ferry from Ireland to Britain. But once in Scotland he seemed unstoppable, approaching any journalist he could find, organizing a reception for a visiting dignitary (helpfully sponsored by Guinness), and producing as a press pack a handsomely illustrated twelve-page booklet that carefully shaped journalists' awareness and understanding of the company and their plays. The beauty of the booklet as a physical object remains striking to this day (there are several copies of it in the Druid Archive at the University of Galway), but its influence on the critical reception of the work can be seen in the fact that much of its text was directly integrated into reviews and other press coverage.

And of course Druid's triumph was noticed in Dublin too. An invitation to the Abbey Theatre soon followed, with *Bar and Ger* and *Island Protected by a Bridge of Glass* being presented on its Peacock stage in 1981.

On 23 September 1980, shortly after Garry returned from the Edinburgh Fringe, she travelled to Derry for the opening night of a new play by Brian Friel, called *Translations*.

At that time she'd been thinking a lot about both her work as a director and the future direction of Druid – and how both were intertwined.

For the first few years, the Druid name usually referred to work that was made by Garry and Marie – and initially with Mick too, of course. But now that word also referred to a venue, and it had suddenly become possible to imagine Druid shows being directed and performed by other people. What might that mean in practice?

The only way to find out was by letting more people in to do the work.

The first time there had been a Druid production *not* directed by Garry had been in the winter of 1979, when Loretta Kelly did *Eternal Triangle*, an adaptation of a Frank O'Connor short story by the American writer Paul Avila Mayer. The show had gone quite well – no one loved it, but no one hated it either, and because it was an Irish story being reimagined by an American dramatist, it confirmed that it was possible for other directors to make work that aligned with what the company had done before.

But from 1980 onwards, Maelíosa started to show an interest in, and a talent for, directing – and Garry was happy to let him at it from time to time. In 1980, he presented a one-act drama called *Sundance* by Meir Ribalow, thus showing that, like Garry, he too had an interest in contemporary American playwriting. And he also began to explore his own interests more. He directed Frederick Knott's *Dial M For Murder* in 1981, in a production that was designed as if it were a black-and-white film – matching the mood of the thrillers that the company had grown up watching on their monochrome TVs (they were all surprised to learn that the original movie had actually been made in colour), but also showing impressive theatrical inventiveness with the lighting, set and costumes. Druid, it was apparent, was able to stretch itself and to evolve, but without losing its core identity.

And there was no better example of that than the ongoing success of Mick Lally. He'd left Druid in 1977 and, while keeping a link with the company, had prospered in Dublin – so much so that he'd been cast in Friel's *Translations*, alongside actors like

Dial M For Murder, 1981.

Ray McAnally, Liam Neeson and Stephen Rea. Neeson and Rea would later go on to have major international profiles (both were nominated for Oscars in the early 1990s), but by 1980 they were already highly regarded in Ireland. McAnally likewise would find a measure of international fame a little later, when he appeared in feature films such as *The Mission* in 1986 and *My Left Foot* in 1989, but he too was immensely respected in Ireland in 1980, as an actor on stage and TV. So even before *Translations* opened, it was being widely said that it featured one of the most impressive Irish casts ever assembled. Mick was a key part of that, just five years after he'd quit his job as a teacher to found Druid.

Garry must also have thought – if only to herself initially – that by premiering a major new play in Derry, Friel was proving something that Druid had been asserting resolutely during the previous five years: that Irish theatre didn't have to happen only in Dublin or Belfast, but that it could be made and staged anywhere on the island. At a time when to speak of an 'Irish audience' was often to describe a Dublin audience, Friel was showing how a theatre for the nation needed to engage with audiences across the nation. Druid had been making the same case.

Friel's thinking was of course deeply political, and was conceived as a direct response to the Troubles. By 1980, that conflict had been underway for more than a decade and had already resulted in more than 2,000 deaths. Some of its victims were members of the army or police, such as Ernest Johnston, an off-duty reservist with the Royal Ulster Constabulary (RUC), who was killed by the IRA in County Fermanagh on the very night that *Translations* premiered. But most were civilians, such as Michael Donnelly, a 21-year-old Catholic from Belfast who had been shot by the British Army in Belfast the previous month, August 1980.

Friel's hope in writing *Translations* was to show that it might be possible for all sides in the conflict – Catholic and Protestant, Irish and British, nationalist and unionist – to imagine new ways of expressing and asserting their identity, their sense of home and belonging, and their ties to the past. He did that by setting the play in the 1830s, at a time when Irish placenames were being 'translated' by the British Ordnance Survey and the British Army, thereby hastening the country's transition from being predominantly Irish-speaking into becoming mostly Anglophone. *Translations* states unambiguously that the loss of Irish was a tragedy – but because the play itself is performed in the English language, it illustrated that the Irish people could change yet still be Irish. And if it was possible to change in the 1830s, perhaps it might be possible to change in the 1980s too, Friel implied.

That plot was given real political power by the decision to stage the play in Derry's Guildhall – which was not a theatre but the home of that city's local government, and therefore a symbol of the unionist domination over Derry's Catholic majority. Because his newly founded company Field Day had presented their play in so contested a place, Friel was showing that physical spaces like the Guildhall could also be 'translated', that a symbol of dominance could become a symbol of unity, shared purpose and a desire for peace. The fact that his plans were carried out with the full support of the city's unionist Lord Mayor was an inspirational illustration of how theatre could create space for new possibilities.

So as *Translations* completed its first performance on that opening night, and as Garry started thinking about the long journey back from Derry to Galway, it was obvious to her and to everyone else in the Guildhall that the Irish theatre had just entered a new era.

The staging of *Translations* in Derry was an indication that theatre could bring about change, that it could resist the catastrophic – not just in what it said but also in where and when it said it. Garry already knew that, of course: she'd seen firsthand how dramas like Synge's *Playboy* meant different things when performed in different places, and her programming choices had used international dramas to open up conversations that needed to happen in Ireland.

But with a new decade beginning, there was so much more now to be said. The Troubles were a national catastrophe – but there were other looming disasters. The Irish economy was deteriorating rapidly, with businesses closing and emigration on the rise again. The advances towards equality made by Irish women in the early 1970s were being resisted and in some cases rolled back, and the discrimination long suffered by gay Irish people showed no signs of being alleviated. Also, although

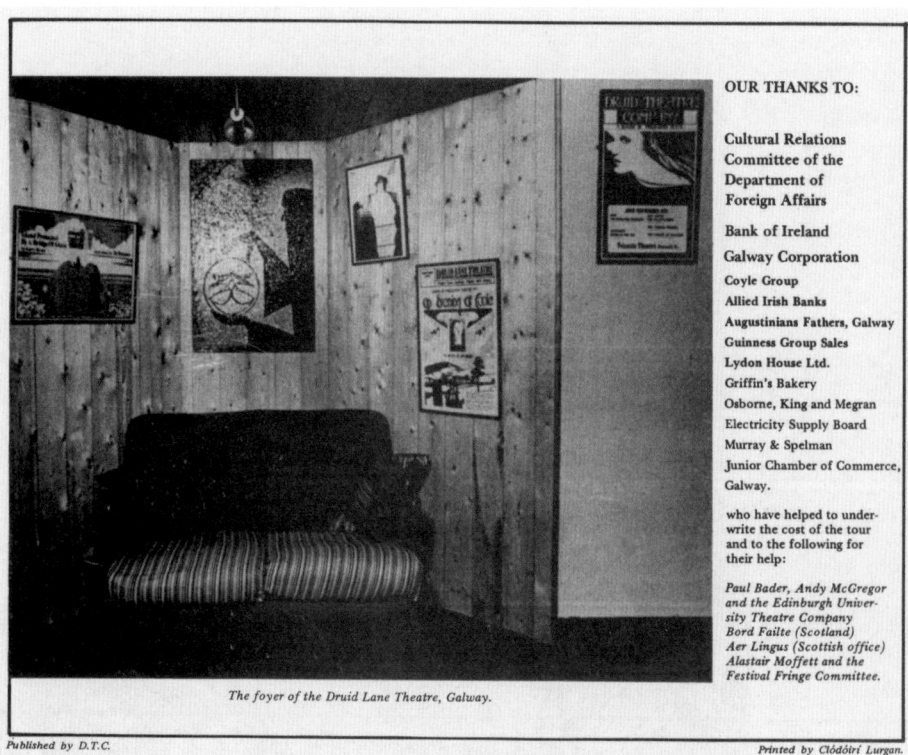

The foyer of the Druid Lane Theatre, Galway.

Edinburgh Fringe programme, 1980.

censorship was no longer formally being imposed upon artists, it was still difficult for many to express themselves freely and fully, whether on the stage, in their workplaces or in the national media.

The shape of the new decade was starting to come into focus, and a different kind of Irish theatre was emerging to face it. Garry knew that Druid would have new opportunities, but she also knew that they would face new challenges – and that they would have to shoulder new responsibilities too.

The Druid company on their way to Inis Meáin.

Chapter 4
Unusual Rural Tours, 1982–1984

IN THE EARLY years of the twentieth century, before he became a famous playwright, John Millington Synge was told a story by the oldest living person on Inis Meáin:

> He often tells me about a Connaught man who killed his father with the blow of a spade when he was in passion, and then fled to this island and threw himself on the mercy of some of the natives with whom he was said to be related. They hid him in a hole—which the old man has shown me—and kept him safe for weeks, though the police came and searched for him, and he could hear their boots grinding on the stones over his head. In spite of a reward which was offered, the island was incorruptible, and after much trouble the man was safely shipped to America.

Synge found that anecdote fascinating, and wondered why the people of the west of Ireland felt such a strong compulsion to protect criminals:

> It seems partly due to the association between justice and the hated English jurisdiction, but more directly to the

primitive feeling of these people, who are never criminals yet always capable of crime, that a man will not do wrong unless he is under the influence of a passion which is as irresponsible as a storm on the sea. If a man has killed his father, and is already sick and broken with remorse, they can see no reason why he should be dragged away and killed by the law. Such a man, they say, will be quiet all the rest of his life, and if you suggest that punishment is needed as an example, they ask, 'Would any one kill his father if he was able to help it?'

Inspired by those insights, Synge went on to write his greatest play, *The Playboy of the Western World*, in which Christy Mahon shows up at a Mayo shebeen, claiming to have killed his father while 'under the influence of a passion'. 'He was a dirty man, God forgive him,' Synge has Christy say:

> and he getting old and crusty, the way I couldn't put up with him at all ... I just riz the loy and let fall the edge of it on the ridge of his skull, and he went down at my feet like an empty sack, and never let a grunt or groan from him at all.

Like the islanders on Inis Meáin who had proven 'incorruptible' when faced with the choice between hiding the man and handing him over to the 'hated English jurisdiction', the villagers in the play feel no need to call for Christy to be tried for murder. Rather than being scandalized or morally affronted, they're actually impressed by him, celebrating him as a hero and encouraging his courtship of Pegeen. Until, that is, the 'dead' father shows up again – at which point the story turns in a direction that is entirely of Synge's own invention.

The play caused riots in Dublin in 1907, but when it had been presented in the west of Ireland itself it was usually received

Arriving on Inis Meáin.

quite warmly. Throughout the twentieth century, it had been staged in visiting professional productions in Galway City, and had also been performed in an Irish translation as *An Buachaill Báire an Domhain Thiar*, by Seán Ó Carra, at An Taibhdhearc in 1973. It was also quite well known in the rural areas of Galway, Mayo and Roscommon – partly due to its inclusion on the school curriculum, but also from performances by local amateur groups.

But when Garry returned her attention to Synge again in the early 1980s, she realized that the play had never been done in the Aran Islands themselves. What would it mean to take *The Playboy* back to the place that had inspired Synge to write it? Would the people there recognize it as part of their own culture – or would it instead feel like a caricature, or maybe even as an appropriation or a kind of theft? Druid thought it was time to answer that question, and so, in 1982, they boarded a boat to make their way to Inis Meáin.

Druid's 1982 *Playboy* has now become legendary, and is considered by many to be the definitive production of that play. It opened in Galway in August and, in a sign of the company's increased stature, it then embarked upon a four-month tour that included several major venues. There was a return visit to Edinburgh, a slot in the Dublin Theatre Festival (where they performed for a week in the 1,200-seat Olympia Theatre), two nights at Derry's Guildhall (where *Translations* had premiered two years earlier), and visits to Sligo, Cork and Belfast. Their tour therefore included performances in each of Ireland's four provinces, and was seen by the biggest audience they'd had up to that point.

And yet, when they were asked years later what they remembered most from those months on the road, almost everyone gave the same surprising answer. They'd enjoyed performing before those huge crowds in those well-equipped venues, they said: it was certainly gratifying to be hailed as a success for a second time in Edinburgh, to play in one of Dublin's biggest venues and to go across the border into Northern Ireland for the first time. But the really special nights had been on the Aran Islands, especially on 19 October on Inis Meáin.

Video footage from that trip shows that everyone in the company was excited about the prospect of performing there, but it's also obvious that they were starting to feel apprehensive as the time for the performance drew nearer. Those feelings had probably been intensified by a very rough journey across Galway Bay, which meant that they had to unpack their set and equipment quickly, while managing the lingering effects of seasickness.

But of course the weight of expectation was a factor too. Upon their arrival on Inis Meáin, Jerome had been told that about 150 people were expected to the island's town hall to see the show.

That was good news ('a full house!') but also worrying because it was far more people than the space could accommodate.

As everyone raced to get the set and equipment from the harbour to the hall, an RTÉ film crew started interviewing some of the actors. Maelíosa was asked how he was feeling about the prospect of playing Christy that night. 'I'm very nervous about it, myself,' he admitted. 'I think they will like it … but it could go the other way.' He quickly shook himself back into a positive frame of mind: 'But I'm really looking forward to it,' he concluded, with a smile that suggested that he'd almost persuaded himself that he really felt that way.

Also interviewed was Bairbre Ní Chaoimh, who had just joined the company and was playing the role of Sara Tansey. Showing the perceptiveness that would later help her to forge a career as an award-winning director, she spoke thoughtfully about what might happen later that night:

> With other theatre audiences, people have criticized us from an artistic point of view or have been surprised with how naturalistic the thing is. But here we're going to have a much more gut reaction from people; they're going to be much more critical in some ways because they're going to expect it to be very real.

Mick Lally was there too, having returned to the company for the first time since 1977 to play the part of Old Mahon, the 'dead' father whose reappearance causes Christy to lose his heroic status amongst the Mayo villagers. 'This is the first time *The Playboy's* ever been seen on the island,' he told the film crew. 'It's bringing it back to its own cradle, and I'm sure they're going to like it.' In the video footage of that interview, there is a lot of bustling and rushing going on behind Mick as he talks – but he himself doesn't seem very stressed about anything.

That confidence probably arose to some extent from Mick's personal disposition, but it had undoubtedly been boosted by his connections to the island, through his wife Peig. He'd come out a few days before the rest of the company, and had been staying with Peig's family, with whom he was very close – so he could therefore gauge the islanders' likely reactions from direct personal knowledge: this to Mick was not an abstract 'audience', but a group of people whom he knew both as individuals and as a community.

Sadly, Peig herself had to stay in Dublin because their second child was too young to travel with them at that time (though she heard a great deal about the performance during the months and years ahead, both from Mick and from her family). She too had felt sure beforehand that the performance would go well. Inis Meáin and Inis Oirr were relatively underdeveloped in the early 1980s – 'we had electricity but that was about all,' Peig recalled – but she knew that the community there would have no trouble engaging with the play, even though it was being performed in English rather than Irish. The islanders were becoming more used to people speaking in English, Peig explained: 'they didn't feel confident about speaking it back themselves, but they could understand it'. And in any case, she also assumed that the acting would be strong enough to communicate anything that might be lost in translation.

So she wasn't surprised when Mick told her that it had been a great success. 'He said it was fantastic,' she recalled. 'Mick was quite taken because the islanders came and spoke to them afterwards,' explaining what they'd liked about the show, discussing the characters' motivations and decisions, and sharing local stories about Synge's time there. One islander had even approached Mick to try to persuade Druid to perform for a second night. 'That was a powerful play,' the man had said, 'and if you do it again you'll get an even bigger audience,' he promised. Mick explained that it wouldn't be possible for them to stay, but that they'd do their best to come back again.

Chapter 4: Unusual Rural Tours, 1982–1984   87

Talking about *The Playboy*, Inis Meáin, 1982.

Marie too would remember the performance on Inis Meáin as an extraordinary night, both in her company's history and in her own professional life:

> The audience had a completely different reaction to the play than anyone else did – they didn't laugh at the same places, and they talked to each other about what was happening as the story was unfolding. But they were completely enthralled.

She attributed those reactions to several different causes, one being that Synge had lived among the islanders: he was remembered by the islanders as someone who had actually

The audience on Inis Meáin.

been there, as someone who had written about their home with respect and affection. It probably helped in that context that Druid had brought their production there in October, long after the islands' nascent tourist season had concluded. By choosing that time, they were making clear that the performance was for the islanders, and only for them.

Marie also admired how freely the audience there had laughed at the many jokes in the play about the local priest (or the 'priesteen', as one of the characters calls him, using the Irish diminutive). 'They had a very healthy disrespect for the Catholic Church,' Marie thought, and that helped them to connect with a drama that she herself had always seen as 'a very pagan play'. And so that night Druid began a relationship with the people of the Aran Islands, and especially with Inis Meáin – which, during the years ahead, would become one of the company's most beloved homes away from home. That performance brought

Chapter 4: Unusual Rural Tours, 1982–1984 89

Druid's poster for
The Playboy, 1982.

something new to their understanding of *The Playboy* – and that new knowledge would also stay with them for many years to come.

Having produced the play twice already, by 1982 Druid at last felt that they were properly coming to terms with *The Playboy*. Garry had thought that their first production, in 1975, had reflected a shared sense of innocence in the company. They were responding to the text and the characters they were playing, she thought – but they hadn't understood how the play worked in its entirety.

That began to change when they returned to it in 1977; Garry was starting to see how the characters' reactions to each other had consequences that reverberated unpredictably into the rest of the action. This made it exciting for her to work on the play as a director – but there was often the uneasy, niggling possibility that she could have chosen a different pathway through the action, maybe even a better one.

Speaking to RTÉ during the summer of 1982, she explained how the play had come to have an almost hypnotic attractiveness for her:

> We're discovering the resonances of the play extend very wide indeed; that, each time you do a scene, there are other ways to interpret it that suggest other things – that it's possible to constantly explore the play. I haven't really found this with any other play in quite the same way.

Druid were constantly finding new levels in Synge's work; every performance of it was not a repetition of something that they had already done but a discovery of something new. This was exhilarating, but also occasionally unsettling, because it raised the question of how to do justice to a play that doesn't ever fully reveal itself in the way most other plays do.

Marie shared that excitement, and was also finding new things in the play herself. That sense of fresh discovery was partly due to the simple fact that she was performing in a new role, having shifted from playing Pegeen in 1975 to the Widow Quin in 1977. 'I wasn't a natural Pegeen; I know that now,' she admitted years later; but she had loved playing the part opposite Mick in 1975:

> Pegeen falls headlong in love with this guy; it's beautiful what happens to her. So I loved the words, and I loved

Marie as the Widow Quin, 1982.

her predicament, and I was as honest a Pegeen as I could possibly be. And I don't think I let the production down. But I wasn't a shining Pegeen. She just didn't come together for me.

But the part of the Widow Quin really did 'come together' for Marie, and has since come to be seen as one of her greatest performances. One reason for that success is that she and Garry made the decision to play the character as Synge had written her – as a young woman, aged roughly thirty, who is both sexually and economically powerful. In Ireland, she had almost never been played that way: from the 1930s onwards, she had been presented as a comic figure, usually as a woman in her fifties who is so much older than the two central characters that her pursuit of Christy seems ridiculous, if not a little pathetic.

That interpretation of the character was so pervasive that Druid had presented the Widow Quin that way themselves when they first did the play in 1975, with Mairead Noone playing the part. 'Mairead was brilliant in the role,' Marie recalls, saying that the audience had found her performance hilarious. But when Druid looked back on that production, they knew that they had chosen to meet the audience's expectations rather than grappling fully with Synge's portrayal of the character.

But now Garry and Marie had determined that Widow Quin needed to be Pegeen's equal: the audience needed to believe fully in the possibility that Christy could choose her instead. In Marie's performance, the Widow Quin had what she thought of as 'a savage kind of sexuality' – and she therefore loved playing the role:

> I was a rival to Pegeen; I was something to be looked at. She was a handsome woman and she had a great freedom about her. She had a swagger.

That meant that Christy was genuinely taken with her, impressed by her exuberance and her freedom. It also meant that when Old Mahon shows up, he too was attracted to the character – which meant that the dynamic Marie and Mick had established in 1975 as Pegeen and Christy could now shift forward into their performances as the Widow Quin and Old Mahon in 1982.

That approach to the character was true to Synge's intentions – but it also added huge emotional force to the Druid production, illustrating the truth of Garry's observation about the play's many possible 'resonances'. By rejecting a woman as impressive as the Widow Quin, Christy is showing that his love for Pegeen is enormous. His choice therefore elevates the play's central love story to such an extent that the ultimate separation of the two characters feels guttingly tragic – an emotional impact that was

Chapter 4: Unusual Rural Tours, 1982–1984

Bríd Brennan as Pegeen, 1982.

heightened by the controlled intensity of Maelíosa as Christy and Bríd Brennan as Pegeen. 'Our approach served the story so well,' Marie observed. 'But it was just devastating playing it.' She had to give life to that swaggering, handsome woman – and then had to show her being rejected.

Having returned to the company, Mick too was finding new things to admire in the play, appreciating in particular how Druid were pushing back against the idea (then still pervasive in Ireland) that Synge had romanticized the west of Ireland. For Mick, Synge 'didn't set out to show the loveliness of Ireland at all', but instead saw it as a place of 'suppressed savagery'.

In interviews at the time, Mick recalled how violence could often burst free unexpectedly in rural Irish life: 'As a child I remember fights every fair day [at Toormakeady] and people going around with blood from getting a crack – and not from a loy – but from a fist or maybe sometimes a bottle,' he said. Synge's play is unsparing and unsentimental in its representation of this aspect of Irish life. 'There are no nice characters in it,' Mick asserted – and it was time for audiences in Ireland to start facing that fact.

So by 1982, Druid knew that it would be wrong to present *The Playboy* as if it were a realistic drama, like something written by an Ibsen or a Chekhov: the language was too heightened, the humour too cutting, the subtext too unsettling. But nor was it a fantasy or a romance; it was rooted in a world that everyone in Druid recognized from their own experiences of life in the west.

So, as an ensemble, they had to find and occupy the space between all those extremes. They had to make sure that the play felt emotionally authentic, but that it was not misunderstood as a faithful recreation of a 'real world' that real people might have lived in. The spoken words had to sound natural without neglecting Synge's elevation of the language – his poetry, his artistry. And they had to be truthful about the violence in the play, but they also were determined to ensure that the beauty of Pegeen's love for Christy would be given full expression.

The trip to Inis Meáin with *The Playboy* had given Druid a lot to think about. One of the discoveries that particularly fascinated them was the authenticity of the reactions they'd experienced there – and they were also preoccupied with the question of why those reactions had differed from the responses in other places on the tour.

Those differences weren't necessarily huge. Audiences everywhere had responded to the core features of the work in much the same way, loving its humour, the beauty of its language and its vivacious characterization, especially of the women. But there were subtle variations from place to place. It wasn't that audiences on the Aran Islands had 'correctly' interpreted Synge's play while audiences in Dublin or Edinburgh had been wrong – or vice versa. Rather, Druid were starting to understand how taking a play to various places could expand its possible meanings. In Inis Meáin and in Dublin, *The Playboy* had meant slightly different things, but both responses were equally valid and equally true.

That realization opened up the possibility of rethinking what it meant to make theatre in Ireland, and for Ireland. The tendency in the country up to that time – as was true in most other places in western Europe – was to think of the national theatrical culture as working with a centralized core (usually the national capital) and a regional periphery. That model brought with it a set of other assumptions: that metropolitan audiences would be more sophisticated than people in the regions, that professional work happened at the centre while the regions tended to be more 'amateur', that work considered 'national' was inherently better than work described as 'regional', and that professional success for theatre artists required them to move gradually from peripheral spaces (like Galway) to the core (in Ireland's case, Dublin).

Druid had been pushing against those assumptions from the beginning anyway, and now that Field Day were touring Ireland too, they were no longer alone in making that case.

But as Druid moved into the 1980s, the question of what it meant to be an Irish theatre was becoming more of a preoccupation. By bringing *Island Protected by a Bridge of Glass* to Edinburgh a year before they brought it to Dublin, Druid had shown that a supposedly 'regional' company could represent Irish theatre on an international stage without first obtaining permission or endorsement from the national capital. That wasn't to express anything negative about Dublin: Druid had been delighted to bring *The Playboy* to the Olympia and also appreciated greatly the support of Dublin-based people such as Joe Dowling, who was then Artistic Director of the Abbey Theatre, and Arthur Lappin at the Arts Council. But they were increasingly uncomfortable with the widely held assumption that artistic success in Dublin was inherently more important than success in any other parts of the country.

So they started thinking more about what it might mean to integrate touring more fully into their activities – by going not just to cities like Dublin and Edinburgh, but also to towns across Ireland. They came to call these visits 'Unusual Rural Tours' – or 'URTs' for short.

Perhaps because they didn't have a venue of their own for many years, Druid had learned early on to be nimble. They first performed outside Galway City as early as 1976, when Garry drove Mick and Marie to a school hall in Athenry (then a small town, about 23 km to the east of Galway) to perform an English play called *An Entertainment on a Marriage*, by David Campion and James Saunders. They also occasionally brought work to Tuam during the same period.

But especially after their success in Edinburgh in 1980, new invitations were coming in all the time. In a sign of how admired they had become, both in the west of Ireland and nationally, they were invited to bring one of their productions to inaugurate the opening of a new theatre in Sligo in January 1982 – the name of which, the Hawk's Well Theatre, was taken from the title of a play by William Butler Yeats. The formal opening of the theatre was to be carried out by the then-President of Ireland, Patrick Hillery – and his speech would be followed by a performance of a Druid show.

Chapter 4: Unusual Rural Tours, 1982–1984

Much Ado About Nothing, 1981–1982.

A theatregoer in Sligo at that time might have predicted that Druid would mark that occasion by staging one of Yeats's plays – they had already done *The Pot of Broth* and *Purgatory* in Galway, so there was a track record of other Yeats productions for them to draw from. Or if not something by Yeats then perhaps a celebration of the artists he'd promoted and defended: Synge, of course – but also O'Casey, Gregory and countless others.

But, just as Druid had done the unexpected thing by staging Brecht at the opening of the Druid Lane Theatre in 1979, they marked the opening of the Hawk's Well by doing something that no one would have predicted: they didn't stage Yeats but instead presented *Much Ado About Nothing* by William Shakespeare. There was an attractive symmetry to this choice: this would be a play by England's great poet in a theatre named after a work by Ireland's great poet. But Druid were also tapping into a long history of Shakespearean performance in rural and provincial Ireland, dating back to (at least) the 1830s, when touring companies and artists performed Shakespeare in places like Galway, Sligo and Castlebar. Older people across the west of Ireland would also have seen Shakespeare regularly, most often in one of the fit-up companies that the English director Anew McMaster had brought around Ireland from the 1920s to the 1960s.

Druid also wanted to challenge the idea that an Irish theatre company should not be staging Shakespeare. Speaking to the *Evening Press* about the play in the winter of 1981, Garry explained their thinking. 'We were all agreed,' she said, 'that if we did a Shakespeare we wouldn't do it in an Elizabethan setting' but would instead present it in a 'parallel society which would mean something to our audiences'.

That parallel society would be nineteenth-century Ireland, they decided. The action would be set in a regional town (much like Sligo) and the characters would be taken from the local Anglo-Irish gentry (the kinds of people whom Yeats liked to associate himself with when he wrote about his Sligo childhood). The names would be unchanged and the language was left mostly intact, so Druid were not really adapting Shakespeare, but were instead showing that he could easily be nudged into a west of Ireland context so that, as Garry had promised, 'it would mean something' specific to their audiences. By doing that, Druid were showing that relevance to a specific place did not have to be direct or literal; it could instead be suggestive, relying on audiences to find the meaning themselves.

Perhaps more importantly, Druid also understood that *Much Ado* is one of Shakespeare's funniest plays – and they therefore trusted the text to bring the comedy to the fore. Marie had a great time playing the part of Beatrice alongside Mike Williams, who played her arch-enemy-turned-true-love Benedick. Garry also showed a willingness to play around with gender (something she'd return to when she staged Shakespeare again) by casting Rebecca Bartlett as Antonia (not the male Antonio that the script calls for), and she also gave the acting company an opportunity to demonstrate its versatility by asking some of them to play multiple roles – indeed, Seán McGinley played three different parts.

The production of *Much Ado* would also prove to be an important moment in the development of Garry's own artistic practice. The success of *Island Protected by a Bridge of Glass* had prompted people both within and outside Druid to ask her when she might write another play. She would usually push back against those questions, saying that she hadn't really written it, that it was a collaboration – and that she didn't see herself as a playwright anyway. Her work on *Much Ado* demonstrated that direction too could be a form of authorship. That didn't mean that Garry had rewritten Shakespeare (she hadn't) but rather that she was literally re-presenting his work, holding it up to new scrutiny, making it feel as if *Much Ado* was a brand-new play. The work she had done in *The Pursuit of Pleasure* and *Island* had been greatly admired, but from 1982 onwards she had firmly chosen her path forward: as a director.

And it all worked brilliantly; *Much Ado* was a huge hit in Sligo, and was revived in Galway in 1982 too.

By the following year, 1983, Druid were ready to think about touring to places that, unlike the Hawk's Well, were not necessarily set up for professional theatre. They had chosen a play, *The Wood* of the Whispering by M.J. Molloy. And they also knew where they wanted to go. They would head back to the Aran Islands, to both Inis Meáin and Inis Oirr; and they would return to Dublin for the Theatre Festival too. But they were also going to embark on a tour that would take them most of the way down the west coast of Ireland, and largely to places they had never been before – from Ballyshannon and Ballybofey in Donegal; to Westport in Mayo; to Clifden, Milltown and Rosaveel in rural Galway; and to Lisdoonvarna in County Clare.

As Druid's publicity material from that time explained, they had deliberately chosen to perform in those places because they were among the least populated parts of the country. That decision was partly an expression of the company's commitment to public service: they wanted to bring theatre to people who wouldn't see it otherwise, because that was just a good thing to do.

But the decision was also a direct response to the crisis of emigration from Ireland, which had largely stopped in the 1970s but by 1983 was increasing again, soon to become frightening in its intensity.

As had happened during the last major wave of emigration, in the 1950s, most of the people who were leaving Ireland in the 1980s were relatively young. And although they migrated from every part of the island, the impact of their departure was felt with particular severity across the small towns of the western seaboard, many of which were not just emptying but in danger of dying altogether.

In that context, the simple act of going to a place that so many people were leaving was important – but so too was Druid's choice of play, because Molloy's *The Wood of the Whispering* was itself about the causes and consequences of Irish emigration.

M.J. Molloy had been born in 1914 in Milltown in north Galway – close to the county border with Mayo and thus very much part of the imaginative territory that Druid were making

The Wood of the Whispering.

their own. The Abbey Theatre staged many of his plays from the 1940s onwards, and although he was more than once on the verge of breaking through to international success, he never quite achieved it – his 1948 play *The King of Friday's Men*, for example, made it to Broadway in 1951, but then closed after only four performances.

The Wood of the Whispering appeared shortly after that setback, premiering at the Abbey in 1953. Molloy would later tell Garry and Marie that he'd hoped that the play might bring in enough money to allow him to marry a woman he'd been engaged to at that time – but the production did only moderately well, and the marriage could not go ahead. He continued to write for most of the rest of his life (he died in 1994), but from the 1960s onwards, his plays were rarely produced professionally.

Those personal contexts might explain the play's strange blend of optimism and despair. It's set in the 1950s and dramatizes the life of a west of Ireland village that is on the verge of abandonment due to poverty and emigration. At its centre is a farmer called Sanbatch who has fallen on hard times but who hopes to revitalize his community by encouraging its youngest members to stay in Ireland, marry each other and repopulate the countryside. Sanbatch also cares for an older woman called Sadie, who was too poor to marry the man she loved and had withdrawn from society and become mute (a situation that would discreetly echo events in Molloy's own life).

There is also a lively blend of supporting characters, including a pair of older bachelors whose bizarre comic interplay coincidentally but intriguingly resembles the characters of Didi and Gogo in Samuel Beckett's *Waiting for Godot*, which at that time was still a couple of years away from its Irish premiere.

The play ends happily, with several marriages ready to take place. But it would be wrong to see it as a comedy along the lines that Shakespeare had laid out in *Much Ado About Nothing*. Molloy wasn't trying to follow the formal rules of theatre, and he wasn't writing a realistic play with a sense of documentary accuracy. Rather, *The Wood of the Whispering* is more like a folk drama, a fable that performs a community back to itself in ways that highlight problems and present new possibilities. Those features were much closer to the oral and vernacular traditions of rural Ireland – which meant that the play was not properly appreciated in its first productions at the Abbey, where it was instead performed in a style of realism that made the comedy feel too broad, and the ending too simplistic. The problem was not that the play was bad, but that it had been misunderstood.

When the Druid company read it, though, they felt that they did understand it. Maelíosa would later say that *The Wood of the Whispering* 'really spoke to us', that it felt like a presentation of a

Mick in *The Wood of the Whispering*, 1983.

world they knew intimately, both emotionally and geographically. Garry agreed: the characters 'were the people of our parents' generation,' she felt. But she saw too that the terrible choice that those characters are forced to make (to leave Ireland and live well, or to stay and stagnate) was now being faced by young people across the west of Ireland, including many of their friends, family members and audience members.

So some of the company drove up to Molloy's house in Milltown to talk to him about reviving the play. He was very

Mary McEvoy in *The Wood of the Whispering*, 1983.

welcoming, offering them a glass of whiskey while they chatted. Garry explained that Druid loved the play and wanted to stage it; Molloy was delighted, and seemed ready to agree. They did want to talk about some cuts, however, said Garry – maybe the removal of some lines that mightn't work now as well as they had done in the 1950s. And maybe getting rid of some repetitions.

M.J. grew a little uncomfortable but asked what they had in mind. Garry suggested that they could start with the first line of the play and take it from there. When asked years later how Molloy responded to that suggestion, Garry's answer was succinct: 'he went bananas'.

But they resolved that problem quickly enough, and soon Druid were in rehearsals. Mick had returned to Galway again, this time in order to play the central role of Sanbatch (one of his

The Wood of the Whispering poster, 1983.

best Druid performances, people would later say). Also present, and working for the first time with Druid, was a young actor called Mary McEvoy, who had coincidentally just been cast alongside Mick in *Glenroe*, where she would play his character's girlfriend, and later wife, Biddy. The cast also included the core Druid actors – Maelíosa, Seán, Ray, and Marie were all in it. They had also hired a professional designer called Monica Frawley for the production: she worked on both the set and the costumes, and would go on to collaborate regularly with Druid in the years ahead.

The play opened in the Druid Lane Theatre in August 1983. Garry and the actors had been nervous about how Molloy might react to the changes they'd made, but they knew that their production was shaping up well, and that audiences were almost certainly going to like it. They watched Molloy as he watched their production, but found his reactions hard to gauge. Jerome decided to take him for a drink in a nearby pub so they could talk about the production privately – and, he hoped, resolve any conflicts. When Jerome came back, he told everyone that Molloy was happy enough: their production 'resembled a play that I wrote once,' he had said. The URT soon followed, and the performance of the play in Molloy's home town of Milltown showed how powerful it could be to bring a play back into contact with the place that had inspired it.

During the years ahead, the company embarked upon many similar URTs, though there was soon a semi-deliberate ambiguity in what they intended by using the word 'unusual' in their acronym. The simple explanation was that the tours were going to places in which it was 'unusual' to find professional theatre companies. But it was also soon apparent that the tours were occasions in which strange things could – and usually did – happen.

The oddness of those tours was a feature from the beginning. Garry recalls that the tour to Sligo with *Much Ado* took place during one of the coldest Irish winters in living memory – so everyone in the company was worried about getting from Galway to the Hawk's Well on time and safely.

But then, a few days before opening, they got word from Sligo that there was a problem at the venue: the newly installed lighting board wasn't working properly, and Druid would need to source an alternative one – and quickly. 'Myself and Seán McGinley got into my car,' Garry recalled, 'and we drove to a convent in Ennis, where we had tracked down a lighting board. We had brought a pickaxe, chocolate and blankets with us, because we didn't know if we'd make it there or back in the snow.' They arrived at the convent, and the nuns greeted them. 'They were wearing dressing gowns,' Garry recalled. 'I had never seen nuns in dressing gowns.' They invited Garry and Seán in for tea, gave them the lighting board, and sent them on their way back to Galway before the weather got any worse.

When they got back to the city, Garry took a phone call from Jerome, who had gone ahead earlier that day to bring several members of the crew and cast to Sligo. 'Do you want the good news or the bad news?' he asked Garry.

The good news, Jerome said, was that they had reached Sligo safely. The bad news, however, was that he was calling from the garda station in Sligo town, because a member of the crew had just been arrested for speeding.

Jerome got that problem sorted out and finally almost everyone who needed to be in Sligo had arrived. But there was one exception: Mike Williams, who was playing Benedick but whose day job was as a lecturer in Geology at UCG, had been delayed at work. He left Galway much later than everyone else, only to have his car's heater pack it in just a few minutes into the long journey northwards. The only way he could get safely to the Hawk's Well without his windows fogging up was to drive for the remaining three hours with all his windows rolled down – in subzero temperatures. 'I remember him staggering into the theatre,' Garry said. 'We had to give him brandy instantly; he was within inches of hypothermia'. But there was no question of delaying the show; the President of Ireland had arrived and was ready to give his speech. Mike just had to get warm, and then get on with it.

Another 'unusual' moment happened in Killasser in County Mayo – which, in later years, some members of the company would remember as 'the night we blew up a whole village'. Druid brought their production of Tom Murphy's *Famine* there in 1984, and shortly before it began their equipment had somehow blown out the local electrical substation, leading to a total blackout in the area. Maelíosa wasn't in that production, but in the years ahead he often spoke about what happened next with a sense of wonder:

> What I love about that story was that the show wasn't cancelled; it went on three or four hours later. Someone went to Galway to get a generator and everyone else went to the pub: cast and crew and audience.

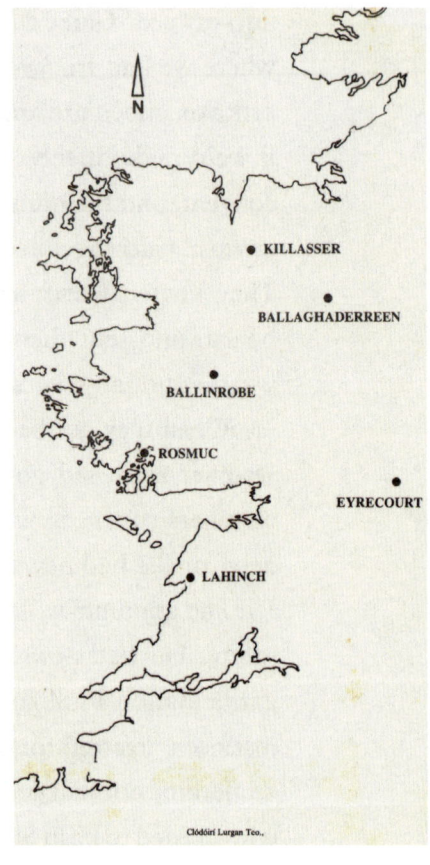

Promotional map of the URT for *Famine*, 1984.

The performance started sometime around midnight, finishing up at around 3 am. And the blackout persisted for a couple of days afterwards.

Those URTs coincided with a growing number of international tours. Druid made their London debut when *The Playboy of the Western World* was staged at the Donmar Warehouse in 1985, and also took it on tour to the Pepsico Summerfare in upstate New York in 1986 and to Sydney, Australia in 1988. In all those international locations, Druid were greeted with great admiration. The quality of the ensemble and the excellence of the direction were always mentioned, but there was also a plainly evident sense that international audiences felt that they were seeing something truly authentic, a marriage on stage between Synge's masterpiece and the places that had inspired it.

But the urban and the international always went together. In the weeks before Druid opened at the Donmar, they brought *The Playboy* on another URT, one which not only brought the company further afield than it had been before (they went to the border counties of Cavan and Leitrim, before then heading south-east into Tipperary, Carlow and Kilkenny), but which also included two nights in Garry's home town of Ballaghadereen. Opening in London for the first time was a great moment for the company, but opening in Roscommon also felt special, though of course for different reasons.

In the show programme for their first season, Garry had quoted Tennessee Williams's urgent encouragement to 'make voyages'. Throughout the 1980s, Druid were doing exactly that – building new audiences, building a reputation and finding new ways of making their work meaningful.

Tom Murphy, Galway, 1985.

Chapter 5
Tom Murphy, a Writer-in-Association,
1984–1987

IN 1958, when Tom Murphy was twenty-four, his friend Noel O'Donoghue suggested that they should write a play together. They were living in Tuam, and they didn't have much money – and they were bored – so perhaps they could try to pull something together and, if it was good enough, bring it to an amateur theatre festival?

Murphy wasn't surprised by his friend's suggestion: 'In 1958 everyone in Ireland was writing a play,' he later explained.

One of the primary reasons for that phenomenon was the existence of a thriving amateur drama scene, especially in the towns and villages outside Dublin. Amateur groups allowed people to mix with each other more than was usually possible in Ireland at that time. Men and women could meet relatively freely, and other boundaries – such as those associated with social class and (in some cases) religion – could also be set aside, if only temporarily.

They also provided an outlet for individuals who wanted to express themselves creatively but had been blocked from doing so, such as women who had been forced to quit their jobs when they had married or had children. And finally, because they so often staged plays from other countries, amateur theatre groups gave

Irish people a space to explore ideas that were not being openly spoken about in other social contexts: ideas about sexuality, belief in God, the family – even Irishness itself.

For all those reasons, Murphy was intrigued by O'Donoghue's proposal – and wondered what their play should be about. O'Donoghue didn't have any precise ideas, but he knew what he didn't want: 'One thing is fucking sure,' he declared. 'It won't be set in a kitchen.'

That was a joke, but a pointed one. O'Donoghue and Murphy didn't want to write the kind of play that was dominant on Irish stages at that time – domesticated, parochial and, in the eyes of many young people like them, overwhelmingly claustrophobic. They wanted to do something new: something bold and maybe even combative – something that would set aside the predictability of the Irish country kitchen play in order to present life as it was actually lived.

The result was *On the Outside*, a play about two young men who can't afford the entry fee into a town dancehall (and are therefore left 'on the outside'). It was successful on the amateur circuit, winning a prize at the Athlone All-Ireland festival in 1959, just as Garry and Marie would do later with *Elizabeth I*.

But, more importantly, *On the Outside* allowed Murphy to prove to himself that he could write drama, and soon he was composing another play, this time written entirely by himself, which he provisionally called *The Iron Men*. By 1961, it had been renamed *A Whistle in the Dark* and had become an enormous if controversial hit in London. That success inaugurated a professional career that would last for more than fifty years, so that, by the time of his death in 2018, Murphy had come to be regarded as one of Ireland's greatest playwrights.

So in Druid's early years, Murphy was both an idol and an emblem. He had shown – as Druid were demonstrating themselves – that building a successful career in theatre means that you have to do the work yourself rather than waiting around in the hope of being discovered by someone else. Although he had to go to London to achieve professional success, Murphy had also shown that Galway could be a starting point for a career in theatre. And, above all, he had shown that it was possible to root drama in the west of Ireland without being imprisoned or inhibited by that place. When they read his plays, Druid understood that they too could be *of* the west of Ireland but could also, when necessary, position themselves 'on the outside'.

And so when the company decided that they were ready to work with a major Irish playwright, there really was only one obvious contender.

―――――

By the mid-1980s, Druid had settled into a regular rhythm of blending Irish plays and international classics in their repertoire. Irish comedies were particularly popular. Dion Boucicault's melodrama *The Shaughraun* opened in Galway in 1982 before transferring to the Peacock in Dublin, while Richard B. Sheridan's *The Rivals* toured from Galway to Limerick, Cork, Sligo and Derry in 1983. Also a popular success was Oscar Wilde's *The Importance of Being Earnest*, in 1985 – a production that starred a young Ciarán Hinds, thus marking the first (but not the last) occasion when a Druid show featured a future Oscar nominee.

Another priority was to give Galway audiences an opportunity to see contemporary Irish plays that had already been done in Dublin. Bernard Farrell's *I Do Not Like Thee, Doctor Fell* is a dark comedy about group therapy – and it had been an unexpected hit at the Abbey when it premiered there in 1979. Druid staged their own version of it twice, in 1981 and 1988. Also in 1988, they staged their own production of Frank McGuinness's first play, *The Factory Girls*, which had premiered at the Peacock just five

The Rivals, 1982.

years earlier. They then brought that play on a tour that included visits to Glasgow and McGuinness's home town of Buncrana in Donegal, placing *The Factory Girls* and its setting into alignment with each other, just as they had already done with the plays of Synge and M.J. Molloy.

Druid were also developing a deeper relationship with Geraldine Aron. Having presented the Irish premieres of *A Galway Girl* and *Bar and Ger*, in 1984 they went one step further by giving a world premiere to *Same Old Moon*. Galway audiences instantly embraced that play – responding warmly to its funny but unblinkered presentation of west of Ireland life, and sympathizing sincerely with the characters' experiences of religion, emigration and thwarted creativity.

And more than anything, audiences loved the fact that Aron's play featured so many great roles for women. The cast had six

Programme for *Same Old Moon*, 1984.

women in it, which was very unusual at that time (and remains so now). Some were new to the company: *Same Old Moon* brought Jane Brennan to Druid for the first time, and the production also included a young Galway actor called Pauline McLynn, who a decade later would become famous for playing Mrs Doyle in the TV comedy *Father Ted*. Mairead Noone returned to Druid for the play, and it also featured Mary Ryan, Marie Mullen and Rebecca Bartlett, alongside Seán McGinley and Ray McBride. The play was revived in Galway several times during the 1980s, selling out almost every performance when it did so.

All that Irish work was impressive, but the list of international plays that Druid staged during the same period is astonishing for its range and ambition, including work by Sam Shepard, Dario Fo, John Gay, Tennessee Williams, Joe Orton and Eugene O'Neill.

Jane Brennan in *Same Old Moon*, 1984.

They also returned to Brecht in 1983, presenting *Mother Courage and Her Children* – though on that occasion, Garry brought in another director, Andy Hinds, to tackle the play. And they continued the experiments they had begun with Shakespeare's *Much Ado* by presenting another early modern play, John Ford's Jacobean tragedy *'Tis Pity She's a Whore*, which was performed in the summer of 1985 – on Druid's tenth birthday.

Ford's title was deliberately provocative when he'd first used it back in the 1620s – but it was fairly shocking in twentieth-century Galway too ('Blood, Cruelty and Lust at Druid Lane' ran one headline, not altogether approvingly). Mairead Noone recalls how in that 1985 production Garry had continued to experiment with the portrayal of gender, and she also vividly recalled its violence and theatricality:

Chapter 5: Tom Murphy, a Writer-in-Association

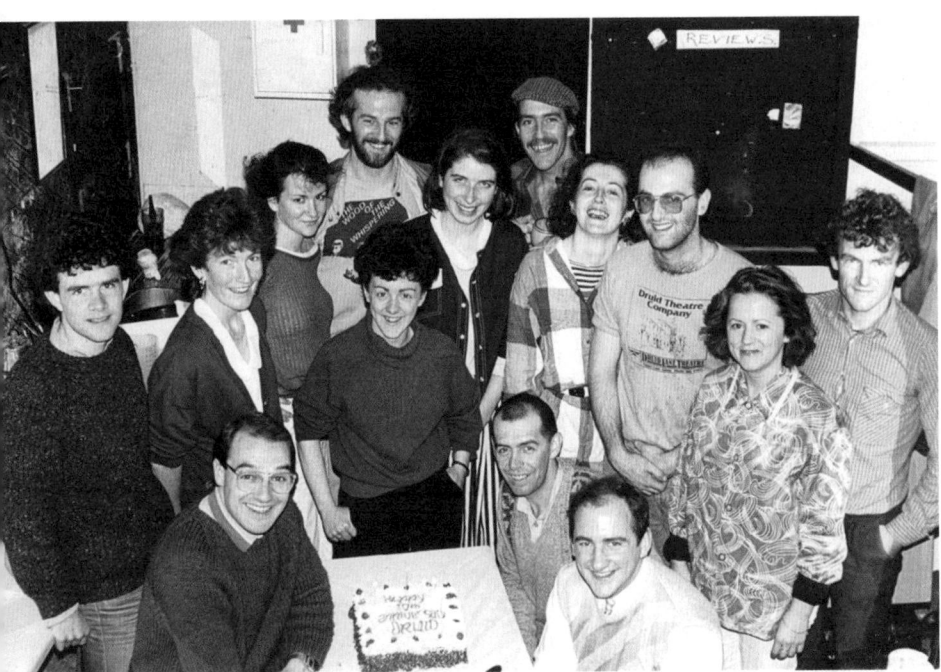

Druid's tenth birthday celebration.

There were bodies all over the place. Marie Mullen and I played two parts each and we kept running off stage to change costumes. I played a man and a woman and I think I had to do my lipstick eight times in the first act.

Jane Brennan was playing alongside Ciarán Hinds as the incestuous lovers at the centre of the play. 'Ciarán and I had no problem recreating the white heat of illicit love between Annabella and Giovanni', she later wrote, explaining that 'we had both just fallen in love – with other people' (the 'other person' Jane had just fallen in love with was Tom Murphy, as it happens). Both actors were praised in newspaper reviews, though it was Maelíosa, in the supporting role of Bergetto, who was most often singled out.

'Tis Pity was appreciated, but there wasn't much fondness for it – audiences could see its ambition but they seem to have found it heavy-going, perhaps because all those newspaper headlines about lust had channelled expectations in the wrong

direction. But when members of the company later looked back on the 1980s, many of them highlighted *'Tis Pity* as a moment when they had pushed themselves further than ever before – and had met the challenge.

The Druid company at that time rarely referred to themselves as an ensemble. But as they worked through that extraordinarily diverse range of productions, they were becoming more cohesive, and increasingly versatile too; by working together, they were learning skills and techniques that they likely wouldn't have discovered by themselves – certainly not as quickly, and maybe not at all.

Perhaps that cohesion arose because working as an ensemble can encourage generosity on stage: the actor who plays the lead role in one production knows they will probably get a supporting role in the next, and is therefore happier to share the audience's attention. And being in an ensemble also forces actors into roles that they (and their director) might not have considered themselves an obvious fit for – and that can drive them to keep learning instead of falling into habits or becoming typecast. The actors' trust in Garry was a major factor in their development, but they were also pushing each other collectively.

Added to the excellence of the acting was an increased professionalization of the technical elements of Druid productions.

Poster for *'Tis Pity She's a Whore*, 1985

Poster for the 1984 *Glass Menagerie*.

In their first years, most of the design was carried out in-house; Garry did a lot of set and lighting design, and Marie continued to work on costumes into the early 1980s. But – leaving aside that neither of them had huge expertise in those areas – the company's ever-intensifying workload meant that they needed to concentrate on what they were best at: directing and acting, respectively. And Druid's growing reputation meant that professional designers wanted to work with them now anyway.

Garry would therefore later say that a significant turning point was in 1984, when Frank Conway designed the set for a new production of *The Glass Menagerie*. Conway had trained with English National Opera and had assisted Tanya Moiseiwitsch at the Met in New York; he had also worked for almost a decade with the Abbey Theatre, designing some of the most popular productions there during that era, including the premiere of *I Do Not Like Thee, Doctor Fell*.

Druid also began to work closely and regularly with Monica Frawley: she designed *Wood of the Whispering* in 1983 and *Same Old Moon* in 1984. Working with Conway and Frawley was a firm statement by the company that they wanted the technical aspects of their productions to be held to the highest standards.

So as Druid approached the end of its first decade, they had a sense of pride for all that they had accomplished – but they were also starting to sense that they had been getting ready for something bigger.

'We wanted to do new work,' Garry would later explain. 'We wanted to be involved in the process of creating an entirely new play because we knew we had a lot to learn.' They were getting regular submissions of scripts in the post, but the majority were not suitable for one reason or another: they were too big, or too bad, or just not the kind of thing that Druid would ever want to do. But instead of working with a novice writer, perhaps they could be more ambitious, Garry thought – why not try to collaborate with someone who had already established a major career, in Ireland and internationally?

The idea of working with Murphy was soon being discussed as a real possibility. Garry had been reading his work since she first began making theatre, and had developed a deep love for it. 'There was also the fact that, as a writer, his imaginative hinterland was the west of Ireland,' she said – and she also knew that Murphy had never professionally produced one of his plays in the west. Doing so might connect him with audiences there in new ways: she knew it would be good for Druid, but she felt that Murphy might consider it beneficial too.

Garry didn't know Murphy personally, but they did have a mutual friend in another playwright, Thomas Kilroy, who was Professor of English at UCG at the time. Garry approached Kilroy, who introduced her to Murphy – and a meeting was soon set up.

Garry's plan was to propose that Druid do three things. First, they would revive a play from Murphy's canon: something that had already been produced somewhere else but that deserved to

Chapter 5: Tom Murphy, a Writer-in-Association

be seen in the west. Second, she would ask Murphy if he was 'less than happy' with any of his earlier works – and, if so, whether they could collaborate on developing it further. And finally – and this was the most ambitious request – she would ask if Murphy would consider writing a play specifically for the Druid company.

They met once and it went well – and over several weeks they continued to meet, getting to know each other better. During one of those meetings, Murphy told Garry that he'd seen *Island Protected by a Bridge of Glass* at the Peacock, and had got into a light-hearted row with a man in the gents afterwards because Murphy hadn't been sufficiently effusive in his praise for the show, leading the man to take offence. Garry wondered who her supporter had been. 'He said his name was Oliver Hynes,' Murphy replied, with a glint in his eye – it had been Garry's father, looking out for his daughter yet again.

With the rapport between them deepening, Garry proposed that Murphy could be Druid's writer-in-residence. He didn't much like that title. He had left the west of Ireland in the 1960s and was happy where he was, in Dublin. But he would be a 'writer-in-association,' he said.

Druid were now ready to start thinking about productions – resulting, in quick succession, in a revival of Murphy's plays *Famine* and *On the Outside* in 1984; a revised version of an older play, which became *Conversations on a Homecoming*, in 1985; and, most significantly of all, the writing of a brand-new drama – one that is now seen as Murphy's masterpiece: *Bailegangaire*.

Famine is set in Mayo, and begins in the year 1846, and thus dramatizes the beginning of the Great Irish Famine of the 1840s, a catastrophe that caused the death of a million people, and the emigration of a million more.

Poster for *Famine*, 1984.

Notably, however, Murphy did not call his play 'The' *Famine*. His setting might have been historical, but his interest was in famine in general – famine as a state that can be emotional, intellectual and spiritual, as well as physical or political. Introducing his play to audiences at the Abbey Theatre when it premiered there in 1968, Murphy wrote that the Great Famine of the 1840s had 'stopped the Irish race in its tracks', which meant that the county was still suffering 'a hangover that had lasted over a hundred years'. Hunger had largely been removed from Irish life by the 1960s, Murphy acknowledged, but other 'poverties' persisted:

> Poverty of thought; wild wisdom and native cunning stalemating a twentieth century need to open out and expand

> ... the natural extravagant vitality of youth being frustrated and made to feel guilty by the smell of too much history.

Murphy concluded that he too was a victim of famine. But so was everyone else in Ireland, he insisted.

By the mid-1980s, those old poverties were asserting themselves again – especially a poverty of opportunity, which was causing growing numbers of people to emigrate from Ireland, mostly to Britain and the United States. But there was a new context now: when Druid made the decision to stage *Famine*, they were doing so in the wake of the 1981 hunger strikes in Northern Ireland, in which ten republican prisoners had starved themselves to death in protest at their treatment by the British government.

Those hunger strikes were political (the first man to die, Bobby Sands, was elected to the UK's parliament while still in prison, for example), but they were also performative – drawing on images of martyrdom, blood sacrifice and starvation in order to situate the prisoners' struggle within the long history of English violence in Ireland. The IRA prisoners were deliberately evoking memories of the Famine during the Hunger Strikes, so it seemed likely that Druid's audiences would in turn find contemporary relevance in Murphy's play: it is, after all, a drama in which many of the characters starve to death. Druid wouldn't place undue emphasis on the potential relevance of the play to the north – but that was partly because they didn't need to.

If the social and political context made a production of *Famine* more immediate but also riskier, there were also serious practical difficulties to overcome. It is simply a huge play, requiring a cast of nineteen actors; staging it in the Druid Lane Theatre was therefore out of the question, and the company instead rented space in the Seapoint Ballroom in Salthill, where they could accommodate an audience of about 400 people each night. That was a new scale for them – excitingly so – but it also meant having to sell more tickets in a month than they would normally sell in a year.

But they definitely felt ready to take on the play's formal and technical complexity. When Murphy had written it, in the mid-1960s, he'd been living in London, where he had seen many productions of Brecht's plays – and the influence of Brecht can be seen in how *Famine* keeps its characters at a distance, denying emotional identification so that audiences can instead think about the play's political relevance to their own lives. Because Druid had staged two Brecht plays during the preceding five years, they were well prepared for the style of acting that *Famine* demanded – as were their audiences.

There was also the fact that Mick Lally knew the play intimately, having translated it into Irish, as *Gorta*, for a production at the Taibhdhearc in February 1975. Mick had played the lead role of John Connor in that version, and was returning to it now with Druid.

Rather like John Proctor in Arthur Miller's *The Crucible* (which Murphy also named as an influence, even though he disliked Miller's tendency towards moralizing), Murphy's John Connor is heroic mostly in his powerlessness: he wants to do the right thing, and he tries to do the right thing, but he ultimately loses everything anyway. It's an exceedingly challenging role for an actor to play: thematically and linguistically, but emotionally too.

The play's first words, delivered by John, are 'How am I to overcome it?' spoken in response to the death of his son – and from there, things get worse for him. Mick needed to ensure that audiences would remain invested in his character, even as he tries to 'overcome' experiences that are progressively dreadful. His earlier experiences with the play proved invaluable in allowing him to give the role the necessary balance of dignity, distance and despair.

Famine opened in Salthill in February 1984, initially for four weeks, but the run was extended for another fortnight due to

Chapter 5: Tom Murphy, a Writer-in-Association

Mick Lally (second from right) in *Famine*, 1984.

strong word of mouth and an intensifying sense that this was not so much a production as an event. Speaking to a reporter at the time, Marie described acting in *Famine* as 'the most powerful experience I've ever had in the theatre', and Galway audiences were telling the company constantly that they felt the same way.

The production then embarked upon a URT that took in many towns that had themselves been decimated by the Famine, such as Lahinch in County Clare and Killasser in Mayo (the town that Druid accidentally caused a power outage in). In organizing that tour, the company again needed to overcome practical difficulties; Jerome told Jim Fahy on RTÉ news that 'Getting an articulated truck around those country roads could be quite a job.' But the experience proved deeply meaningful for the actors: audience members in each of those communities stayed behind after the performances to share local memories and stories about the Famine, and to tease out the play's consequences for the present.

That sense of meaningful immediacy was mentioned everywhere the play went. Audiences understood that Murphy had written about a specific moment in the Irish past, but they also saw that, if *Famine* was about the 1840s, it was also about the 1960s and the 1980s, and much more besides. In an Ireland that felt increasingly unstable, audiences knew what it felt like to measure themselves against forces so vast as to feel unstoppable; they too had found themselves asking more and more frequently, 'How am I to overcome it?'

With the tour finished, Druid wanted to explore a different facet of Murphy's work, and thus decided to stage *On the Outside*, a play that was well known in Galway (it had been appearing regularly in amateur productions since the early 1970s), but which had never before been produced there professionally.

Garry was unable to direct it, so she turned instead to Paul Brennan, who had already been directing regularly with Druid, doing Beckett's *Endgame* with them in 1981 and Seán O'Casey's *Bedtime Story* in 1983. Pauline McLynn, Seán McGinley, Maelíosa Stafford and Ray McBride were all in the cast; and so was Jane Brennan who was not only appearing in a production directed by her own brother, but also acting for the first time in a play written by the man she'd eventually marry. Also appearing was Páraic Breathnach, who up to that time had been stage-managing and building sets for Druid. Now he was actually appearing *on* one of those sets, playing the bouncer who refuses to let the two young men into the dance.

That willingness and ability to move people into and out of different roles within the company was another example of the

Chapter 5: Tom Murphy, a Writer-in-Association 127

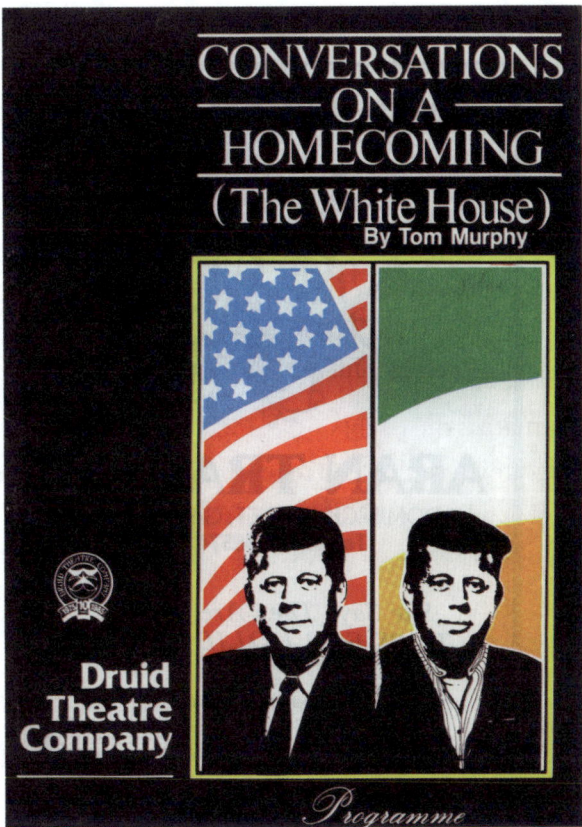

Conversations on a Homecoming poster, 1985.

cohesion and flexibility of the ensemble. It would be evident again when Druid turned to their next Murphy production – where Paul Brennan would feature once more, but this time as an actor rather than a director.

That production was *Conversations on a Homecoming*. It was a reworked version of a 1972 play called *The White House*, which Murphy had originally written in two acts – one set in a period of optimism in the early 1960s (that optimism caused partly by the election of the first Irish-American president, JFK) and the other during a period of disillusionment a decade later.

Murphy had never been fully sure about how to order those two acts. He wanted to start in the 1970s and then move backwards in time, but audiences at the Abbey (where the play premiered) seemed to find that confusing – and during its original run at that theatre, both approaches were attempted, but neither very successfully. In the following years, Murphy occasionally tried to redraft the play, but he remained unhappy with it.

The new relationship with Druid gave him an opportunity to try again, however. Garry had told him how much she liked the part of *The White House* that had been set in the 1970s and, as he thought more about what she'd said, he decided to jettison the other act altogether, instead developing a one-act play that would dramatize the events of a single night in a single place – a pub in Tuam, where the 'conversations' of the new title take place.

He also decided to shift the geographic focus. *The White House* had been about an Irishman who returns to Galway after emigrating to England, but in *Conversations* the emigrant is coming back from New York. That change arose because Murphy wanted to respond to what he saw as a 'great erosion of culture' in Ireland during the 1980s, one indicator of which, he thought, was the popularity of American country and western music: 'the awful sentimentality in most of the songs is hostile towards the idea of an Irish culture,' Murphy complained. In expressing that frustration, he wasn't proposing a return to a nationalistic version of Irish culture; he just wanted to insist that art should be intellectually ambitious, that instead of pandering to people emotionally it should ask something of its audiences. *Conversations* would do exactly that.

At the heart of the play is a dispute between two men: the returned migrant Michael, who was played in the premiere by Paul Brennan, and Michael's old friend Tom, who was played by Séan McGinley. The fact that one of the characters shares his first name with the author might suggest that Murphy had already picked a side in their debate, that he wanted the audience to identify more with Tom's cynicism than Michael's idealism. But it becomes apparent during the play that each man is the

Chapter 5: Tom Murphy, a Writer-in-Association

Seán McGinley in *Conversations on a Homecoming*.

other's alter ego, and that both are using public performance in the pub to cover up a deep-rooted sense of personal failure – Tom is less cynical and Michael less optimistic than either of them is willing to admit. Both Ireland and the artist needed to find a way of balancing extremes, Murphy shows: open conversation has to overcome rigid conviction.

The subtlety and depth of that characterization required the Druid company to think intensely and intensively about the script – a responsibility that was aided by Murphy's presence in the rehearsal room. When she was asked years later what Murphy contributed to Druid's practice, Garry's answer was simple: 'Rigour was the main characteristic of the relationship':

From the very beginning, there was a pattern where Tom was present in the rehearsal room for that first exploration of the script. From that time onwards, I learned how I had to read his plays as much for their musicality as their meaning. I had been aware of that from reading them anyhow, but having Tom with us showed how the music of the plays is in the meaning, and the meaning is in the music.

Maelíosa, who was playing a character called Junior, also saw Murphy's rigour as formative. 'Being in *Conversations*,' he said, 'was a milestone for me as an actor':

> To use a football analogy, we had moved into the Premier League. As Tom would give notes, or just a thought about the language, or even if he started singing – I realized he'd written an opera. He had the whole play in his head musically.

But the musicality of the language meant that seemingly minor mistakes in one part of the play could have a disproportionately severe impact minutes later. 'The whole house of cards used to fall down regularly' in rehearsal, Maelíosa recalled. 'But I found Tom really helpful with those smaller points; he was almost singing the parts to you. I found that not intrusive; I found it necessary'.

Garry agreed. With Murphy, she had come to understand, there is the 'absolute discipline of knowing that if a line is written as three words, then that is absolutely how it must be said':

> That knowledge would stand me in great stead not just in Tom's work, where it's a rule that you absolutely have to obey, but when I was looking at other writers later on as well.

Marie Mullen and Paul Brennan in *Conversations in a Homecoming*, 1985.

Marie was also enjoying the challenge. Playing a character called Peggy, she too had to focus on the musicality of the language – but she also had to act in several periods of silence that are in their own way very meaningful. When she looked back on that rehearsal process, Marie remembered working hard to ensure that her line delivery combined accuracy and speed with rhythm. But she also understood that the play needed to be believable; it might be written like an opera but it couldn't be performed as one. 'The acting style was very realistic' as a result, she said, adding that it was therefore 'very scary in a lot of ways'.

A further challenge during the rehearsal period was that the company was so busy with other productions. 'We rehearsed *Conversations* all over the place,' said Garry. 'We were on tour, so we rehearsed it in Limerick, and then we rehearsed it in London when we were doing *Playboy* at the Donmar Warehouse.' That meant that they didn't get to do a run-through in the Druid Lane

Maelíosa Stafford (left) as Junior in *Conversation on a Homecoming* 1985.

Theatre until a week before they were due to open. Garry found herself deeply unhappy with how it was coming together when they got back to Galway. 'I was absolutely terrified,' she said: the rhythms weren't right yet, both for individual lines and the overall shape of the piece. She thought it was going to be a disaster.

They kept working on it of course, but *Conversations* is a play that – to an unusual extent – needs to be put in front of an audience before it can fully come together. Murphy had adopted a daring approach to the representation of time in the play, which was to mark the passing of a night's drinking by the regular chiming of a clock, each chime representing another passing hour. Thus, although the audience is sitting in the theatre for only about ninety minutes, they must believe that they have witnessed the passage of several hours. An acting company can never really be sure that this technique is working until they run it right through with an audience.

Murphy's use of time also had the practical impact that the actors need to get through a lot of drink in a short period; Maelíosa's performance as Junior was thus remembered for many years afterwards in part because he had to work his way through seven or eight pints of stout each time they did the play.

It opened in April 1985 in the Druid Lane Theatre and, as Marie later recalled, 'Galway loved *Conversations*' straightaway. Druid brought it back for that year's Galway Arts Festival – with one performance happening in a real Galway pub, Rabbitt's Bar, just around the corner from the train station. And from there it went to the Dublin Theatre Festival, and would stay in the Druid repertoire for the next three years. Murphy was delighted. 'One feature of my association with Druid was that they were all twenty years younger than me,' he explained. 'In mixing with such talented young people, I achieved a rejuvenation, because there is tremendous energy in *Conversations*.' That rejuvenation would lead him to his next play – which went into rehearsal even as *Conversations* was finishing its run in Dublin: *Bailegangaire*.

―――

With *Conversations* on its feet, Tom was now ready to send a copy of that new play to Garry. 'When I started to read *Bailegangaire* at first I was absolutely astounded at the radical nature of the dramaturgy,' she said. 'The concept of the play was so huge.'

It is written for three women – a grandmother called Mommo and her two granddaughters, Mary and Dolly. And it involves the compulsive retelling of a story from Mommo's past, about how a town in Galway was renamed 'Bailegangaire', the 'town without laughter'. Night after night, the bedbound Mommo retells her story, looping back and forward in time, often coming close to revealing the truth about a tragedy from her past. Partly because she suffers from dementia, but also because it's just too painful

Siobhán McKenna in *Bailegangaire*, 1985.

for her to do so, Mommo never finishes that story, until one night Mary and Dolly finally help her to bring it to a conclusion. It was an amazing play, Garry thought: 'complex, angular, and extraordinary in its ambition'.

Tom had written it for Druid but he had also imagined the role of Mommo being played by Siobhán McKenna. Siobhán by that time was in her sixties, and was massively admired in Ireland for her career as an actor, whether as Saint Joan in the Taibhdhearc and on Broadway, Pegeen Mike in the film version of *The Playboy*

Chapter 5: Tom Murphy, a Writer-in-Association

Marie Mullen and Siobhán McKenna in *Bailegangaire*.

of the *Western World*, Anna in David Lean's film adaptation of *Doctor Zhivago*, or in countless other roles on stage and screen.

But she was also respected for her activism: she had even given a speech against apartheid to a United Nations committee in 1982. The prospect of bringing her into a Druid production was tremendously exciting, especially given her Galway roots. But it was a major step up for the company too.

Garry had met Siobhán several times before, but had never directed her in anything. 'Working on a new play of that kind, working with Siobhán McKenna – it was very daunting,' Garry remembered. Her trepidation was completely understandable: the part of Mommo is one of the longest roles on record for a woman, so they were staging a play that was asking Siobhán to do something that had almost never been done before. 'We know

now that it is possible to perform the part,' Garry said. 'But in rehearsals I'm not sure any of us were sure that it could be done':

> Like with any new play, after its premiere it always seems eternally obvious that it was always going to be the way it is. But it is never like that beforehand, and it particularly wasn't like that in the case of *Bailegangaire*.

Nevertheless, said Garry, 'it turned out to be a wonderful rehearsal process'.

But as opening night drew nearer, everyone was starting to register that the play was much too long. On the night of its first dress rehearsal, it took them almost two hours to get to the end of the first act alone. Murphy, who had come down to Dublin for the night, went to Garry's office while the actors took a break. He wasn't inordinately worried about the length, he told her: 'I know what's wrong and how to fix it'. He suggested that they could stay up all night working together on making cuts.

Garry thought it would be better for Murphy to work alone. She was also thinking about how her cast would react to the changes: they all knew that the play was too long, but she would be asking the three of them – and Siobhán especially – to do the one thing that actors absolutely don't want to do so close to an opening night: to forget their lines.

Murphy was staying in the Great Southern Hotel on Eyre Square, about a five-minute walk from the theatre, and he got back to his room around midnight. He poured himself a large brandy, got into bed and started cutting – stopping six hours later for a short nap. At nine o'clock, he went back to Druid and told Garry that he'd been able to cut twenty-five minutes from the first act; Garry agreed to bring the changes to the actors.

Murphy watched the performance again later that day: 'Siobhán was magnificent in dealing with twenty-five minutes of cuts,' he recalled, 'so I went home to the hotel and I cut five to eight minutes more.'

The next night was their first time playing *Bailegangaire* before an audience. Murphy arrived early to the theatre and slipped backstage to the dressing rooms. 'Siobhán was already in costume,' he said.

> And she had her back to me and I leaned against the door and she turned around, walking slowly, rivetted on the cuts and on the script, and I thought she didn't hear me come in or was unaware. She looked up when she was passing me, abreast of me, and she said – 'great cuts'.

And then she went back to working on her lines. Murphy was tremendously moved, he said – and he left the dressing room and prepared himself for the audience's reaction.

———

People in Galway would later joke that if everyone who claimed to have been present for the opening night of *Bailegangaire* had actually been there, Druid would have filled the theatre dozens of times over. And while Marie and Mary McEvoy were hugely admired as the two granddaughters, that production's legendary status is mainly attributable to Siobhán's performance.

Early in rehearsals, Garry had become aware that there was something powerful about having Siobhán play Mommo not as an actor 'impersonating a semi-old woman' but instead as herself. That approach might have seemed counterintuitive: often, productions that feature well-known actors seek to play down, or even play against, that person's public persona. But for *Bailegangaire*, having Siobhán *be* Siobhán was the right approach. 'It enabled us to see more quickly that the play is a metaphor rather than a reality,' said Garry. 'And that helped the audience to understand the same thing quickly in turn':

> Despite the very strangeness of the set-up – of a woman telling a story that she won't finish – there's something, as in all Tom's work, that is viscerally recognizable to an audience. You can never say exactly what that is but you know it's scraping away at something that is about *you*.

And that was how audiences found it – they knew it was doing something to them, even if they couldn't necessarily define or understand what that something was. Because they were watching Siobhán McKenna perform her own encounter with the play, they could in turn open themselves up to it.

After its Galway run, the play moved to the Gaiety in Dublin. It was met mostly with positivity there but, as Murphy himself would later admit, that enormous Victorian theatre was probably too big for the play, which had worked much more effectively in the intimacy of the Druid Lane space.

It fared better in February 1986 when it went to England, to the Donmar Warehouse – which is a West End venue but one small enough to allow the audience to connect directly with the play, as they had done in Galway. Murphy had not had a hit in London since *A Whistle in the Dark* almost twenty-five years

Bailegangaire at the Donmar Warehouse, 1986.

earlier – but with *Bailegangaire* the critics there were suddenly taking him very seriously again.

The production finished its London run on 15 March. By then there was huge demand from audiences to see it – and Druid began planning a tour to Sydney for 1987.

But then, shockingly, in November 1986 Murphy took a phone call from Garry, who told him the terrible news that Siobhán had just passed away: she had gone to the Blackrock Clinic in Dublin for a lung operation but had had a cardiac arrest while being operated on. They were devastated, of course – and the idea of doing *Bailegangaire* with anyone else in the role felt unthinkable. Plans for the tour were immediately set aside.

Murphy would eventually return to the play in 2001, directing it in an Abbey Theatre production that featured Jane Brennan as one of the granddaughters. But the lingering memory of Siobhán's performance as Mommo haunted the play for many years to come.

By 1986, Druid and Tom Murphy had done what they set out to do: they had revived a play, revised a play and premiered a play – and in doing so Murphy had been rejuvenated, while the Druid company had further matured. The ending of the formal writer-in-association relationship after *Bailegangaire* didn't mean that they would stop working together, however.

Conversations on a Homecoming was revived, touring to New York (not to the city but to a festival upstate) in 1986 while also being performed in Australia and in three Irish prisons in 1987. That juxtaposition – between playing in Sydney in one month and then playing before audiences who had been locked away a few weeks later – offers another encapsulation of Druid's egalitarian attitude to their audiences.

And then a new idea came forward: that the Abbey and Druid could work together on the revival of a Murphy play.

To anyone working in Irish theatre, such a combination made sense. Even as Murphy was working with Druid, he had continued to stage plays at the Abbey, premiering *The Gigli Concert* there in 1983 and a play called *A Thief of a Christmas* (which stages the story that Mommo narrates in *Bailegangaire*) in 1985. A co-production between Druid and the Abbey would bring the two strands of his recent career together, for everyone's benefit.

But that moment also represented an acknowledgment of Druid's growing national status. At the start of the decade, they were being invited to the Abbey as guests, but now they were to be its co-producers – an indicator of their parity of esteem in artistic terms, even if the Abbey was of course vastly better funded.

Conversations poster, 1987.

Their joint production was a revival of *A Whistle in the Dark* – a play that the Abbey had rejected when Murphy had sent it to them in 1960. By giving it a long-overdue place on the national stage, the Abbey was, rather like Mommo in *Bailegangaire*, going backwards in order to go forwards – reaching into its past to signal that its relationship with Irish dramatists like Murphy had changed for the better.

But it was a similarly momentous production for Druid and, in particular, for Garry. She had brought Druid's work to the

The cast of *A Whistle in the Dark*, 1987.

Abbey's smaller Peacock space before, but was now making work on the main stage of the national theatre. With Druid's reputation continuously expanding, Garry was more frequently being spoken of as a future Artistic Director of the Abbey. A production of *A Whistle in the Dark* on the main stage was an opportunity for her to consider what it might mean to work there in practice.

The Abbey had certainly been wrong to reject Murphy's play back in the early 1960s – but there is no denying that it is brutal and unforgiving, both on the page and on the stage. It's about a Galway family called the Carneys, who have emigrated to Coventry, where most of them thrive through violence and criminality. But one of them, Michael, has married an Englishwoman and is trying to live a 'respectable' life – and as the play begins he is preparing to welcome his father and youngest brother, who are visiting from Ireland.

What follows is a tragedy in the formal sense, in that *Whistle* is structured in a similar way to *Hamlet* or *Oedipus*, showing how the faults of a well-meaning man can bring about a disaster that feels both inevitable and inescapable. But it is also tragic in the simple sense: that it is completely devastating to watch.

That co-production opened in the Abbey during the 1986 Dublin Theatre Festival before returning to Galway for a summertime performance in the Jesuit Hall the following year. And Garry and Tom Murphy continued to work together regularly for much of the next decade – but they were to do so mainly at the Abbey, rather than in Druid.

In 2016, just two years before he passed away, Tom Murphy sat down with the Druid Literary Manager Thomas Conway to record a series of interviews about his work with the company. Shortly before they wrapped up, he told Thomas about an incident that captures well his feelings about working with Druid.

It was 1989, and the Abbey/Druid *Whistle in the Dark* had opened at the Royal Court Theatre in London. Critics and audiences were raving about it, finding it unbearably tense but also unbearably moving. And they were full of praise for the acting, both by the Druid regulars (Seán, Maelíosa, and Ray) and by Godfrey Quigley, who was playing the Carneys' father.

But the critics kept coming back to Garry's direction – her ability to keep such a tightly coiled play under control, and to combine the play's musicality with its inherent violence, was astonishing, they said. Murphy was of course delighted.

At the opening night, he had found himself standing outside the Royal Court – probably having a cigarette. He could hear the cheers coming from the auditorium, where the ovations were still going on. Garry came out to join him. He knew that she would be expecting him to say 'well done', and indeed that this would have been the right thing for him to do: it had been 'well done' – indeed, much more than that.

But he decided to take a different approach. 'It's a great play,' he told her, no doubt somewhat mischievously.

Garry would tell that story back to Murphy again in the future – and while she would have been entitled to tell it with a good dollop of frustration, it's probably fair to say that Murphy was paying her a compliment. Many of his plays *are* great – but they haven't always had great productions, perhaps because directors hadn't understood them, or maybe because audiences weren't ready for them when they first appeared.

Garry's production had demonstrated the greatness of Murphy's writing – and her ability to do that was a vivid example of her own growing greatness as a director.

Chapter 6
A Transforming Galway, 1987–1990

IN THE LIFE of any artist there inevitably comes a moment when a reputation becomes a kind of straitjacket.

Everyone involved in the company had tended to resist the idea of Druid becoming an institution – because an institution is something fixed, something that must be kept going because of what it did in the past rather than what it might do in the future. So it was both natural and inevitable that the core members would eventually want to explore other ways of making theatre. As the 1980s came to a close, the established acting company therefore began to dissolve, while Garry started working more frequently with other theatres.

And so a question that had been looming for a while was now being asked more insistently. What exactly was Druid Theatre?

One way of answering that question was to say that it was a building in Galway – that, so long as there were plays being performed in the space in Chapel Lane, then there was a Druid Theatre.

For others, 'Druid' meant the company of actors – Marie, certainly, but also Seán, Maelíosa, and Ray, as well as the many others who had been drawn in over the years in order to replenish and revive that core group.

But for most people, 'Druid' simply meant Garry. True, she hadn't directed everything that Druid had done, and audiences had enjoyed the company's shows when people like Maelíosa, Paul Brennan, Ben Barnes, and Andy Hinds had taken her place. But Garry had chosen those productions, had chosen those directors; even when she was not directly involved, she had still shaped and defined the work.

So if a Druid show was not directed by Garry Hynes, did not feature any members of the original ensemble, and was not being performed in the Druid Lane Theatre, was it still a Druid show? If so, how? And if not, what did that mean for the future of the company?

It was time to start answering those questions.

The first person to go was Maelíosa.

He had already left Druid once, when Joe Dowling offered him a two-year contract at the Abbey Theatre in 1984. Maelíosa had been delighted to get the opportunity to work in the national theatre, but had quickly become frustrated — and he quit halfway through his term, leaving the Abbey with Dowling's blessing. He returned to Galway simply because he felt that he could learn much more with Druid.

But then in January 1987, the possibility of leaving came up again. He was on tour with Druid's production of *Conversations on a Homecoming*, which was playing at the Belvoir Street theatre in Sydney. And that was where he met and fell in love with the woman he'd share the rest of his life with, Carolyn Forde.

He was happy, of course — but he was also unsure what to do. The run of *Conversations* had finished and he wanted to stay with Carolyn, but he had commitments back in Ireland: a tour with Druid, a freelance gig with the Abbey during the summer. 'I'll

Maelíosa and Pauline McLynn, *Bedtime Story*, 1983

come over for a few months and we'll see how we go,' Carolyn told him.

So they lived in Ireland for a time, and they had their first child together in 1988. But Carolyn had her job as a teacher waiting for her back in Australia, and Maelíosa knew he could continue acting there – so they decided to make their life there instead.

In 1990 Maelíosa and Caroyln married in a ceremony that was held in the back garden of Carolyn's mother's home in Sydney; and in the same year, Maelíosa set up a theatre company of his own, O'Punkskys, together with his friends John O'Hare and Patrick Dickson. Their first show was Frank McGuinness's *Observe the Sons of Ulster Marching Towards the Somme*, a play about Irish soldiers in the First World War that had premiered at the Peacock Theatre in 1985. The production was very well received, and O'Punkskys soon became an essential part of the Sydney theatre scene, staging the Australian premieres of many Irish plays.

As he moved to Australia, Maelíosa assured everyone that he wasn't finished with Druid, or with Ireland. His parents were still living in Galway, and he expected that, like Mick Lally before him, he would come back and appear in Druid shows from to time. But, as the new decade began, he was looking forward to a new life with his young family on the other side of the world.

———

Jerome too was ready for something new, and in 1988 he left Druid to become the managing director of Wexford Festival Opera.

Over the years, newcomers to Wexford would sometimes express surprise that it was the home of an opera festival. It's a relatively small town (its population in the mid-1980s was about 35,000 people), and although the south-east of Ireland had a long tradition of amateur musical performance, it seemed an unlikely spot for an opera house. Yet, under the stewardship of Dr Tom Walsh, the festival had not just survived since its foundation in 1951 but had developed an international reputation for staging neglected or forgotten operas, usually over a fortnight in October every year, and usually to a very high standard.

But by the mid-1980s it was facing many challenges. Its grant from the Irish Arts Council was temporarily withdrawn in 1986, and a renovation of the Wexford Theatre Royal in 1987 had increased the festival's seating capacity at a time when it had very little money to do anything – including the intensive marketing that was needed to sell all those additional tickets. The entire arts sector was in a state of crisis at that time, with the rapid deterioration of the Irish economy pushing arts funding way down the list of government priorities. But while many companies were muddling through, the relative expense of opera left the Wexford Festival in a particularly vulnerable position.

It was a tough job for anyone to take on, but Jerome threw himself into it determinedly, applying all the knowledge he had picked up at Druid – about developing audiences, building an identity, keeping a committed (but sometimes demanding) local community on board, and getting by with nowhere near enough money. Garry had asked him to stay on with Druid as a member of their Board of Directors, and he agreed to do so, remaining in that role until 2003. But Jerome quickly made his mark in Wexford, cementing an identity in his own right as one of Ireland's leading arts managers. Under his leadership, the festival quickly stabilized – and from there it began to grow.

Garry too was thinking about what to do next. She had spent more than a decade working with a tight-knit group of actors; people came and went, but the core group had stayed more or less the same. She knew them well, and they trusted her – and it had been enormously successful for all of them.

But most directors don't work like that: the norm in the 1980s was to hire a group of freelancers who would gather for a production and then go their separate ways. Given her widening international reputation, Garry was getting regular offers of work away from Druid – which meant directing new actors in new ways. That would be a challenge, but an appealing one.

The co-production of *Whistle in the Dark* with the Abbey had gone well, and in 1988 they offered Garry the opportunity to work directly with them. She might have been ambivalent about the idea of Druid being an institution – but she understood that she could learn a lot from working in one, and there was none bigger in Irish theatre than the Abbey. So she agreed, and her first production for that theatre was of another Murphy play, *A Crucial Week in the Life of a Grocer's Assistant*.

In the early 1960s, that play had been called *The Fooleen* and, like *Whistle*, it had been rejected by the Abbey. But they had been much faster to rectify their mistake, staging it under its revised 'crucial week' title in 1969. For his new production with Garry at the Abbey, Murphy had reworked the play – not to the extent that he had done with *Conversations*, but enough for it to need actors who would be able to handle the challenge of working on it.

Fortunately, the cast was dominated by Druid actors (including Seán, Ray, Maelíosa, Jane Brennan and Joan Sheehy), most of whom had already worked on at least one of Murphy's plays; and to add to that sense of familiarity the set was designed by Monica Frawley, who by then was a regular Druid collaborator. It was widely remarked upon that, although the Abbey show programme didn't mention Garry's name on its title page, it did include a hand-drawn image of a Galway street that was literally around the corner from Druid's theatre on Chapel Lane. *Crucial Week* thus looked and felt a lot like a Druid production, notwithstanding the inclusion of actors from the Abbey company.

In contrast, Garry's next production for the Abbey, in 1989, included many actors whom she had never worked with before. One of that group was Brendan Gleeson, who was making his Abbey debut. Her production there was a revival of Eugene McCabe's *The King of the Castle*, which had been a success at the 1964 Dublin Theatre Festival but had fallen into neglect in the intervening years.

It's a ferocious play, focused on sexuality and religion, and (like so many of the plays that Garry was directing at that time) it is almost obsessive in its rage about how young people's energy and hope is sapped and exploited by older generations. Once again, Garry was demonstrating her distinctive ability to bring old plays into contemporary contexts.

Chapter 6: A Transforming Galway, 1987–1990

Abbey Theatre show programme for *A Crucial Week in the Life of a Grocer's Assistant*, 1988.

In 1990, she returned to the Abbey for the third year in a row, on that occasion for Boucicault's *The Shaughraun*, a play that she had presented in the Peacock in a Druid production in 1982. Again she was working with many new actors, some freelance and some from the Abbey company: the cast included vastly experienced actors such as Anna Manahan and Joan O'Hara, alongside younger performers like Bríd Ní Neachtain and Catherine Byrne, both of whom had just earned rave reviews for their performances in the premiere of Brian Friel's *Dancing at Lughnasa*.

But in *The Shaughraun* there was a greater balance between Garry's past and present: she was giving Marie a (long overdue) debut on the Abbey mainstage, Ray McBride was choreographing the show, Monica Frawley was designing it and Seán McGinley played the lead role of Conn. Her new *Shaughraun* was therefore noticeably different from the Druid version – partly because the Abbey's bigger stage allowed for a more expansive style of performance, but mostly because of the mix of personalities and styles in the acting company.

Garry's work at the Abbey might have seemed similar to her work at Druid, but she had also taken the opportunity to do something (almost) completely different – which was to spend a year working at the Royal Shakespeare Company (RSC) in Stratford-upon-Avon in 1987–1988. She was joined there by Marie, who was hired for the acting company at the same time.

While working with the RSC, Garry directed the world premiere of *The Love of the Nightingale*, a version of a Greek legend by the British-American playwright Timberlake Wertenbaker. She also took on a Restoration comedy for the first time, directing George Etherege's 1676 play *The Man of Mode*. Playing one of the main roles in the latter production was Simon Russell Beale, who was then at the start of his career but who is now considered one of the leading Shakespeare actors of his generation. Beale later praised Garry for allowing him to mix the inherent silliness of his character (the aptly named Sir Fopling Flutter) with a moment of pathos that most other directors probably wouldn't have permitted. In doing that, Garry was demonstrating the evolution of a skill that she had honed by directing plays like *Bailegangaire*: the ability to mix theatrical modes that other directors would have kept apart for fear of creating discordance or incoherence.

Marie, unsurprisingly, was in both of Garry's productions in Stratford, but she also had the opportunity to play Goneril in an RSC staging of *King Lear* in 1989. She was directed in that role by Cicely Berry – someone who was respected as a director but revered as a vocal coach. Working with Berry offered Marie the opportunity to develop her already formidable technical skills,

Chapter 6: A Transforming Galway, 1987–1990

while also broadening her range. And playing a character who has an iconically difficult relationship with an elderly parent would also prove useful in the future, notably when she came to play Maureen in *The Beauty Queen of Leenane*.

Garry hadn't left Druid; she was still directing productions in Galway, and she was still the Artistic Director. But as the 1980s concluded, she was doing other things too, exploring different ways of being a director. And she was also contemplating future possibilities: she was now regularly being spoken about as a likely Artistic Director of the Abbey Theatre – and very soon she would have a choice to make.

With Garry spending more time in Dublin and Stratford, there was now space for Druid to try new things. One of the company's most exciting innovations during that period of transition was to invite Jim Sheridan to direct Brendan Behan's play *The Hostage* for the company. It opened in Galway in October 1987 before going on a fifteen-venue URT that finished on Inis Meáin shortly before Christmas.

Hiring a Dubliner to stage a play by a Dubliner in Galway, and then bringing it on tour to rural Ireland – that was an appealingly mischievous reversal of the usual theatrical traffic from the west of Ireland to the capital city. But it was also a reflection of the fact that Sheridan had been an important influence on Druid from their early days; his work with his brother Peter at Dublin's Project Arts Centre had given Garry and Marie an inspirational model of what might be possible in Galway.

There was also a feeling that a Galway-based production could crack open new features of Behan's classic play. *The Hostage* had started life as an Irish-language one-act play called *An Giall*, which had been performed at the Damer in Dublin in 1958. Later

Eanna MacLiam and Rachael Dowling, *The Hostage*.

that same year, it was produced in English in London – but in a markedly different version that some thought was more the work of its director, Joan Littlewood, than of Behan (a suggestion that, depending on his mood, Behan sometimes agreed with and sometimes rejected angrily). Either way, Littlewood's influence had indisputably helped to make *The Hostage* a worldwide success, but there had been a lingering suspicion that *An Giall* was closer to Behan's intentions. The Irish version was shorter, simpler, more tragic – and maybe even a better play.

Because of the strength of the Irish language in Galway, there were many people there who knew *An Giall* already, some of them because Maire Stafford had translated the Littlewood/ Behan version back into Irish for An Taibhdhearc in 1970. For the new Druid production, Maire was involved again, preparing a new translation of Behan's original *An Giall* into English – and

Sheridan interspersed parts of her version into the text of *The Hostage*. That resulted in an intriguing hybrid, a staging of the play that retained the anarchic humour of the Littlewood production but which also found space for the honesty and simplicity of the original.

Maire herself appeared in Sheridan's cast, playing an elderly prostitute called Ropeen, but most of the other actors were new to Druid. There was also live musical accompaniment from a young accordion player called Sharon Shannon, who went on to become one of Ireland's most popular traditional musicians. Her presence demonstrates how Galway's music and theatre scenes remained closely intertwined in the late 1980s – but also shows how Druid's productions could foster the development of careers in many different art forms.

No one knew it at the time, but Sheridan's own career was also about to take off in a major way, though as a filmmaker rather than a theatre director. Shortly after *The Hostage* completed its run, he began shooting his debut film, *My Left Foot* – which in 1990 was nominated for five Academy Awards, winning two of them, for the performances of Daniel Day-Lewis and Brenda Fricker. That film has since been credited with reinventing Irish cinema, and it certainly gave Irish culture a much higher international profile than it had enjoyed at any time since the heyday of the Irish revival, at the start of the twentieth century. Sheridan's achievement would have a major impact on the reception of Irish theatre too – as Druid would go on to discover during the 1990s.

In 1989, Druid linked up with another filmmaker, staging Anthony Minghella's *A Little Like Drowning*, his adaptation for the stage of his first film. The Galway production was directed by Jane Prowse, a freelancer from the UK – and it featured a

A Little Like Drowning by Anthony Minghella.

cast who were mostly unfamiliar to audiences in the city, with the exception of Jane Brennan. Also featured in one of the lead roles was Katherine O'Toole (now better known as Kate). She had some connections to the west of Ireland through her father, the actor Peter O'Toole – and while she of course wanted to be judged as an actor in her own right there was inevitably some interest in her famous dad in pre-publicity for the show.

Jane Daly, who had replaced Jerome as General Manager in 1988, thought highly of that production. 'It was beautiful,' she said: 'beautifully produced, and the design was gorgeous.' She was also pleased that Minghella had visited Galway: he liked the city and the production, she thought. But the front of house and administration staff in Druid were picking up on a feeling in Galway audiences that the show lacked something – that there

Chapter 6: A Transforming Galway, 1987–1990

Sabina Higgins in *St Patrick's Day*.

was no sense of familiarity or connection in it, that it just didn't feel like a Druid show. Even so, it received complimentary reviews, with Fred Johnston describing it in the *Sunday Press* as 'probably one of the best things Druid have presented' – though that might have been a backhanded compliment, given that it was one of the few shows not to have been directed by Garry.

Another England-based director, Jon Tarlton, came to Galway in 1990, but this time for an Irish play: Richard Brinsley Sheridan's *St Patrick's Day*. Again there were plenty of actors new to Druid, but on that occasion there was also a positive sense that Galway audiences were getting to see people who had made a recent impact in Dublin. The cast included Arthur Riordan, one of the founding members of Rough Magic theatre company, a Dublin-based ensemble that had been inspired by Druid. There were also actors from Passion Machine, another new company that had been creating a buzz with its productions of new plays about working-class life by Paul Mercier and Roddy Doyle.

But returning to Druid in Sheridan's play was Sabina Higgins (now going by her married name), who played the role of Bridget Credulous. By then, Sabina's husband Michael D. had been elected to the Dáil as a Labour Party TD; he therefore needed to arrange a 'pair' (an agreement with a politician from another party that both would absent themselves from any votes that might be taken) so that he could attend the opening night.

For that production, Druid had removed all the seats – which had been built so carefully by Seán McGinley eleven years earlier – from the Druid Lane theatre. They had done so from necessity (they were in dire need of repair), but as ever Druid were making the most of the situation, arranging for the play to be performed twice a night and in promenade style, with audiences walking to different parts of the building to see different scenes. It felt like a return to form, a production that was attuned to recent developments in the rest of the island, but which was giving Galway audiences what they had come to expect.

By 1990, Druid was Galway's most famous arts organization – but it certainly wasn't the only one.

The city's annual Arts Festival had begun in 1978, initially as a weeklong celebration that combined readings, a screening of Bob Quinn's film *Poitín* (Mick Lally's first film role), visual art and theatre. Druid's production of Chekhov's *The Proposal* also featured that year, thus initiating a relationship with the festival that has continued ever since.

Els Comediants in Galway, 1985.

Under the leadership of Ollie Jennings, who stayed as its Artistic Director until 1990, the festival quickly began to bring international work to Galway – often for the simple reason that it was brilliant and therefore deserved to be seen, but also because there was an understanding that new ideas from abroad could inspire the development of work by local artists. Thus, the travelling theatre company Footsbarn first came to Galway in 1981 and became regular return visitors; and the Quebecois director Robert Lepage staged his *Dragon's Trilogy* in an improvised venue in Galway in 1987 as part of a tour that would soon make him an international star.

But perhaps the most influential visiting production during the festival's early years was by the Spanish street theatre collective Els Comediants. Noeline Kavanagh, who would herself go on to be a director of street theatre in Galway, recalls the impact of that performance on her:

> I was ten … a kid from Renmore watching naked Spanish people come down the town with a dragon and breathing fire. I remember standing on the street in the lashing rain and there was this pandemonium; you could hear these drums, but you couldn't see anything. You could hear this roaring and you could smell the smoke. And then, out of nowhere, these masked crazy demons and devils dancing with bare arses were weaving their way down the street. I remember sitting in the back of the car on the way home and saying to mum and dad, 'What else would you want to do with your life? Isn't that just brilliant.'

Kavanagh was not the only person who felt that way. In 1986, Páraic Breathnach, Tom Conroy, Ollie Jennings and Pete Sammon came together to found Macnas, which grew into a much-loved street theatre company whose annual parades became an essential fixture in the cultural calendar not only of Galway but of Ireland. Their work aimed to complement Druid's rather than competing against it: Druid was focused on professionalism, but Macnas would do community-based work; Druid was a literary theatre, while Macnas was more interested in visual impact; Druid made performances for theatres and Macnas made them for the street.

The Arts Festival also placed theatre in dialogue with other art forms, often resulting in the creation of spin-out festivals and companies. Its support of film resulted in the foundation of a separate festival exclusively dedicated to that art form, the Galway Film Fleadh. Beginning in 1989, it developed into an important showcase for Irish filmmaking, and was instrumental in Galway being named a UNESCO city of film in 2014. Similarly, in 1985, the poet Fred Johnston formed the Cúirt Festival, working with Dick Donaghue, the director of the Galway Arts Centre, and with advice and support from Tom Kenny and Ronnie O'Gorman.

Chapter 6: A Transforming Galway, 1987–1990

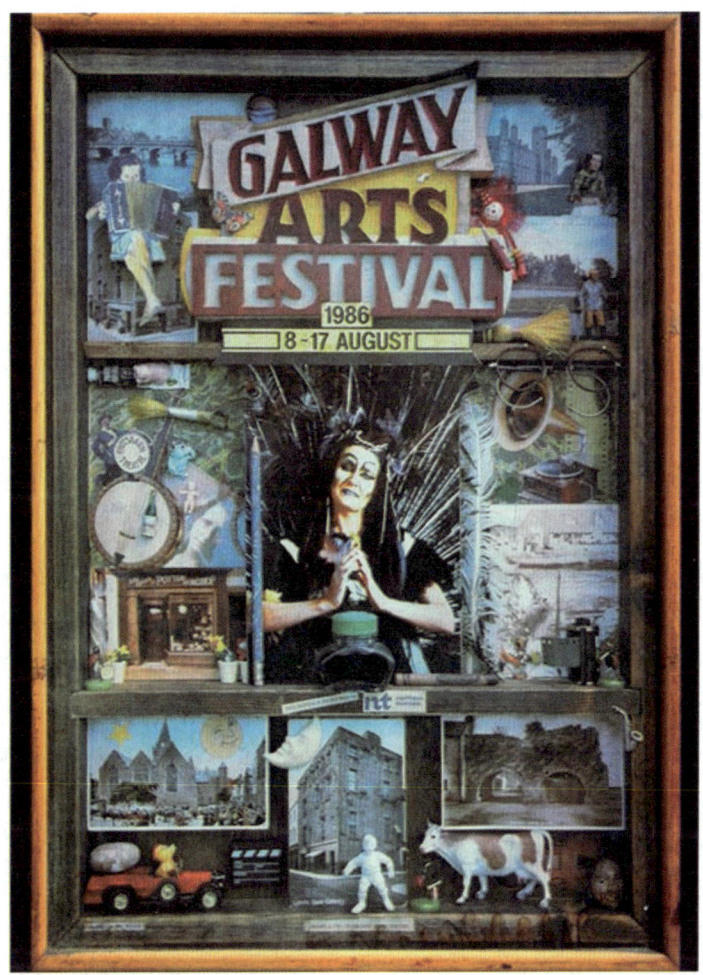

The Arts Festival poster for 1986.

Initially focused on poetry, Cúirt soon expanded to include all kinds of literature, including playwriting.

There was lots of other theatre happening in the city too. John Arden and Margaretta D'Arcy had established the Galway Theatre Workshop in 1976, and their combination of theatre, public performance and radical activism remained an important current in Galway's cultural life for decades thereafter. In 1984, for example, they had protested the visit to Galway by the US president Ronald Reagan by placing themselves in two chairs at the top of Eyre Square for several days beforehand – where they engaged passers-by in conversation about the American government's attacks on Nicaragua. As the journalist Jeff O'Connell later recalled:

> It was a peaceful, dignified, and principled protest, and many people did stop to talk. Arden and D'Arcy, throughout their lives and careers, were firm believers in the crucial importance of local community involvement and activism, and their protest was of a piece of this.

There was also a growing number of other theatre groups, professional and amateur, across the city and region. In 1989, David Quinn and Sean Evers founded Punchbag Theatre Company, which went on to produce Patricia Burke Brogan's *Eclipsed*, an important exposé of the abuses suffered by Irish women in Magdalene laundries run by the Catholic Church.

Then, in the early 1990s, the Kings Head pub became home to the Flying Pig theatre company and comedy troupe, which combined improv, stand-up comedy and live music. Their early productions (which featured a young Tommy Tiernan) included *Playboy of the European Community* and Julian Gough and Gary McSweeney's *Peig – The Musical*, both of which made good-natured fun of the Irish-themed work that Druid specialized in.

And of course, theatre wasn't being made in isolation in the city. Shortly after her arrival in the city, Jane Daly found out just how intertwined the Galway arts scene was. 'I was twenty-seven when I moved to Galway ... I started in November 1988 and Maureen Hughes had arranged a room for me in a house on St Mary's Terrace,' she recalled. Among her new housemates were Ollie Jennings, Joe Wall (who had just set up a band called the Stunning), and Leo Moran, whose band the Saw Doctors had been set up in Tuam in 1986. 'I lived there for about six weeks,' Jane recalled, 'and I never looked back.'

Chapter 6: A Transforming Galway, 1987–1990

As the 1990s began, Druid was part of a thriving cultural ecosystem – and Galway's reputation as a cultural city was having a major economic impact, driving tourism and leading to the regeneration of the city.

Somewhat paradoxically, however, that regeneration was making Druid's occupation of their own theatre space more uncertain. When the McDonoghs had leased their warehouse to Druid, they were giving the company a largely derelict space in a rundown part of the city that many Galwegians tended not to visit very often. But with increasing prosperity, a growing number of pubs and restaurants, and rising real estate prices – much of which was driven by Druid's presence in that part of the city – that warehouse was now worth quite a lot of money.

The removal of the seats from the Druid Lane Theatre had intensified local audiences' speculation about the future of the venue. Garry felt compelled to address the local media about that anxiety:

> All the growth going on in this town is not unrelated to the growth of the arts here. The arts have created a kind of special atmosphere in Galway, causing people to want to invest here and to live and work here. This very growth, which has been wisely ordered by our local authorities, is in fact, in a curious way, creating problems for the generators of all this in the first place, the people involved in the arts. All the building that's going on is making us homeless.

There had been lots of talk around the city about the eventual development of a municipal theatre for Galway – one that might (or might not) provide a permanent home for Druid. But in the meantime the company's activities were being conducted under the constant threat of eviction, the prospect of which Garry described as 'obviously traumatic':

> It's like leaving a home where you have lived for a long time and raised a family and been happy. We were very lucky to have it. We were housed by the kindness of the McDonogh group for ten or twelve years. If they hadn't come to the rescue it's doubtful there'd be a Druid today. Now we're apprehensive about the future.

Most people in Galway knew that, when Garry spoke about those apprehensions, her own future with the company was also uncertain.

In August 1990, the news that everyone was expecting finally came through: Garry had accepted the offer of the Artistic Directorship of the Abbey Theatre, after several months of negotiation. Jane Daly told *The Irish Times* that Druid was 'very happy and very proud for Garry', and the announcement was greeted with enthusiasm in Irish theatre circles – and with quite a lot of relief too.

She had been offered that role at least once before, in 1986, but had turned it down; and since that time the Abbey had found it difficult to keep anyone in the job: Joe Dowling had left in 1985; then, Christopher Fitz-Simon had been replaced by Vincent Dowling in 1987 only to be replaced in turn by Noel Pearson in 1989. The theatre received much more money than any other arts organization in Ireland, but was still chronically under-funded relative to its responsibilities, and it had major problems with its structure and governance.

With the news of Garry's appointment, there was a widespread feeling – naively, it would turn out – that those problems could be

Chapter 6: A Transforming Galway, 1987–1990

The advertisement for Garry's replacement.

overcome simply by hiring someone new. She would be 'Bringing the Druid Spirit to the Stage of the Abbey', as one newspaper headline had it – as if the Abbey's problems were to do with 'spirit' rather than more tangible matters. It just wasn't that simple.

Donagh O'Donoghue and the rest of the Druid Board had known that Garry's departure was likely, and they moved quickly to replace her, posting an ad in *The Irish Times* on 22 August to find her successor.

And with that done, it was time for a farewell production.

Lovers' Meeting by Louis D'Alton opened in Galway in October 1990, and was followed by a URT. Gesturing to the future, the cast featured a promising young actor – Aidan Gillen – in the lead role; but the production was widely seen as the final bow of the company that had made Druid great.

Lovers' Meeting with Ingrid Cragie and Marie Mullen, 1990.

Yet again, Garry was retrieving a forgotten Irish play – this time from 1941; and yet again, she had chosen a revival that told a story about young Irish people being mistreated and abused by their parents' generation. Seán and Marie were sharing a Druid stage together as a married couple for the first time; Maelíosa had come back from Australia, and Ray McBride was there too. Garry was working again with the designer Frank Conway. There was novelty in the production too: the film-maker Thaddeus O'Sullivan was employed as lighting designer, emphasising the deliberately cinematic style of the production. But even in the

Chapter 6: A Transforming Galway, 1987–1990

choice of venues on the URT, the show felt like a final farewell, especially when it finished the tour on Inis Meáin a few weeks before Christmas.

Meanwhile, the Board of Directors had some decisions to make. That *Irish Times* ad had been widely noticed – but they had been disappointed that they hadn't received applications from many (or, some claimed, any) suitably experienced directors. It wasn't clear why that was. Maybe there was a feeling that Garry just couldn't be replaced? Or perhaps there was a belief in the theatre sector that the job had already gone to an internal candidate, that the ad had been placed for the sake of appearances? Or maybe all that speculation about Druid being on the verge of homelessness had put people off? Whatever the reason, Garry was leaving and the role had to be filled – and it was time to do something about it.

The Board knew that Maelíosa had moved to Australia, that his production of McGuinness's *Observe the Sons of Ulster* in Sydney had been a success, and that he had a young child and a new wife who loved her own job – so it seemed unlikely that he would take up the role of Artistic Director if he was offered it. But there was only one way to be sure. And so, in October 1990, while Maelíosa was on the URT with *Lovers' Meeting*, he got a phone message. Donagh O'Donoghue wanted to have a conversation with him about the future of Druid Theatre.

From *The Increased Difficulty of Concentration* by Vaclav Havel.

Chapter 7
A New Artistic Director, 1991–1995

MAELÍOSA DIDN'T need to think for very long about whether he wanted to be Artistic Director – but he was certainly taken aback by the offer. 'I didn't expect to be asked,' he admitted. 'It was quite a surprise to think that Garry was leaving in the first place.'

He'd been living in Australia and was supposed to be in Galway only from August to November 1990, first to rehearse and then to act in *Lovers' Meeting* – but his plan had been to return to Sydney afterwards.

But of course he wanted to be Druid's Artistic Director. He had already shown that he could run his own company by setting up O'Punkskys, he had been directing plays for over a decade, and he believed in Druid and wanted to keep it going. And yet ... He had just moved to Australia, he was making contacts in the theatre scene there – and he was happy. Was this the right time?

During the following days, he ran up a large phone bill talking things over with Carolyn. He was being offered a contract for four years, to lead the theatre until 1995. It wasn't what they had planned but, as they talked, Maelíosa felt sure that it was too good an opportunity to pass up.

So they agreed that he would take on the role, and that they'd stay in a house that he owned on Wood Quay, near Eyre Square.

But at the end of the four years, they'd sell the house in Galway, and would use the proceeds to buy a new home in Sydney – and that's where they would settle. From the beginning, therefore, Maelíosa knew that he would have four years with the company and that, at the end of that time, he would definitely leave again.

From there everything moved quickly. 'We started talking about me doing the job in October,' said Maelíosa, 'and I was appointed in November. Then I had to go back to Australia for Christmas, pack up and bring the family back for January.' And somehow, while all that was going on, he had to programme a year's worth of theatre for 1991.

Maelíosa started making plans with Jane Daly, talking to her mostly by phone during December. 'I have one idea that can take us up to March,' he told her, 'and I'll have to do the rest when I get to Ireland.'

Like almost everyone else in Ireland at that time, Maelíosa had watched with surprise and delight as the Berlin Wall fell in 1989 – after which, one after another, the countries of central and eastern Europe gradually freed themselves from totalitarian rule. Observing those unfolding events, he had been particularly inspired when the playwright Vaclav Havel had been elected president of Czechoslovakia in 1989, calling his country's first free elections since the Second World War shortly afterwards.

Havel had been a hero to many Irish theatremakers, both as an artist and a political dissident; Samuel Beckett, for example, had dedicated his 1982 play *Catastrophe* to Havel, both as a sign of esteem and as a protest against Havel's continued imprisonment by the communist regime. Yet now that dramatist was not only free but leading his country towards freedom. To Maelíosa it seemed not only appropriate but necessary to mark

Chapter 7: A New Artistic Director, 1991–1995

that transformation by staging one of Havel's plays. 'I didn't want it to seem pretentious,' he explained. 'I just felt it was important that we honoured him. Here was a man who had been hounded by his government – so let's celebrate him.'

During his time in Sydney, Maelíosa had met the Czech writer Katerina Ivak, who had directed her own translation of a Havel play at the Belvoir Street theatre in Sydney in August 1990. Maelíosa had read her version and, although he appreciated its politics, he also saw that it was simply a very enjoyable play, that it would be fun to do. And so it was agreed: Maelíosa's first production as Artistic Director would be Havel's *The Increased Difficulty of Concentration*. There was of course some evidence of continuity in that choice – with Druid once again marking a major occasion by doing something that hardly anyone would have predicted.

To be ready for the play's opening night on 6 March 1991, Maelíosa needed to finalize his cast very quickly when he arrived back in Ireland. Kate O'Toole would return to Druid for the show, but he also gave debuts to several young actors – among them a young man from Sligo who had trained at the École Jacques Lecoq in Paris and who went by the name Mikel Murfi. Maelíosa was therefore bringing someone to the company who would go on to have a major impact on it later (especially in his collaborations with Enda Walsh) – and that would become one of the defining features of his tenure as Artistic Director.

Rehearsals began in late January. 'I just dived into it,' Maelíosa recalled, 'and I had fun.' He was feeling confident that audiences would like Havel – despite the seriousness of what had happened to him, his plays *are* very funny.

And he was proven right. The audience hadn't known quite what to expect but within a few minutes of the play beginning each night they were enjoying themselves, and it had a successful run first in Galway and then in Limerick. 'It was a good production and I knew it would be,' said Maelíosa afterwards, though of course he was also relieved to have been proven right.

And, showing that things were changing in Ireland too, its opening night had been attended by the newly elected President of Ireland, Mary Robinson: the first woman to fill that role, and also the first nominee of the Irish Labour Party to be elected to it. She would later agree to become Druid's patron – a ceremonial role but a huge honour for the company.

Things were looking a little more promising for the Druid venue too. Donagh O'Donoghue and the McDonaghs has been able to arrange that Druid could stay in Chapel Lane until there was somewhere else for them to go: they definitely would not be made homeless. And Galway's local politicians really did seem serious about building a new theatre; their commitment to culture in the city had been signalled by the appointment in 1990 of a new Arts Officer, James C. Harrold – and it seemed possible that a new theatre building could be built and opened as soon as 1993.

With so much optimism in the air – the Cold War over, Ireland showing signs of progress – there was a sense that Druid's future might be a little more secure than it had been for some time. The new Artistic Directorship was off to a good start.

But even at that early stage, Maelíosa was already a little frustrated.

After getting underway with Havel, his next idea had been to draw on the connections he'd made in Australia by staging a play called *The Golden Age* by Louis Nowra. He brought that idea to the Board. 'It's set in the remote Tasmanian Bush,' he explained:

> It's about a lost tribe that were found there speaking old Cornish English. It's based on fact, but it's really a play

about experimenting on human beings, fascism, white Australia ... And it needs a cast of eight actors.

The initial idea was to bring Australian actors over to Galway, and that Druid would do a return season with the same team, maybe producing Seán O'Casey's *The Plough and the Stars* or *The Playboy* and taking it to the Sydney Festival, where they had already had so much success with *Conversations on a Homecoming* and Garry's production of *The Playboy*.

In Maelíosa's recollection, the Board's response was immediate and painfully short: 'Too risky, too much money. No.'

He was disappointed, of course. He didn't remember ever hearing anything about the Board saying no to Garry – shouldn't he be treated the same way? Already feeling isolated, he knew that he'd need help if he was going to make his time as AD a success.

Jane Daly had been with Druid for a little over two years when Maelíosa was appointed.

She'd been disappointed upon her own arrival to learn that the company of actors who had so excited her (and everyone else) were beginning to drift away: 'I joined an administrative team and I came to a venue, but I didn't come to a company,' she later said. Most of Jane's working time was therefore spent with Druid's administrator, Anne Butler, and with its Artistic Administrator Maureen Hughes, who had been developing an unusually strong talent for working with actors (she would soon join Garry at the Abbey as the theatre's casting director before setting up her own casting company).

Jane, Anne, and Maureen quickly formed a close bond. 'Their passion for Druid was exemplary,' said Jane, 'and I think that passion carried us through an awful lot of the darker days, the trickier days to come'.

Those 'darker, trickier' days were caused to a considerable extent by anxiety about the future of the venue. 'We were forever living under the threat of eviction from Chapel Lane,' Jane recalls; and when the building behind the Druid Lane Theatre was sold, they had to move their administrative offices to a vacant warehouse nearby. The new administrative space was windowless and constantly freezing; it was difficult to bring people in for meetings – and it was just a terrible place to work. The ongoing uncertainty was a definite strain.

But there was a bigger problem, Jane realized – the difficulty of managing success:

> We were so busy. We were doing four shows a year, and we were touring, and we were doing revivals. We just didn't have enough time to stop and reflect. And to be honest, in those days there wasn't an awful lot of talk about strategic planning and business plans and action plans. You were doing shows all the time and you were trying to balance the books and … We were just in this maelstrom.

The arrival of Maelíosa inevitably meant that that there would be more disruption, for a time.

'It was a learning period,' Jane acknowledged. 'It took a while for us to work out the rules of engagement for an Artistic Director working with a General Manager.' For her part, that was partly because she'd developed so much autonomy during the preceding years, and now had to adjust to working with an Artistic Director who was around on a daily basis. But there was also an adjustment to be made for Maelíosa: he was so used to working with other actors, to thinking instinctively and maybe even impulsively, that he was occasionally making long-term

Chapter 7: A New Artistic Director, 1991–1995

decisions about the company not in an office with Jane but in a rehearsal room.

So they both quickly had to learn to collaborate rather than presenting each other with decisions that they had already made by themselves.

It helped that they liked and respected each other. Jane particularly appreciated what she saw as Maelíosa's humility:

> He never claimed to be something he's not. He's an actor, he's a director. He would never have claimed to be a producer or a manager. What we did develop quite quickly was a sense of mutual respect, in that I couldn't direct a show, and I couldn't perform in a show, and he couldn't write a compelling funding application, or negotiate contracts with actors and agents. So we found a good place in many ways, and we relied on each other in a way that might have surprised us both at the start.

In a curious way, the fact that Maelíosa's time with the company was limited to four years gave everyone a necessary sense of certainty. They didn't know what might happen after 1995, but for now, they could all agree on a plan: 'Let's just try and do the best work we possibly can while we're here.'

That attitude created space for others in the company to come forward with new ideas. Anne Butler had been with Druid for several years, and had been watching their audience grow older as the company itself matured. She could see that there was now a bit of a problem: as the audience was aging, the next generation wasn't necessarily following them to Druid shows.

Yet there was so much evidence of an enthusiasm for theatre among young Galway people. Rebecca Bartlett had set up Galway Youth Theatre in 1991, Macnas parades usually had lots of students in them, and the university DramSoc was as strong as it had ever been. Why weren't more of them coming to Druid? 'I felt I wanted to do something about that,' said Anne, so she started talking to Maelíosa about starting a schools programme:

> It was initially very simple. Basically my job was to go to schools and find somebody, usually an English teacher, who had an interest in theatre, and to get them excited about the possibility of maybe coming and seeing rehearsals, or maybe bringing their class in.

Anne started putting together education packs for shows, and arranged a special student rate. They did need to keep the balance right – putting a class of thirty teenagers into a space limited to a hundred audience members in total would have thrown the energy of any performance out of balance. But, gradually, small groups of students started appearing in the theatre, initially accompanied by their teachers and then more often just coming along by themselves. Anne also began to organise the open submissions of plays to the company, overseeing the new writing process (Martin McDonagh would later credit Anne with bringing his work to Druid's attention).

By supporting those kinds of initiatives, Maelíosa was trying to find a balance too, trying to reconnect the company with Galway, while also trying to bring in new people – both into the company and into the audience.

As he built up a solid working relationship with Jane, Anne and the rest of the company, he was able to focus more on the artistic programme. The biggest question for him was how to do that in a way that would work for the distinct groups he had to contend with, including funders, the Board, audiences and the rest of the theatre's staff. It wasn't going to be easy.

Chapter 7: A New Artistic Director, 1991–1995

When he looked back on his first year in the job, Maelíosa claimed that he had been lucky, that things started to work out for him mostly because of serendipity.

Maybe that claim was another example of the humility that Jane had noticed in him – but it is true that his successes as AD were bolstered by chance meetings, stray conversations and acts of seeming impulsiveness that somehow worked out brilliantly.

In the years before Maelíosa's appointment, Druid had been working a lot with freelance directors – often from the UK, where Garry had developed good contacts. Maelíosa knew that he couldn't direct a full season of shows himself (nor did he want to), but he also wanted to hire directors who had a stronger sense of Druid's identity, and who might form a stronger bond with their audiences. He encouraged the company's stage manager, Moya McHugh, to start directing – but he was also interested in working with up-and-coming Irish directors.

In early 1991, he'd been in Dublin to cast a show and got talking to the agent Lisa Richards – who told him that there was a young director in Cork who was generating a lot of buzz. He was still in college, still making shows at the University College Cork Drama Society, but his brother Bob was already doing amazing work in London as a theatre designer. His name was John Crowley and he was worth checking out.

So that's exactly what Maelíosa did. He travelled to Cork to see one of Crowley's shows – and quickly made him an offer. Maelíosa had hired Roland Jaquarello, the director of Belfast's Lyric Theatre, to do a summertime show called *Cheapside* by David Allen (which Maelíosa himself would play the lead role in). Crowley would be a trainee director with Jaquarello, and he would then be given the opportunity to direct a lunchtime production, of a play called *John Hughdy and Tom John* by a new writer, Vincent Woods.

Crowley of course said yes, and he went on to direct throughout Maelíosa's time as AD – a key step in the development of a career that would eventually see him become a Tony-nominated director, for Martin McDonagh's *The Pillowman*, as well as a filmmaker whose movies include the 2003 Irish hit *Intermission* and, in 2015, a much-praised adaptation of Colm Tóibín's *Brooklyn* that starred Saoirse Ronan.

But an even more serendipitous meeting for Maelíosa had happened in late 1990 in Australia, when he had found himself talking to a young Irish backpacker at a poetry reading in Sydney – Vincent Woods. 'I just went up to him and we got chatting,' Maelíosa recalls:

> You know the way you find sometimes with people: you just get on. I was interested in his poetry and I felt I understood it. He was an intelligent man who was interested in theatre, and he said that he'd been in New Zealand, had taken a couple of years off, and had been writing. He showed me a series of three monologues. 'I don't even know if you'd call it a play,' he said, but that was the beginnings of *John Hughdy*.

Maelíosa took the stories back with him to Ireland and the two men met there again in the spring of 1991. Showing a talent for dramaturgy that would form the bedrock of their relationship, Maelíosa told Vincent that two of the three stories connected well together, but that the middle one felt like something separate – maybe it could work as a radio play, he thought? So they came up with the idea of bringing the first and third parts together into an hour-long lunchtime drama. And that was how *John Hughdy and Tom John* found its way into production, with John Crowley directing.

And then, as Maelíosa and Vincent got to know each other better, they started talking about Vincent's home county of Leitrim.

Leitrim is within Druid territory – which is to say that it's in the province of Connacht and lies close to Marie's home county of Sligo and Garry's of Roscommon. But it was also somewhat different from those places because of its proximity to Northern Ireland, with which it shared what was at the time a highly militarized border.

It was also a place that had performance traditions of its own. Maelíosa knew Leitrim as what he called 'the heart of mumming territory'. Mumming is part of the vernacular Irish performance tradition and usually involves members of a local community visiting homes in disguise, often around Christmas time or on other festive occasions, to perform simple plays or other entertainments. Their costumes are often elaborate but are made from everyday items; the masks that hide the performers' identities, for example, are often made of straw. And they usually perform plays that have been handed down through an oral tradition, and which feature various stock characters such as a Captain, a Doctor, Beelzebub, Miss Funny and Oliver Cromwell (that last character was very much a villain).

Mumming is similar to other European amateur performance traditions, especially in countries that have a tradition of Carnival. But it was also a strong example of the ongoing vitality of a distinctively Irish tradition, especially around the border counties.

Both Vincent and Maelíosa knew about that tradition – the latter remembered his father participating in mumming when he was a child, and he had also read (and loved) the books of the American folklorist Henry Glassie, who wrote about Irish mumming. Maybe there was something there, they both thought – a play that might blend that old Irish tradition with an exploration of the impact of the Troubles in the present?

Vincent started thinking about writing a drama that he would call *At the Black Pig's Dyke*.

The Mummers in *At the Black Pig's Dyke* (1992).

Maelíosa had been keen to engage more with audiences in Northern Ireland anyway. The collapse of the Berlin Wall had created a sense of optimism around the world, a belief that seemingly intractable conflicts could at last be set aside. But in the north, the Troubles seemed as far from resolution as they had ever been. Maelíosa therefore felt it was important for Druid to spend more time with audiences there, but he had also come to the conclusion that people in the south also needed to face the reality of that conflict more fully.

That conviction led him to decide that his first URT – of a play from the 1930s called *Shadow and Substance* by Paul Vincent

Shadow and Substance, set and costumes by Francis O'Connor.

Carroll – should include visits to the north: alongside stops at regular venues such as the Hawk's Well in Sligo and the Belltable in Limerick, Druid would also travel to Armagh and Strabane for the first time.

That production didn't succeed in the way that Maelíosa had hoped it would. Druid had a reputation for finding contemporary resonances in old plays, and he had a hunch that audiences might respond to Carroll's suggestion that Irish Catholicism was in danger of losing its status as a personal faith and instead becoming a vehicle for intolerance and oppression.

But Druid's audiences didn't warm to the play, maybe because it was too melodramatic, or perhaps because its warnings about religion felt redundant in a country that was rapidly secularizing. 'Even in rehearsals I knew something wasn't right,' said Maelíosa. He didn't know what that something was, but he knew it wasn't working. Jane agreed – she would later recall the feeling of deflation when the show opened in the Cork Opera House to an audience of only fourteen people.

But there was one particularly important outcome, which is that the production marked one of the first times that the designer Francis O'Connor worked with Druid (he had designed for the company only once before, for Ken Harmon's *Wild Harvest* in

1989, directed by Andy Hinds). His set and costumes were realistic enough to ground the play, but also had a heightened quality that brought out its metaphorical and even spiritual qualities. It was obvious that he was an immensely talented designer, and from the mid-1990s onwards he would become one of Druid's most important contributors.

The two visits to Northern Ireland had been a positive feature of an otherwise disappointing tour. But Maelíosa wanted to maintain his focus on the north – and that gave rise to the idea of reviving Frank McGuinness's play *Carthaginians* for his season in 1992.

That play had premiered at the Abbey in 1988, where it had been met with praise but also a degree of uncertainty in the audience response. It's set in Derry City, in a graveyard where a group of local people gather every day to remember their loved ones, perhaps hoping that somehow they will be resurrected – and is McGuinness's theatrical response to the events of Bloody Sunday, when the British Army opened fire on a Civil Rights march in Derry in 1972, murdering thirteen civilians.

Yet despite its serious and politically charged context, *Carthaginians* is an often light-hearted and occasionally hilarious piece of theatre, especially during the performance of a play-within-the-play, *The Burning Balaclava*, which is led by a drag queen called Dido. That use of humour explains the uncertainty in the audiences' reaction in Dublin. Bloody Sunday was one of the biggest tragedies in recent Irish history – wasn't it wrong to laugh so much at a play that was responding to those events?

But McGuinness knew exactly what he was doing. He was using comedy to show how the conflict in Northern Ireland had been fought not only through acts of physical violence but also

From *Carthaginians*.

through the imagination: through the promulgation of sectarian stereotypes, the misuse of national and religious symbols, and the insistence upon a rigid loyalty to cultural images that were causing more harm than good. His proposition in *Carthaginians* was that humour could undermine those pieties, and thus offer a way forward. And he was arguing specifically that the queer performativity embodied by Dido might bring liberation from ways of living that had until then seemed inescapably fixed.

It's worth recalling that homosexuality was illegal in the Republic of Ireland when McGuinness wrote the play, and that in the north homophobia was a constant on both sides of the sectarian divide. *Carthaginians* was, to put it mildly, giving audiences a lot to think about.

So with the twentieth anniversary of Bloody Sunday looming, Maelíosa wanted to bring that play to audiences in Galway – and he thought it was important that it should be seen in Derry too. It was decided that McGuinness would direct it, and that it would include three Druid regulars: Maelíosa, Pauline McLynn and Joan Sheehy. And for the role of Dido, they cast a young actor from Cork, Pat Kinevane – who would later go on to be an important playwright himself.

McGuinness had never directed his own work before, but Maelíosa was confident that it would work out well: 'What Frank brings,' he told people, 'is an open heart' – and if that statement was vague it was nevertheless reassuring. It was McGuinness's story, Maelíosa said; he knew the emotional arc of the play better than anyone – and anyway, Maelíosa would be in the rehearsal room too.

They started thinking about how the production should appear visually. McGuinness had an idea: maybe they could have a chat with Brian Bourke, a major Irish artist who was living in Connemara? 'So I said "absolutely",' Maelíosa recalled, and he asked Jane if she could arrange a meeting:

> We met up for lunch and Brian drew the set. He just took out a packet of cigarettes, opened the box out, and started filling in different colours.

Maelíosa and McGuinness were blown away – both by Bourke's ideas and by how deeply he had thought about the play. And soon he was painting the inside of the theatre. During the run, art dealers would show up at Druid asking if they could buy parts of the set afterwards – the answer, of course, was no.

Bourke's design ensured that the production was not misunderstood as documentary realism but that instead it was revealed as something closer to the Greek theatre that had so inspired McGuinness. Dido was a drag queen but was also like Dionysus, a god(dess) of misrule; and the small group of people in the Derry graveyard were in some primal way a microcosm of their entire community, even though McGuinness had created them in such a way that they also felt like real people. Bourke's design was essential to the realization of what McGuinness had been trying to do in writing the play.

McGuinness had of course been nervous about bringing *Carthaginians* to Derry. Druid had done some groundwork by seeking advice from local activists such as Bernadette McAliskey, and they also liaised with the office of the Lord Mayor of the city. 'They were ready for it,' Maelíosa said later. 'And maybe it softened the blow by having obviously southern actors putting on northern accents. So anyone who didn't want to believe it could go "well, what do they know?"' But the reaction was unreservedly positive: audiences in Derry found the production moving, respectful and powerful.

Druid would return to Derry once more during Maelíosa's time as AD – though their next visit would have a vastly different outcome.

But first there was another moment of serendipity to be savoured. Maelíosa had been approached by a Galway-based traditional musician called Seán Tyrrell, who had come up with the idea of doing a musical version of *The Midnight Court*, an English-language translation of the eighteenth-century poem *Cúirt An Mheán Oíche* by the County Clare poet Brian Merriman.

The 'court' of the title involves a hearing in which the women of Ireland complain that their men are refusing to get married – and are also failing to meet their conjugal responsibilities. It's bawdy, playful, energetic and also a wonderful work of art that had deep roots in Druid's imaginative hinterland. Maelíosa thought it was an exciting proposition, though it wasn't immediately evident how Merriman's thousand-line poem could be made to work in a live performance.

The Midnight Court, 1992.

But when Jane looked back on the production that emerged from those initial conversations, she described it as one of Maelíosa's great artistic successes. 'Seán had read David Marcus's translation of the poem and he could hear it in his head,' she said. 'But he didn't know how to get it out of his head and onto a stage.' Working together, Seán and Maelíosa started to understand how it might be made to work in a theatre: they would do it as a late-night show, starting at around ten at night, so that it would feel almost like a gig or a trad session rather than a play. Jane was deeply impressed by the results:

> I think Maelíosa actually pulled off a miracle. There was an alchemy, where you had a disparate group of musicians

Chapter 7: A New Artistic Director, 1991–1995

who for the first time were actually sitting and playing in front of an audience that was paying to see them, that weren't getting up and going to the bar every five minutes for a drink and talking over them, as happens at a trad session in a pub.

Maelíosa was having fun with it too. On some nights they'd try segregating the audience into men and women, letting the poem's division of genders spill into the auditorium. The music was great, and the poem felt just as relevant in 1992 as it must have been 200 years earlier.

The musicians were delighted with the experience, but, as Jane observed:

> Everybody got something out of that show. The audience had got something. The artists got something. The company completely got something, in that *The Midnight Court* brought in a whole new audience for Druid.

The sales from those new audiences generated some much-needed income after the disappointment of *Shadow and Substance* – and that, combined with a successful blending of conventional theatre with traditional Irish performance styles, meant that the time was now right to move forward with *At the Black Pig's Dyke*.

Maelíosa had learned a lot from watching Garry and Tom Murphy working together in rehearsal rooms, and with his relationship with Vincent Woods he was starting to form a sense of the strength of his own dramaturgical skill.

For *Black Pig's Dyke* he and Vincent had already worked through a number of drafts – but as they came closer to producing it, Maelíosa felt it was important to bring a designer into their discussions early on, and therefore engaged Monica Frawley. He also brought in a musician, Brendan O'Regan. 'So once we started sharing the visual ideas, the music ideas, the writing got sharper,' Maelíosa said: 'The next draft would be clearer because we'd all see what we were doing, particularly Monica, myself and Vincent.' Woods had been writing the play at home in Leitrim, where he'd returned when his mother had become seriously ill. He knew that the plan was to write a play that would 'use the device of mumming and tell some story of political conflict in Ireland'. But as he talked to his parents about their memories – both of mumming and of the conflict over the border – the play began to take shape.

Certainly, he agreed with Maelíosa about the need for audiences in the Republic to face what was happening in the north:

> It still seems very strange to me that there was this savage war going on so close to us all, and we were able to almost ignore it – except that it was there, except that it was a reality. But a reality that we could stay away from.

He therefore used mumming as a way of thinking about how communities use performance – both in the theatrical sense and in a more sinister way – to understand themselves, to express their values, and sometimes to exploit or even harm each other.

Maelíosa could see how powerful Vincent's approach was. The play explored how violence in Ireland followed deeply ingrained cycles. That offered an important way of thinking about the Troubles, Maelíosa knew, but he also saw that the play had something to say about other patterns in Irish life, such as the cycle of abuse against young Irish women in the Magdalene laundries. The use of mumming, both as a performance style and

Show poster, *At the Black Pig's Dyke*, 1992.

as a metaphor, would allow audiences to think about how the Troubles intersected with multiple other elements of Irish life.

They began to assemble a cast. Marie was mostly working at the Abbey with Garry by then, but Ray was still in Galway – so he not only took on the role of the Captain Mummer but also choreographed the show. The rest of the actors were freelancers, but some were appearing semi-regularly with Druid, providing the basis for what might almost have been a new ensemble, including actors such as Deirdre O'Kane, David Wilmot, Frankie McCafferty and Peter Gowen. Maelíosa thought it was also important to draw in actors from the north, and so Stella McCusker was cast in the lead female role of Lizzie Boles.

At the Black Pig's Dyke opened in Galway in September 1992 – and it was Druid's 100th production. The play received instant acclaim, and plans for an all-Ireland and international tour were soon underway. In 1993, the play went to Derry and to the Tricycle Theatre in Kilburn in London, and the following year it went to Canada, Scotland and Australia.

More than with any other production during Maelíosa's tenure, *At the Black Pig's Dyke* showed that there could be a life for Druid after Garry and Marie.

The play definitely felt like a Druid production. It had begun life in the west of Ireland, and it featured a tightly knit ensemble of actors who had developed a deep understanding of how the playwright was using language.

But it also placed emphasis on characteristics that would have been less prominent in Druid's past. It was drawing on oral and vernacular traditions more than literary ones; it was squarely addressing the contemporary political situation rather than coming at it indirectly or form an obtuse angle; and it had been created through a deeply collaborative interplay between direction, design, playwriting and musical composition. Maelíosa was starting to put his mark upon the company.

Not everyone appreciated the play's approach to politics, however. Woods received some direct criticism, both from acquaintances and members of the public, for his treatment of republican violence. If it is read superficially, it is possible to interpret the play as a suggestion that the IRA's campaign was based not on ideology or idealism but that it was instead driven by the selfishness of flawed, damaged men. In that analysis, the Troubles were depoliticized, driven by acts of individual criminality and dysfunction rather than historical injustice.

Woods's defenders rejected that interpretation, arguing that *Black Pig's Dyke* instead shows the historical roots of Irish colonialism (that's one of the reasons that Oliver Cromwell features as a villain in mumming plays, after all). Woods's aim, they suggested, was to highlight the human costs of communal violence. He was trying to make people think rather than telling them what to think: this was a work of art, not a political tract or manifesto.

In Derry, however, the negative interpretations of the play came to the fore when a local group staged a protest during its performance, doing so in a way that looked initially as if it might be an ambush from a paramilitary group. 'In retrospect,' Maelíosa said, 'it was a storm in a teacup: the protesters were a young, active republican group with strong political views'. But, he said, 'they did fuck up the show. They scared the crap out of some of the actors and people in the audience who ended up running away.'

Maelíosa knew what the protesters were trying to do; he understood that they were motivated by ideas about performance-based protest from the Brazilian director Augusto Boal, and he certainly didn't want to silence them. He just thought that they were going the wrong away about making their point:

> If they had said to us, we really disagree with this play, I would have said 'If you want to do a protest play, you can use our set. You can come on after we're finished and we'd invite the audience to stay.' But you don't come in and scare a bunch of actors who are guests of the city. It's not their politics. It's not their opinions; they're actors. If you want to have a go, have a go at me or Vincent.

It was suggested to Maelíosa that no harm had been done, that the protest had generated a great deal of free publicity. But for many years afterwards, he continued to feel protective of the actors, suggesting that they shouldn't have been on the receiving end of so negative an experience.

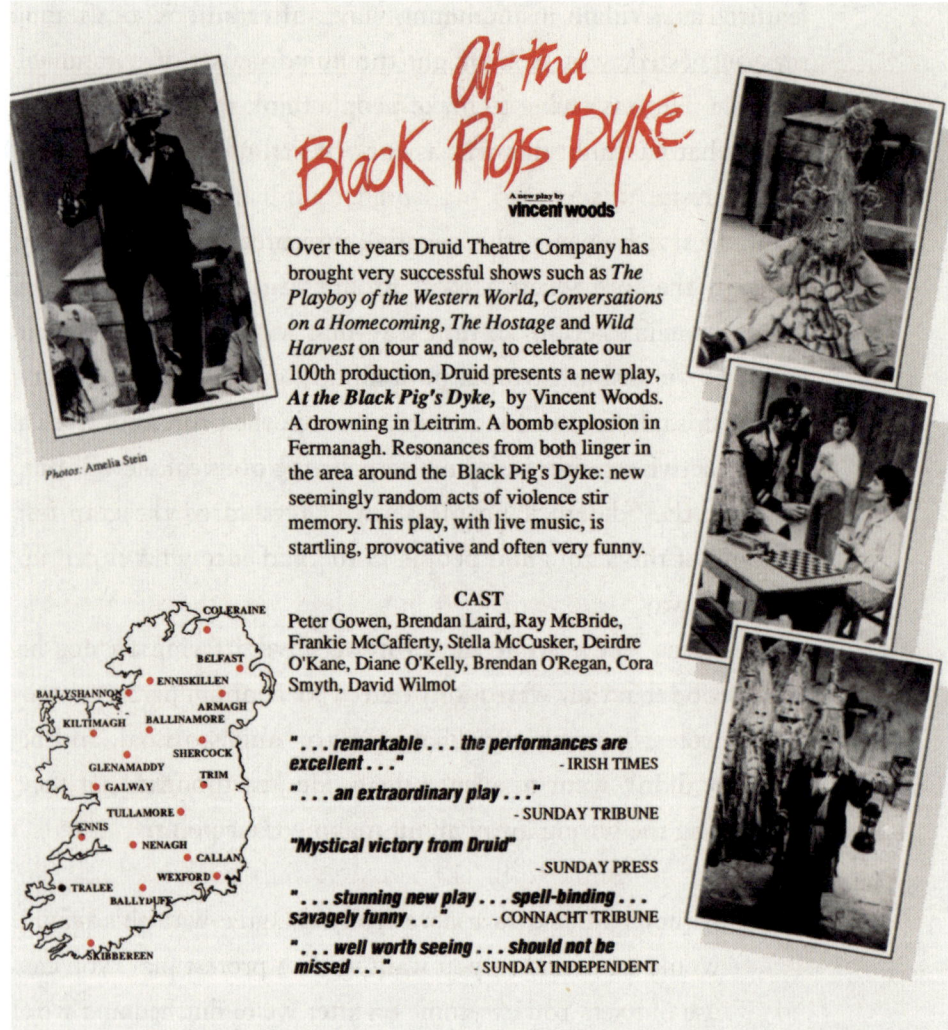

Nationwide tour of *At the Black Pig's Dyke*.

But the history of Irish theatre is in many ways a history of great plays being disrupted by protests and even riots – and *At the Black Pig's Dyke* had written its way into that history in Derry.

There was one other important legacy from the production. Vincent Woods and Monica Frawley's artistic collaboration during the creation of the play had brought them closer together – and soon they were partners in life too, becoming one of a growing number of couples who had been brought together by their work with Druid.

Chapter 7: A New Artistic Director, 1991–1995

By 1994, Maelíosa had found his stride as Artistic Director. *Black Pig's Dyke* was touring the world; there was continued demand in Ireland for tours of *The Midnight Court*, and Druid had begun another relationship with a contemporary Irish writer: Billy Roche – whose play *Belfry* they had staged to immense success in 1993.

And although Maelíosa's early idea of collaborating with Australian actors had been considered too risky to go ahead at the start of his contract, by 1994 Druid were again collaborating internationally, notably with the Tricycle, which brought a co-production of Mustapha Matura's *The Playboy of the West Indies* from London to Galway in 1994.

That was an adaptation of Synge's play, but relocated to Trinidad in a way that brought to the fore the histories of racism and colonialism that in Synge's original are definitely present, but obliquely so. In the first decade of the twenty-first century, Irish theatre companies would attempt to reflect the diversity of the Irish population by adapting Synge – in one case setting *The Playboy* in China and in another re-imagining Christy Mahon as a Nigerian asylum seeker. Maelíosa was therefore considerably ahead of his time in bringing Matura's work to Galway.

With a combination of critical success, a renewed international profile and a relatively healthy box office, it was only right that the Druid Board asked Maelíosa if he would consider staying on for another year or two. But he had been consistent from the start: he would stay until 1995 – but then he would definitely leave.

Of course he felt torn when the new offer came his way. His relationship with Vincent Woods had resulted in another new play, *Song of the Yellow Bittern*, which was due to go on in November 1994. And he'd brought a lot of new people into the

Show poster, *Song of the Yellow Bittern*, 1994.

company. They were now hosting a steady stream of young arts administrators, many of whom would go on to be major figures in the Irish sector, including Maureen Kennelly (an eventual director of the Irish Arts Council) and Loughlin Deegan (a future director of the Dublin Theatre Festival). They had hired a script adviser, Charlie McBride, demonstrating their ever-growing commitment to the development of new Irish playwriting. And they were also working regularly with some great young actors.

But Maelíosa had made a commitment. He told the Druid Board that, although he would programme a year's worth of work for 1995, he was heading back to Australia.

The Beauty Queen of Leenane at the Walter Kerr Theatre, New York, 1998.

Chapter 8
The Leenane Trilogy, 1996–2001

IN NOVEMBER 1995, the designer Francis O'Connor took a meeting in London with Garry Hynes. She had recently sent him a copy of a new play, *The Beauty Queen of Leenane*, by an unknown writer called Martin McDonagh – and Francis was excited: 'I just thought it was such a great play, a great bit of writing,' he recalled. He already had lots of ideas about how it might look on stage.

Francis and Garry had never collaborated before, but they both knew each other's work. He had seen some of Garry's productions at the Abbey and had been impressed – he had 'absolutely loved' her staging of John McGahern's *The Power of Darkness* there, he said. He was also familiar with Druid, having visited Galway several times during Maelíosa's tenure – first to design *Shadow and Substance* and then to meet up with the friends he'd made in the company. He had also come to know Jerome Hynes quite well from designing operas for the Wexford Festival. 'I loved Jerome,' Francis explained. 'And I'm pretty sure that he had said to Garry "You should talk to Francis"' when they were making plans to do McDonagh's first play.

The Beauty Queen is set in a cottage in Connemara, where the forty-year-old Maureen cares for her mother Mag. Maureen is lonely and isolated – but she begins to imagine the possibility of escape when she spends the night with Pato Dooley, a local man who has returned to Leenane for a short holiday from the London building sites where he normally works. Afraid of abandonment, Mag sets out to thwart her daughter's chances of finding love, thus bringing about a tragic and volent conclusion.

If described solely in terms of that plot, *The Beauty Queen* might seem very old-fashioned. It's set in a country kitchen, and shows a parent's pitiless exploitation of her child – and thus resembles one of those plays that Tom Murphy and Noel O'Donoghue had felt compelled to rebel against back in the late 1950s. But as Francis immediately realized when he read it, McDonagh's writing has a decidedly contemporary feeling to it, mainly because of its blend of humour and violence and its distinctive dialogue (features that would later draw comparisons with the screenwriting style of Quentin Tarantino), but also because it had a visceral quality that would make the action feel emotionally immediate for audiences. So as Francis and Garry discussed how to capture that strange blend of the old-fashioned with the edgily innovative, he felt happy that they were hitting it off, both creatively and personally.

'We were talking about the sense of heightened reality in the play,' he recalled. 'We agreed that it has to feel like it's happening in a real room but that, in the same way that Martin's language was heightened, the design needed a little push just to elevate it' beyond the real. The set, Francis proposed, would be full of the things that one might expect to see in a Connemara bungalow: 'It would be a cottage but – I didn't want to say it would be a crypt – but it would have a prison-like feel without it being a prison.'

> They also talked about a possible colour scheme – grey walls and a custard-yellow floor – that was based both on Francis's research and on his intuitive sense of how to convey the mood of bleakness and oppression that runs

through the text. He also suggested that the house's electric wiring should be exposed: doing that would suggest that it had been built quickly and badly. There might also be an encroaching dampness along the walls, something to convey a feeling of looming decay.

He also wanted to include subtle symbols of how this seemingly dreary environment might crack violently apart at any moment:

> One of the things we spoke about is that I wanted to put LEDs in all of the plug sockets, and on the kettle, as a little signature of what might occur later in the play.

That design feature would be in keeping with the naturalism of the script – 'we all flick a switch and a red light comes on' in our own lives, Francis explained. But he also knew that when a red light comes on in a completely dark space – such as a blacked-out theatre – it can be more than just a representation of the real world. It would create an image of impending danger, he thought, one that could be 'both realistic and theatrical: it just sets a little charge up for later in the play':

> And so we would have those red lights dotted around the set as if in some way they might represent a spatter of blood.

By the time they finished their meeting, Francis had drawn a rough sketch of the set. He felt that it had been a 'fantastic dialogue':

> She didn't say *you've got the job* or anything, but it had been such a good creative meeting I thought, 'My God, she's *got* to ask me to do it.'

Francis went away, and a couple of days later he got a call from

Garry – but it wasn't with the news that he'd been hoping for. She'd thought carefully about it, she told him, but she was going to go with someone else:

> And I was genuinely disappointed. I can't remember what I said to her. I'm sure I was courteous – 'that's disappointing but it's fine' – and that was the end of it. My career was taking off by then and I had plenty of other stuff going on, so I wasn't upset for that reason. I was more bothered because I thought we'd had a really good conversation.

A few weeks passed.

Then, just a couple of days before Christmas – or maybe even on Christas Eve? – Francis got a phone call, and was surprised to hear Garry on the other end of the line. 'I've made a mistake,' she told him – and she asked if he might be willing to join the production as its set and costume designer. Rehearsals were due to start in the first week of January, she added.

Francis told her that he really wanted to do it because he had loved the play so much – but it was Christmas, and there wasn't much time. 'Are you asking me to do the show in the way that we discussed at our meeting?' he wondered. If so, he could work up the sketches that he'd already developed, and might just be able to make it all come together on time.

Garry said yes.

So Francis got to work. He called a friend, asking for help with making a model of the set, and they began building it on the twenty-sixth of December.

Just over a week later, he arrived in Galway. 'The model was the set we'd discussed all those weeks before', he said. 'And that was pretty much exactly what wound up on the stage.'

Chapter 8: The Leenane Trilogy, 1996–2001

When Garry arranged that meeting with Francis towards the end of 1995, she had just returned to Druid – but was insistent that she was doing so only as a temporary arrangement.

With Maelíosa's return to Australia, the company was again in need of artistic leadership, especially because the long-awaited municipal theatre for Galway – to be called the Town Hall Theatre – was due to open in early 1996. Druid had decided against being that new theatre's anchor tenant, fearing that they would spend all their time and money managing the building rather than making theatre and bringing it on tour. That decision made sense to many (but not all) of their funders and supporters, but it inevitably introduced pressing questions about Druid's future place in the artistic ecosystem of both Galway and Ireland.

Maelíosa had shown that the company could survive without Garry and, having left the Abbey at the end of her contract in 1993, she was looking forward to a period of freelancing anyway. But she saw the importance of stepping in at a time when Druid needed strong leadership, and therefore agreed to take on the role of 'Consultant Artistic Director' in early 1995.

That extra word in the job title – 'consultant' – could mean different things to different people, but it did seem to imply that Garry's relationship with the company was provisional, and maybe even that her true artistic home was outside Druid rather than in it. But any sense of hesitation conveyed by the job title was understandable: it made sense that Garry might be reluctant to resume the management of one theatre company when she had just endured a difficult period in charge of another.

Before taking the job of Artistic Director at the Abbey she'd been uneasy about the well-documented problems with that theatre's governance, finances and structures – and despite assurances that she would be supported in introducing reforms that would address those problems, she eventually concluded that the theatre's board weren't backing her in what she was trying to do.

She had also faced a gradually intensifying level of media criticism, which meant that she was soon spending more time defending the theatre than building towards its future. It therefore felt like something of an inevitability when she announced in April 1993 that she wouldn't be seeking the renewal of her contract when it finished at the end of that year.

The negative criticism of her tenure had not initially been very widespread – but it was often noisy, and it soon became markedly hostile. Her first production as the Abbey's AD was of Seán O'Casey's *The Plough and the Stars*, a 1926 play that had (like Synge's *Playboy of the Western World*) provoked riots upon its premiere, before being defanged by a tradition of sentimental productions that played up its comedic elements while ignoring its treatment of social class and gender.

In contrast, Garry's staging of *The Plough* was uncompromisingly direct in its presentation of the characters' poverty, while also showing how the so-called 'heroism' of O'Casey's men was a cause of utter misery to the women and children in the play. Appearing during the seventy-fifth anniversary of the Easter Rising, it was doing quite pointedly what O'Casey had done: asking audiences to consider seriously whether that rebellion had achieved what it set out to do; whether Ireland could really consider itself free when so much inequality persisted.

That approach and interpretation were bold, but they were also in keeping with what O'Casey had actually written. Nevertheless, many critics had a problem with how Garry had strayed from their expectations. The playwright and newspaper columnist Hugh Leonard was particularly incensed by the production, describing the people who made it as 'the Brechtians'. He did not mean that as a compliment.

Garry's subsequent productions at the Abbey were often criticized in similarly harsh terms. Francis O'Connor may have loved McGahern's *Power of Darkness* – and it was well reviewed by visiting British critics – but several of the Dublin reviewers argued that it should never have been staged at all.

There were also increasing complaints about the programming in general. Having expressed delight about Garry's appointment on the basis that she might do at the Abbey what she had done with Druid, some commentators began to complain that she was … well, doing at the Abbey what she had done with Druid – that there were, in other words, too many plays set in the west of Ireland, especially by Tom Murphy. There was even a suggestion from one of the Sunday newspapers that she had 'feminized' the Abbey by hiring women to key administrative roles. Again, that was not meant as a compliment.

The Abbey had its defenders during her time there, and there were also voices of moderation. For example, Patsy McGarry, who was then a theatre critic for the *Irish Press*, marked the end of Garry's term of office by expressing his opinion that some of her productions hadn't worked – but he was still able to praise her willingness to take risks and her determination to introduce new voices into the theatre. He was also completely clear in stating that the real problem lay with the way in which the Abbey was set up. His attempt at fairness stood out in an otherwise polarized debate.

Garry's time at the Abbey would eventually come to be viewed very differently, partly due to the influence of academic commentary by scholars such as Brian Singleton, who in 2004 praised her *Plough and the Stars* as one of the most radical productions ever staged at the national theatre, not just of an O'Casey play but of any Irish classic. And another factor in that reassessment was the increasing visibility of the impact of Garry's decision to bring new people into the Abbey, among them the actor Aisling O'Sullivan and the playwright Marina Carr.

But that change of perspective would happen later. As she finished at the Abbey, Garry quite understandably told interviewers that she was looking forward to taking some time off: 'It'll be the first time in twenty years that I'll have no executive function in a theatre,' she noted. And she was transparent about her intentions – she might go back to Druid to direct a play from time to time, but 'I will not be going back there permanently. I want to move forward.'

While Garry's time at the Abbey was ending in 1993, over in London Martin McDonagh was busily writing one play after another.

He was then in his early twenties, was in love with film, and was desperate to build a career as a writer. As he tried to put together screenplays, short stories and (eventually) plays, he found that his writing was showing too directly the influence of the dramatists he most admired, Harold Pinter and David Mamet. He wanted to retain the style of dialogue that those writers excelled in – which he thought of as 'strange and heightened' – but he also felt that his own dialogue needed to be distorted in some way, so that the influence wouldn't be so obvious.

In an interview with Fintan O'Toole, he explained what happened next:

> And then I sort of remembered the way my uncles spoke back in Galway, the structure of their sentences. I didn't think of it as structure, just as a kind of rhythm in the speech. And that seemed an interesting way to go, to try to do something with that language that wouldn't be English or American.

Once he had made the breakthrough of drawing on his parents' roots in the west of Ireland, McDonagh wrote

Chapter 8: The Leenane Trilogy, 1996–2001

Martin McDonagh in Galway, 1997.

quickly, producing drafts for six plays that would eventually be produced professionally, among them *The Beauty Queen of Leenane*. He then started sending his work out to theatre companies in Ireland and Britain.

Some of those theatres sent McDonagh rejection letters – if they bothered replying at all (the Abbey was one of the theatres that passed on his work). But, as it would turn out, Garry just happened to be in the right place at the right time for both of them.

When she had returned to Druid in 1995, one of the first things she did was ask if there was anything interesting in the company's pile of unsolicited scripts. She soon found herself reading the play that eventually became the second part of *The Leenane Trilogy*, *A Skull in Connemara* – and she couldn't believe how funny it was. She then read the other two plays that McDonagh had sent in. 'Straight away I asked, *Who is this guy?* – and within a few weeks of reading the plays I arranged to meet him, and we optioned all three of them.'

The original playbill for *The Beauty Queen of Leenane*, 1996.

But which of them would Druid produce first? 'The first question was which was the best play to introduce this writer to the world,' Garry explained – but she was also aware that the play would be the opening production at the Town Hall Theatre, and that it was therefore important to consider which one 'could stand up to that occasion'. And, as always for Garry, a decisive consideration would be casting: she knew that the role of Maureen was ideally suited to Marie, and she also knew that Marie happened to be available in early 1996.

And so *The Beauty Queen of Leenane* was chosen. It would open at the Town Hall on 1 February 1996, marking Druid's twenty-first year in operation with the inauguration of a new 400-seat venue for Galway.

But Garry also felt that the play could have a life beyond the west of Ireland:

> I wanted the production to have an English element because of Martin's background. A lot of the play is very Irish, but there are fragments of English speech too – an English presence because that's where he grew up. So I contacted Stephen Daldry, who was in charge at the Royal Court Theatre in London at the time; I was an Associate Director there too, so there was a good relationship.

Her plans developed quickly. After *The Beauty Queen* opened in Galway it had a short Irish tour, and then it transferred to the Royal Court.

Maureen Hughes would later vividly recall her first impressions of Martin McDonagh when he arrived in Galway for rehearsals of *The Beauty Queen* in early 1996.

By that time, Maureen, like Garry, had left the Abbey; she had then set up her own casting agency. But during a visit back to Galway, she and Anne Butler had taken the young writer out for a few drinks:

> It was like taking someone gently out of an attic who hadn't seen daylight for a long time. We were all a bit wild at that stage, and we thought: this kid arrived now from London – God, he was as innocent! But even from that point you could see in him there was steel, there was ambition. There was a knowledge, a self-knowledge, which is kind of amazing in someone who looks like they hadn't seen daylight for four years. There was such a deep awareness about how good he was himself.

Garry also found herself feeling increasingly impressed by McDonagh. There's a particularly tricky scene in the play in which Pato must write a long letter to Maureen and, as Garry recalls:

> When Martin wrote it he had it literally as an old-fashioned letter scene, where somebody's at a desk and the lights go down and he just articulates the letter. Now, this was a scene which was going to last ten or fifteen minutes and I absolutely knew that this was not going to wash.

In a film, such a scene could be accompanied by a voiceover, but that approach just wouldn't work in the theatre – and having the actor say the words aloud while writing would have been unrealistic, and old-fashioned too.

Garry worked hard with Brian F. O'Byrne, the actor who was playing Pato, to find a way to stage the scene. First they removed some of the props, then they brought him out to speak directly into the auditorium; sometimes they tried the scene with him at a table but then moved him to the front of the stage … And then McDonagh had a suggestion. As Garry remembers it,

> One of the incredibly wonderful things about the process was that this man – Martin – had never been in a rehearsal room before, and here he was in the rehearsal room throughout. I remember when doing that scene with Brian, where Martin would say about moving the chair out, and Brian would move the chair out by a foot from the table, and Martin would lean over and say, 'I wonder if we moved it just a bit further out?' and I'd go 'Yeah, try it, try that, a bit further.' And suddenly – he was right: a bit further out was just critical. And I remember thinking, 'He's a theatremaker – he's not just a writer, he's a theatremaker.'

Chapter 8: The Leenane Trilogy, 1996–2001

Within a couple of months of its opening night in Galway, *The Beauty Queen* was attracting major international notice, and it already seemed likely that, after its run at the Royal Court, it could expect to transfer to the West End in London. There was no guarantee that a New York production would follow, but that was being actively discussed too.

With that success, there were also personnel changes at Druid. Having spent seven years at the company as its Managing Director, Jane Daly felt that it was a suitable time to move on – and therefore handed in her resignation a couple of days after *The Beauty Queen* had opened. She had overseen a major period for the company – taking it through the dissolution of the first ensemble, its second Artistic Directorship and the beginning of the new phase signalled by *The Beauty Queen*. She would later say that she was glad to have left at a time when the company's future seemed so bright.

But there was also a sense of homecoming when the company staged Brian Friel's *The Loves of Cass Maguire* at the Town Hall in July 1996 – Druid's twenty-first birthday. That had been one of the three plays in their first season, and again Marie and Mick were starring in it, as was Anna Manahan, who had been getting rave reviews for her performance as Mag in *The Beauty Queen*. It was a celebratory occasion, with the show programme featuring an essay by Tom Kenny (from the local booksellers – long-term Druid supporters who had themselves shown Galway's capacity for innovation when they became the first Irish company to launch an e-commerce website in 1994). Tom's memories of Druid – and his exploration of its importance to Galway – offered a timely encapsulation of what the company had come to mean for Galway's sense of itself.

Garry Hynes in the *Beauty Queen* rehearsal room.

As they moved into the second half of the year, however, everyone's attention was focused on the future, and specifically on McDonagh's work. First, *Beauty Queen* went on a URT that – following the pattern established during Maelíosa's time as AD – included several performances in Northern Ireland: in Enniskillen and Derry, and on Rathlin Island, off the Antrim coast. The company also returned to old haunts such as each of the Aran Islands. They even performed the play in Leenane itself.

For that tour, Jane Brennan stepped into the role of Maureen at short notice (Marie had just had her second child, so had withdrawn), and Jane would later recall how, when the play was staged in Leenane, the company noticed the imposing figure of an older woman who was sitting in the front row. It was explained to them that the woman was a local character who in the 1970s had been pronounced the 'Cailín Deas of Connemara'. She had therefore thought that McDonagh's drama was a celebration of her. 'When she realized it wasn't,' Jane said, 'she fell asleep for the rest of the play.'

Chapter 8: The Leenane Trilogy, 1996–2001

A week later, *The Beauty Queen* opened in the West End.

By that point, plans were underway to stage the three plays as a single event – the idea being to perform them individually on separate nights and then have 'trilogy days', usually at weekends, which would involve audiences watching *The Beauty Queen of Leenane* at one o'clock, *A Skull in Connemara* at 4.30, and then *The Lonesome West* at 8.

Garry's idea had originally been to do *A Skull in Connemara* by itself in 1997, but the tremendous success of *Beauty Queen* gave rise to a challenge: how to measure up to a debut that had drawn unprecedented praise and attention? That was a good problem to have – but it still needed careful consideration.

McDonagh hadn't originally written the plays as a trilogy, but they were sufficiently close in setting and tone to suggest that possibility. As he further developed *Skull* and, in particular, *The Lonesome West*, he began to impose a new uniformity upon them. Characters mentioned in one play started to appear in the others; he explicitly named Leenane as the setting of all three, and he introduced a formal consistency by giving each play four characters and the shared setting of the interior of a cottage.

Francis O'Connor had returned to design the *Trilogy*, and he too had to think about how to ensure that they could work both individually and as a unified day-long performance. *Beauty Queen*, he felt, had established how the other two plays should look:

> It seemed quite apt that all three plays happen in a cottage. It was a happy accident, but I knew that they could all exist within the same aesthetic. The three plays all had the concrete walls and the bleak grimy surfaces, but they also had slightly different furnishings – a big orange range in *The Lonesome West* as opposed to the old-fashioned one in *Beauty Queen*.

Promotional poster for *The Leenane Trilogy* in Galway, 1997.

But now he needed to factor in two exterior scenes – a graveyard in *Skull* and a jetty beside a lake in *Lonesome West*. 'When I do any new play, I try and do what I imagine the writer wants,' said Francis:

> So when the character is digging a grave in the script, we need to really dig a grave on the set, and we need to go deep down, and the audience needs to see that we've done that.

Again he had to ensure that the play felt real – but that it was also suitably heightened.

Other practical problems needed to be solved. The orange range in *Lonesome West* had to explode under fire from a shotgun; thirty-six religious figurines were to be smashed to

Chapter 8: The Leenane Trilogy, 1996–2001 213

A collection of religious figurines for *The Lonesome West*, waiting to be smashed.

pieces every night (but without injuring any of the actors); and a local artist was required to sculpt a steady supply of skulls that could be crushed with a mallet in every performance of *A Skull in Connemara*.

While all that was happening, McDonagh's reputation was growing. Another of his Irish plays, *The Cripple of Inishmaan*, opened at the UK National Theatre in early 1997 (where its cast included Ray McBride), and Druid had also shown McDonagh's versatility by giving a staged reading to *The Pillowman* – a play about a writer in a totalitarian state – at the Cúirt Festival in Galway in April 1997.

Understandably, expectations for *The Trilogy* were getting higher all the time. Garry of course was thinking carefully about casting, and with the idea of a trilogy came the opportunity to place a key Druid actor in each of the three plays.

Marie had already starred in *Beauty Queen*, and Garry knew that Mick was right for *Skull*, in which he would play the

Brian F. O'Byrne and Maelíosa Stafford in *The Lonesom(e) West*, 1997.

role of a Connemara man (also called Mick) who is accused of murdering his wife. The final play was about a pair of brothers whose incessant fighting with each other draws the concerned attention of a local priest. One of those brothers would be played by Brian F. O'Byrne (who was also continuing in the role of Pato in *Beauty Queen*), but Garry thought the other role could be very well suited to Maelíosa – and she therefore invited him back to Galway to play it.

He jumped at the chance – though one of the first questions he asked when he got back to Galway was whether McDonagh's plays had arrived before or after he'd finished as Artistic Director. 'I often wondered,' he later mused, as if feeling slightly haunted, 'if I'd have seen them for what they were?'

There was a long rehearsal period of twelve weeks for the three plays – but, to his surprise, Maelíosa struggled with his role at first. He had read the script and thought it was brilliant – but as rehearsals began he found himself strangely uneasy.

> And I looked around me at some of the actors, like Brian, who had already done *Beauty Queen*, and he was playing my brother. And I just felt intimidated. He seemed to be doing something that I didn't get.

As he discussed the play with Garry, he began to comprehend that he had been wrong to approach McDonagh's work as if it's a comedy: 'You have to play like it's life and death,' Maelíosa said,

> And the comedy comes from somewhere else. It's hilariously funny, but you can't see it as comedy at all. So it took me a few weeks to adjust to that.

Garry would later elaborate on her approach to directing McDonagh's work, explaining that the audience of *The Lonesome West*:

> must absolutely believe that Valene will not allow his brother to eat a packet of his Tayto. If you think of that as a joke, and take that attitude to it in rehearsal, then the play doesn't exist.

'All of McDonagh's plays have to be rooted in reality,' she explained. 'Otherwise, you don't have permission for the craziness.'

The Trilogy opened in Galway in June 1997, before transferring to the West End, where *The Cripple of Inishmaan* had also transferred – which meant that McDonagh had the unusual distinction of having four of his plays on in the West End during a single year.

The *Trilogy* was then performed at the 1997 Dublin Theatre Festival, where it was named 'Play of the Year' by a three-person voting panel that included Marina Carr. By travelling to Dublin,

The Leenane Trilogy at the 1997 Dublin Theatre Festival.

the company was meeting a pent-up demand in Ireland's capital – which had been so strong that in May of that year *The Irish Times* had published a letter from a theatregoer who was angry about having to wait to see McDonagh's plays (the option of going to Galway seems not to have occurred to him).

Louise Donlon, who had taken over the role of General Manager after Jane Daly's departure, wrote to the newspaper to reply that the complainant 'might now have some understanding of the frustration felt by theatre lovers' outside Dublin. Druid's first commitment, she went on, 'is to its audiences in Galway and its touring venues in Ireland', and it would be wrong to bear any resentment towards:

the people of Cork, Kerry, Kilkenny, Limerick, Clare, Galway, Westmeath, Mayo, Donegal and Antrim (not to mention all three Aran Islands) who were afforded the opportunity, through an extensive touring policy on the part of Druid, to see Martin's work before him and his neighbours in Dublin.

But, Donlon added, the show would find its way to Dublin. Eventually.

That demand to see McDonagh's plays was driven in part by his celebrity. The UK tabloid press seemed keen to present him as the 'bad boy of British theatre' after he had a well-publicized argument with the actor Sean Connery during an Awards Ceremony in late 1996 (McDonagh later joked that his mother was so embarrassed by the furore that she wouldn't speak to him for a week). And he was being spoken of as part of a movement of 'in-yer-face' playwrights that included Sarah Kane and Mark Ravenhill – artists who were using shocking violence, bad language and disturbing plotting to shake their audiences out of complacency.

But in Ireland there was also a backlash to McDonagh's success – some of which was driven by an insecurity that he was not an Irish dramatist who was inviting audiences to laugh *with* him, but that he was (yet another) Englishman who was making money by presenting the Irish as a nation of violent and feckless morons.

Garry had expected that criticism to come up. Even when she was directing *Beauty Queen*, she had been aware of the risk of the plays being misunderstood as pastiche:

> Because they use a gloss of naturalism as the way of telling their stories, the plays could be seen as stating that they were realistic representations of Irish life, whereas it was

very clear to me that they weren't – they were utterly theatrical pieces.

Even so, she was shocked when some of the critics of McDonagh began to argue, in some cases with a vituperative ferocity, that he shouldn't be seen as Irish at all.

It's possible that some of that negativity arose because of McDonagh's willingness to expose taboos that remained sensitive in Ireland at that time, especially about the place of Catholicism in the society. For instance, there's a line in *The Beauty Queen of Leenane* about a priest who has had a 'babby with a Yank', which is a direct reference to the Bishop of Galway, Eamonn Casey, who – it was revealed in 1992 – had indeed fathered a child with an American woman. Bishop Casey was a well-known figure to Druid's audiences, especially in Galway; he had even written the programme note for Druid's 1984 production of Tom Murphy's *Famine*. The line about him in *The Beauty Queen* would be received as a slightly risqué joke when the play was staged in London – but in Ireland it landed with the force of a secret that had for too long been suppressed.

The Lonesome West went even further in its treatment of Irish Catholicism. It is literally iconoclastic, in the sense that it shows the destruction of dozens of statues of saints, but it also includes a priest whose sense of powerlessness leads to his suicide. Coming at a time when the first revelations of clerical child abuse were being made in Ireland, Father Welsh's characterization felt painfully close to the bone.

That relevance hadn't been deliberate, Garry later explained. 'Catholicism is definitely part of Martin's landscape as a writer, but he'd never set out to be relevant deliberately or intentionally – if anything, he'd be quite against that.' Nevertheless, the appearance of *The Leenane Trilogy* at a time of painful change in Ireland meant that it was drawing strong reactions, both for and against it.

Few of those controversies accompanied Druid when they made their New York City debut with *The Beauty Queen*, which opened at the Atlantic Theater on 11 February 1998. Instead, the American response was unequivocally positive, partly because (in true American fashion) they saw McDonagh's sudden success through a 'rags to riches' frame that emphasized how he had been on unemployment benefit when his plays were plucked from the obscurity of the Druid slush pile,

The American critics loved the play. Writing in *The New York Times*, Ben Brantley said that 'sometimes you don't even know what you've been craving until the real thing comes along', and that watching *The Beauty Queen* was 'like sitting down to a square meal after a long diet of salads and hors d'oeuvres'.

The subsequent opening night at the Walter Kerr Theater on Broadway was of course a huge occasion for Garry and Marie, and for Druid and the Irish theatre generally. Messages of congratulation were sent to the company not only from the President of Ireland, Mary McAleese, but also from Bill and Hillary Clinton. And, in a sign of the Irish state's expanding interest in using culture as a form of diplomacy, Galway's Lord Mayor came along to present the cast with gifts of Galway crystal – and he was quoted in news reports the next day as having hailed Druid as 'ambassadors of Irish theatre, of Galway, and of Ireland'.

Those same press reports carried comments in praise of the play from Mick Lally and Jennifer Aniston – and if the juxtaposition of the star of *Glenroe* with one of the stars of *Friends* seemed improbable, it was in keeping with the tone of McDonagh's play, which itself was a blend of rural Irish tropes and international pop culture references. 'I think it is a wonderful play,' Aniston was quoted as saying. 'It brings a new element to Irish theatre.'

The playbill for *The Beauty Queen* in New York, signed by the cast.

And then things got even better. The move to the Walter Kerr had brought with it the expectation that the show might be nominated for a Tony Award – but all concerned were stunned when it received six of them: one for Garry as director, one for McDonagh as the playwright, and the others for the four actors in the cast. Garry told *The Irish Times* that:

> It is exciting that this is exactly the same production that opened in the Town Hall Theatre, Galway, on February 1st, 1996, and was seen in Skibbereen and Inis Meáin.

And she again spoke about the importance of her time in New York in the early 1970s, where she 'discovered theatre could be made for low budget. So winning a Tony nomination here is important to me.'

The nominations for the actors were particularly important to Garry. When the idea of a New York run had been mooted, the producers had considered it necessary to have at least some American actors in the company, but Garry had been insistent about the need to keep the original cast intact. The fact that all four of them were nominated was a vindication of that strategy.

At the Tony ceremony in June 1998, the production won four of the six awards that it had been nominated for. Brian F. O'Byrne and Tom Murphy (an actor in the production, and no relation to the playwright) had both been nominated in the same category of best featured actor, so they had known beforehand that at least one of them would lose out. As it turned out, it was Murphy who won, getting one of the biggest laughs of the night when he thanked McDonagh for 'his great feckin' story and his great feckin' lines'.

McDonagh himself missed out on the award for best play, losing – to widespread surprise – to Yasmina Reza's *Art*, an enjoyable if dainty play that sets out to puncture its characters' pretensions, whereas *The Beauty Queen* was inclined to bludgeon its heroine to death with a poker. But Anna Manahan and Marie did win, for Best Actress and Best Featured Actress, respectively; Marie was presented with her award by Liam Neeson, in a further sign of how the night was dominated by Ireland and the Irish.

And then Garry became the first woman to win a Tony Award for directing. She recalled that,

> As I walked to the stage all I could think was *please don't let me stumble or do anything stupid* and then halfway through the speech, right from the back of this hall with about 6,000 people in it, from up in the gods someone shouted: 'maith an cailín thú' ['good girl yourself!']. I never found out who it was but it was fantastic to hear.

In her acceptance speech, she said that 'the Irish theatre is blessed with very many talented and extraordinary people, and I've been blessed to work with many of them'. She thanked everyone she'd worked with in Druid, past and present, before concluding with a short sentence of her own in Irish: 'Agus míle buíochas le gach duine i nGaillimh' – a thousand thanks to everyone in Galway.

Most of the New York audience didn't understand her, of course – but somewhere from the audience came a whoop of recognition. Garry smiled and left the stage, carrying her Tony with her.

Later that year, there was tragic news back in Galway.

Bernie Walsh had started working with Druid in 1983, initially part-time, by doing stage construction work and carpentry before gradually taking on more responsibility. By 1989, he was the company's full-time stage manager and had even appeared as an actor in Maelíosa's production of *Shadow and Substance*. He had been the production manager for *The Leenane Trilogy* in 1997 and had continued working on Druid's productions during 1998.

But while on his way home from work in August of that year, he was killed when his motorbike was in a crash with a van. The driver of the van was later charged with dangerous driving.

Everyone who knew Bernie was devastated – not just his colleagues in Druid but others in the Galway arts scene who had worked with him in the Arts Festival and the live music scene. Louise Donlon issued a statement on behalf of the company, saying that Bernie was:

> From Galway and knew everyone in Galway. Any problem we ever had he could sort it. Bernie was one of those people who worked behind the scenes to make everything happen.

Garry would later describe him as a 'a lovely man with a quiet still presence' and recalled how, during rehearsals for *The Beauty Queen*,

> when no technical solution proved convincing enough as steam for the oil heating on the range, Bernie hit on the idea of smoking a cigarette through two precisely drilled holes in the scenery. It worked a dream!

'When some tech/light fix needed sorting, he was always there,' Garry said. He had been making 'everything happen' at Druid for fifteen years, and would be an enormous loss.

The Lonesome West followed *Beauty Queen* to Broadway, opening there in 1999 with its original cast of Maelíosa and Brian F. O'Byrne as the brothers, and Dawn Bradfield as Girleen, a young woman who falls in love with the ill-fated priest Fr Welsh, who was played by David Hanly.

Despite those ongoing Irish fears about misrepresentation, audiences in New York understood Druid and McDonagh's intentions without any problems. Speaking to an Irish journalist, Maelíosa was keen to refute the suggestion that American theatregoers would think that *The Lonesome West* was an accurate depiction of life in rural Galway. 'New York audiences get everything,' he said. 'They are with us; they understand Martin's dark humour'. Dawn Bradfield agreed, stating that she was surprised more by the conservatism of American audiences than their interpretation of the Irish material: 'there was a huge reaction to the bad language and to us taking the piss out of the priest,' she said.

Pat Shortt and Jon Kenny in *The Lonesome West*, 1998.

The Lonesome West was less successful than *Beauty Queen* had been, but again there were Tony Award nominations for Garry, McDonagh and O'Byrne, while Bradfield also received a nomination. None of them won, but the nominations themselves represented an extraordinary achievement.

Garry would later express regret that the play hadn't been as popular in New York as *Beauty Queen* had been; she eventually came to think of *The Lonesome West* as her favourite of the three *Leenane* plays. That preference also seemed apparent in Ireland, where audiences had flocked to *The Lonesome West* when it went on an eleven-venue URT in the winter of 1998, with the two brothers being played by Pat Shortt and Jon Kenny of the comedy-duo D'Unbelievables. After its Broadway production, it

Chapter 8: The Leenane Trilogy, 1996–2001

enjoyed a long run at Dublin's Gaiety Theatre in 2001 before coming back to Galway for a fortnight in October of that year – bringing Druid's five-year odyssey with the *Leenane Trilogy* to a conclusion.

The period from 1996 to 2001 was dominated by the *Leenane* plays. But there was still an audience back in Galway; and while McDonagh's plays were being performed in London, New York, Sydney, Toronto and elsewhere, the company was also showing a strong inclination for working with new playwrights, new directors and new actors – both at their original Druid Lane Theatre and in the Town Hall.

The first example of that tendency was the appearance of a new play called *Shoot the Crow*, which was produced in Druid Lane in 1997. Directed by David Parnell, it was a comedy set on a building site, and was therefore exploring territory that might have drawn comparisons with Pato's story in *Beauty Queen*. But its author – the Belfast playwright Owen McCafferty – showed a dramatic style that was distinctively his own. He would go on to become one of the major Irish playwrights of the twenty-first century, charting the evolution of ordinary life in Northern Ireland as the Peace Process took root.

During the following year, Druid returned to Friel, this time reviving his 1964 play *Philadelphia, Here I Come!*, which was directed by Paddy Cunneen. Cunneen was probably better known at that time for his work as a composer for theatre productions – including *The Leenane Trilogy* – but his version of Friel was well received. And in December 1998 he returned to Druid to direct *The Way You Look Tonight*, a new play by the Clare writer Niall Willliams. Cunneen also gave a Druid debut to a young actor called Sonya Kelly. She would act in future Druid productions,

As You Like It, 1999.

but her biggest impact on the company would be as a playwright, from 2017 onwards.

But there was also new work by Druid's longstanding members. Maelíosa directed Shakespeare's *As You Like It* in the spring of 1999 – a daring way for him to warm up for his run as one of the actors in the Broadway production of *The Lonesome West*. And in the same year Garry revived a 1959 play about emigration called *The Country Boy*, by Johnny Murphy. She again asked Francis O'Connor to design the production, and she also cast a young Cork actor who'd been getting a lot of attention for his performance in an Enda Walsh play called *Disco Pigs*. That was Cillian Murphy, earning one of his first professional roles with a major Irish theatre company.

Chapter 8: The Leenane Trilogy, 1996–2001

The Leenane Trilogy had done many things for Druid. It had demonstrated their ability to work on new Irish writing, thus bringing to fruition a process that they had begun by collaborating with Geraldine Aron and Tom Murphy in the 1980s. It also showed that going back to Druid could be a step forward – that, even as the company continued with traditions like the URTs, it could also find new audiences around the world, including on Broadway.

The *Trilogy* had also shown that the idea of a Druid ensemble was still meaningful, not just in the sense that McDonagh's work had showcased the actors' ability to move from play to play but also because it had included artists like Francis O'Connor in the creative process.

And finally *The Leenane Trilogy* demonstrated that a Druid show could be an *event*. It wasn't just a night at the theatre, it was an entire day at the theatre – but, more than that, it was an occasion, something to remember, something to tell people about, to savour forever.

When Garry looked back at the path her career had taken during the 1990s, she saw that her choices had benefitted herself and the company as well. 'Druid needed to know that it could survive without me, and I think I needed to know that I could survive without Druid,' she explained. She had proven that both of those things were true – but she had also shown what she and Druid could do together.

With the demand for productions of the *Leenane* plays starting to wind down as the new century began, Garry was no longer referred to as the 'Consultant' Artistic Director in the company's promotional literature. She was its Artistic Director, full stop – and it was now time for her to decide what Druid might do next.

Chapter 9
Druid Debuts, 2000–2007

AS THE twenty-first century began, it was becoming increasingly apparent that Irish drama had entered a new phase. Irish playwrights were gaining international acclaim and attention like never before, and in the country itself there was a sense that something extraordinary was happening.

A punctuation mark had been set down in Irish theatre history – and it had been imposed by the emergence of a new generation of dramatists, most of them born in the early 1970s. They wrote in a style of harsh but energetic lyricism, and they saw Ireland as a place that was fragmenting as its most cherished myths – about the family, religion and the cohesion of Irish society – were falling apart. Martin McDonagh was a major figure of course, but so were Conor McPherson, Marina Carr, Mark O'Rowe and Enda Walsh – and they had all gone from anonymity to international prominence in little more than five years.

Alongside those young writers was a somewhat older group, mostly born in the 1950s, that included Sebastian Barry, Marie Jones and Frank McGuinness – and they too had been receiving high-profile international productions, especially of plays that explored Irish history and Irish identity, such as Barry's *Steward of Christendom,* Jones's *Stones in His Pockets* and

McGuinness's *Observe the Sons of Ulster Marching Towards the Somme*. And of course, Friel and Murphy were still writing plays too.

The dynamism of Irish drama at that time was unprecedented in historical terms, and unmatched in international terms – and for Druid, the awareness of being at a moment of historical transition provided an opportunity to think again about the company's role in the evolution of Irish playwriting. Whether they were reviving old dramas or staging new ones, a Druid rehearsal room was a space where plays would be read with care and precision – and by the year 2000 that was one of the main reasons that Irish actors, young and old, were so keen to work with them.

With *The Leenane Trilogy*, they had also demonstrated their skill in bringing new writing into production. That meant helping writers to shape and refine their ideas, from the first draft right up to (and sometimes even beyond) the opening night. But they had also developed a singular curatorial sensitivity: they understood the need to stage a new play at a time and place that would allow it to be seen as fully and fairly as it deserved.

Sometimes that would mean producing work as part of a major event, such as *The Leenane Trilogy*. But for most new plays, the level of expectation and scrutiny that comes with being part of an 'event' would have been inappropriate and inhibiting; what is needed instead is a production that is equal parts ambitious and protective. Druid knew the difference, in other words, between supporting a play and setting it up for failure.

Throughout the early 2000s, the company would commission several new dramas, working closely with many of those young writers who had been gaining international notice; they also actively sought out new writers. Some of their productions would be controversial; others would be remembered with affection – and some would go on to be regarded as contemporary classics. It was a period of prodigious creativity, resulting in the creation of a body of new work that would do much to explain a rapidly changing Ireland to itself.

The first evidence of an intensified concentration on playwriting was the creation of the 'Druid Debuts' series, which, beginning in the summer of 2000, gave rehearsed readings of plays that in most cases had been sent in under an open submissions process.

The scheme might at first have seemed somewhat romantic in its conception. Most plays are not discovered through open submissions; they instead tend to be commissioned and then nurtured over a period of time through workshops. The seemingly serendipitous 'discovery' of Martin McDonagh was therefore highly exceptional. Yet with the Debut series, Druid were betting that the exception could become a rule, that there were writers 'out there' who were making plays that could resonate with Irish and maybe even international audiences. They just needed to be found, and then given a chance.

As the series developed, Druid always received many more submissions than they could ever stage. And, naturally, many of the plays that they did give readings to were never read or performed again – because sometimes you have to stage a play in order to understand why it's not working; sometimes a writer has to get their work before an audience in order to understand how to make their next play better.

But, especially when viewed in retrospect, the list of writers who appeared in the Druid Debut series shows that the initiative was not just worthwhile but important. It includes Abbie Spallen, Christian O'Reilly, Meadhbh McHugh, Cristín Kehoe, Sonya Kelly, Erica Murray and Shane Mac an Bhaird – all of whom went on to full productions, either with Druid or other Irish companies.

By general agreement, one of the most exciting figures in that new phase of Irish drama was Marina Carr, so Druid's announcement in May 2000 that they would stage her latest play, *On Raftery's Hill*, was seen as a big moment both for the Irish theatre and the culture more generally.

Carr had never worked with Druid before, but she had known Garry for almost a decade. One of her earliest plays, *Ullaloo*, had been staged at the Abbey when Garry was AD there, in 1991 – and although the production wasn't successful, the experience had prompted Carr to reassess her artistic goals in a way that later led to a breakthrough.

Starting in 1994 with *The Mai* (which Garry had commissioned before she left the Abbey), Carr began to draw on the dialect of the Irish midlands, where she had grown up. Her plays started to take on a tragic, mythic quality, but they were also anchored in a recognizable version of a real Ireland. One of them, *Portia Coughlan*, was directed by Garry in a production that opened at the Abbey in 1996 before transferring to the Royal Court, appearing there during the same summer as *The Beauty Queen of Leenane*. And in 1998 Carr wrote *By the Bog of Cats* for the Abbey, where it was acclaimed almost universally as a contemporary masterpiece, a status that it has retained ever since.

By 2000, Carr was known as a writer of brutal plays that resolutely depicted murder, suicide, infanticide and other forms of violence; she required her audiences to imagine a world that was loveless, hopeless and Godless, and seemed to be writing Greek tragedies that had been transplanted to the Irish boglands. Her plays were unforgiving but had a beauty and grandeur too, especially in their use of a dramatic language that was simultaneously harsh and elevated.

The cast of *On Raftery's Hill*, 2000.

As *On Raftery's Hill* opened in Galway, audiences would have seen all of those traits in action. Again, there was a heightened and poeticized dialect, and again the setting felt like contemporary Ireland overlaid with ancient Greece. But there were differences too, the main one being that this new play was so unrelentingly bleak as to stand apart not only from Carr's other works but from everything else on the Irish stage.

The character who gives the play its title is Red Raftery, an elderly farmer who was played by Tom Hickey, one of Ireland's most beloved actors. Raftery has brutalized his family, and his land is more like a decaying slaughterhouse than a farm – the carcasses of his livestock, dead from neglect, rot in his fields, while his house seems to be in a state of imminent disintegration. His children are not just wary of him but manifestly traumatized: they skulk and cower in his presence, more like kicked animals than humans.

Yes, there had been many oppressive fathers and dysfunctional families in the history of the Irish stage before; there's no shortage of interfamilial violence in *The Leenane Trilogy*, for example, and *The Playboy of the Western World* would not exist without a father's bad behaviour towards his child. But as Carr's play

Tom Hickey in *On Raftery's Hill*.

unfolded, it became clear that she was trying to bring Druid's audiences somewhere they hadn't been before, especially when her first act concluded with the graphic presentation of Red Raftery raping his granddaughter, who (it was revealed) is also his daughter, conceived in another act of incestuous rape years before. In the play, most members of Raftery's family treat that crime as an inevitability: they do nothing to prevent it, and in the second act they display limited sympathy for the victim.

That scene was presented with an extreme and, for Druid, an uncharacteristic literalism – albeit a necessary literalism. The audience witnessed the lead-up to the rape directly and, even if they looked away from the stage or closed their eyes, they could not ignore the character's howls of pain and terror. There was no attempt to present the rape as a metaphor or as a symbol; there was no attempt to hide the violence from view. There was only one question for the audience to consider: why do we sit here, doing nothing?

Of course there were walkouts and complaints, but there was also a broad understanding of what Carr and Druid were trying to achieve. Audiences knew that *On Raftery's Hill* was not a realistic play, but that it was trying to show them a reality: this is what really happens when someone is sexually assaulted, this is the kind of violence that is really experienced by women in their homes every day, in Ireland and elsewhere.

The posters that were used to advertise the show around Galway present a hilltop farmhouse in silhouette against a full moon – and thus make the play seem more like an American horror movie than a representation of rural Irish life. That design choice was justified, however: *On Raftery's Hill* in some ways really is an Irish horror story in a way that can be compared with Sheridan LeFanu's nineteenth-century novel *Uncle Silas*, or even Bram Stoker's *Dracula*.

But it was also being staged at a time when the people of Ireland had been confronted with the realization that abuse – sexual, physical, emotional – had been endemic in the society for decades: that although Red Raftery might have been monstrous, he had many real-life counterparts. Those revelations had started to emerge during the 1990s, culminating in 1999 with two major interventions by the journalist Mary Raftery (who shares her name with the family in Carr's play, but by coincidence). In that year, RTÉ broadcast her documentary *States of Fear*, which was

Show poster, *On Raftery's Hill*.

followed by a book called *Suffer the Little Children* (co-written with Eoin O'Sullivan). In a way, both works seemed like horror stories too, except that they were presenting facts – undeniable facts – about the abuses that had been suffered by Irish children in state- and religious-run care institutions from the 1930s to the 1970s.

As a result of those and many other revelations, the Irish government established a national Commission to Inquire into Child Abuse on 23 May 2000, exactly a fortnight after the opening night of *On Raftery's Hill*. That commission was focused on abuses that had been perpetrated in institutions, mostly those run by the Catholic Church – but there was also an understanding that the entire society was to blame for what had happened, if only in choosing (like Raftery's family) not to see the abuses that were being planned and executed right in front of them.

It had rarely been Druid's way to comment directly on social or political matters; they have tended to allow their work to speak for itself, trusting audiences to draw their own conclusions, while also respecting their right not to draw any conclusions at all. Thus, when Garry spoke in newspaper interviews about *On Raftery's Hill* she only said that:

> Marina has returned again and again to the family, to that central unit by which we organize our society, and has challenged how it works. What she's doing is extremely courageous.

But at that particular place and time, the extreme courage of the play was obviously related to the broader societal contexts, to the difficulty and necessity of facing those painful facts. Audiences didn't necessarily *want* to be confronted with the truths that Carr was showing them, but they knew that they had to face them anyway. *On Raftery's Hill* thus felt to many like a necessary reckoning.

But then Druid brought the play to America – and the response was very different.

'An atrocity upon the Ireland of the imagination' – that was how the academic Melissa Sihra later described America's reaction to *On Raftery's Hill*.

In Ireland, the play had offered an opportunity to confront a difficult truth, but for many in the Irish-American audience, the reaction was instead of denial: this is not us; this should not be happening. Some of those reactions were undoubtedly caused by (justified) Irish-American insecurity: the fear that plays such as *On Raftery's Hill* would confirm longstanding prejudices against the Irish, who had often been depicted as brutal, animal-like, inbred and uncivilized within American culture. But there was also a sense in which the audience were unable to face the facts being conveyed by Carr.

The tour of Carr's play to the US was as part of the May 2000 'Island: Arts from Ireland' festival at the John F. Kennedy Center in Washington, a venue that had of course taken its name from an Irish-American hero.

That festival had been the idea of JFK's sister, Jean Kennedy Smith, who had been the US ambassador to Ireland for much of the 1990s. She had persuaded the governments of both the Republic and Northern Ireland to support what was intended as a celebration of Irish art; it also aimed to mark the achievement of peace in Northern Ireland through the Good Friday Agreement, in which the US government – and Kennedy Smith herself – had been centrally involved. The festival opened with a performance of *Riverdance*, and then over the following fortnight it included readings (including by the recent Nobel Laureate Seamus Heaney), musical performances and theatre productions.

Three plays had been scheduled for the festival, and two of them had the kind of political themes that Irish-American audiences usually warmed to. The first was Donal O'Kelly's one-man show *Catalpa*, which is about a daring jailbreak by Irish rebels in the 1870s; and the second was Rough Magic's production of Stewart Parker's masterpiece *Pentecost*, a deeply moving exploration of the impact of the Troubles on the lives of ordinary people, both Protestant and Catholic, in the north. They were considered to be excellent productions, and it was noted that both were conveying the idea to the Kennedy Center audience that Ireland was moving away from a period of violence to one of peace, that it was a place to be admired and to feel proud of.

The third production was *On Raftery's Hill*, and it was of course aiming to do something altogether different. Many members of the audience at the Kennedy Center were horrified – and as the interval came, many left the theatre altogether, refusing to come back. Reviews were strong, but there was also a definite sense of shock amongst the audience – and a question of how a play like this could be included in a seemingly celebratory event. That question started to be asked back in Ireland too, perhaps due to some of the country's own lingering insecurities, especially about how Ireland is perceived internationally.

The answer was that Druid were again challenging expectations about what they ought to do. Countries around the world at that time were starting to think about nation branding – the use of culture as a form of soft diplomacy, as seen in Tony Blair's embrace of the 'Cool Britannia' movement that had emerged in English music, film and sport in the late 1990s. An event such as the 'Island: Arts from Ireland' festival might have tried to do the same thing, demonstrating that (as one newspaper put it) it's 'hip to be Hibernian'. But what Carr and Druid had shown was that, perhaps paradoxically, the strength and health of Irish society could be revealed in its willingness to confront its failures and traumas.

When things eventually quietened down after *On Raftery's Hill*, Druid staged a new play by Geraldine Aron: a one-woman show called *My Brilliant Divorce*.

To casual observers, Aron's new comedy might have seemed like the polar opposite of *Raftery*, both in scale and tone – but it too was pointing out to audiences that they were living in a new Ireland. Divorce, after all, had been legalized in the country only in 1996 and, although the rate had been increasing since then, it remained low by international standards, with only 2,817 divorces granted in 2001, the year that Aron's play premiered. Divorce was

Glenne Headly, *My Brilliant Divorce*, 2001.

a reality in Ireland – but a brilliant one? Druid's audiences might have needed a minute or two to think about that one.

At the beginning of Aron's relationship with Druid, the company had presented Irish premieres of plays that she had written for other theatres. But from *Same Old Moon* onwards she began writing plays for them to premiere – and, in 1990, that had resulted in a double bill of new works, *The Donohue Sisters* and *The Stanley Parkers*. Speaking about them to *The Galway Advertiser*, Aron explained that she'd been worried that her writing had become 'a bit safe' but, while at a writing retreat at the Tyrone Guthrie Centre in Monaghan she had formed a friendship with Marina Carr, and was thinking about how to take more risks.

The Stanley Parkers certainly was a risky play for Ireland in 1990, depicting the relationship of a couple of gay men when one of them has just been diagnosed with AIDS. Homosexuality

Marion O'Dwyer, Kate O'Toole and Ingrid Cragie, *The Donohue Sisters*, 1990.

in Ireland remained illegal until 1994, and stage representations of gay Irish characters had tended to be coy if not downright dishonest before that time. Aron's attempt to focus on the human dignity of her characters meant that her writing was both topical and well ahead of its time.

The Donohue Sisters might have seemed more conventional by comparison – it could easily have been called *Three Sisters* had that title not been taken ninety years previously by Anton Chekhov. But it too was doing something new, not least in the fact that Aron gives the stage over fully to her three sisters, centring the lives of ordinary Irish women in a way that allowed many in Druid's audiences to see themselves and thus to feel seen.

Aron's many fans in Galway would have guessed ahead of the premiere of *My Brilliant Divorce* that it too would, like those earlier plays, illustrate the truth of Brendan Behan's famous claim that comedy could be a subversive genre: that, while the audience 'were laughing their heads off, you could be up to any bloody thing behind their backs'. And that's exactly what *My Brilliant Divorce* did: it was very funny but also had important things to say.

Garry had cast the American actor Glenne Headly for the play – and although she was a respected stage actor, she was best known in Ireland for her role as a table-turning con artist in the Steve Martin/Michael Caine comedy *Dirty Rotten Scoundrels* from 1988. Audiences therefore arrived at the theatre predisposed to laugh – and they were given plenty of opportunities to do so by a script that was undeniably witty, both in its observation of human vulnerability and in Aron's use of language.

But the action also had an underlying poignancy, showing how the breakdown of a marriage can be both liberating and devastating, often simultaneously. Also surprising was the play's frankness about sex and sexuality. Before that time, the Irish theatre had tended to present sex as a problem to be solved rather than an intimacy to be shared. Aron's play de-pathologized it, showing that sex can be spoken about, laughed about and savoured without guilt or apology. That was new, to the Irish stage anyway.

Like Aron's earlier works, *My Brilliant Divorce* was also significant in creating space for the experiences of women. There had been a glut of Irish monologue plays during the 1990s, but they were almost exclusively focused on men's stories; when women appeared at all, they usually did so to elaborate upon a man's pain, guilt, betrayal or dysfunction. The simple act of staging a one-woman show in Ireland in the year 2001 was a

Deirdre O'Kane in *My Brilliant Divorce*.

quietly revolutionary assertion of the need for women's stories and voices to be listened to. *My Brilliant Divorce* went on to be staged in the West End, with Dawn French in the lead role, in 2003 – and then Druid revived it in Galway in 2007, on that occasion with Deirdre O'Kane as the star. O'Kane had worked with Druid as an actor during Maelíosa's directorship of the company – but after she left, she had gone on to form a reputation as one of Ireland's leading stand-up comedians. Her appearance in *My Brilliant Divorce* provided an opportunity for her to wed those two aspects of her career in one performance. The play proved an ideal vehicle for her talents, allowing her to find and control the humour in the script while giving her audience a fully realized character to engage and empathize with.

It went unremarked at the time, but *My Brilliant Divorce* is notable for the fact that the lead role was played in those productions first by an American, then an Englishwoman and then an Irishwoman – and that all three played the role in their own accents and without making major changes to the script. There had been some mild criticism of the 2001 production with Headly, that the play was insufficiently grounded in a Galway context. But that rootlessness may have been the most important thing about it: in its three productions there was a suggestion that the experience of an Irish woman in the twenty-first century could align with that of women elsewhere in the western world, that the situation of Irish women was no longer inherently anomalous. And that too was a quietly revolutionary statement.

―――

In 2002, Garry sent a copy of a new play to Derbhle Crotty, the actor she'd directed in the lead role of Marina Carr's *Portia Coughlan* at the Abbey six years earlier. They'd been talking for a while about Derbhle performing with Druid, perhaps in a Synge play – but now Garry had a different suggestion.

The play was *The Good Father,* by a young playwright called Christian O'Reilly. He had been given a reading in the Druid Debut series in 2001, for *It Just Came Out,* a play about racism. It had been seen as promising but not suitable for a full production – but Christian had told Garry that he was already writing something else, something better; and she assured him that she wanted to read it once it was ready.

That 'something else' was a drama for two actors. They would play a man and woman – one working-class and the

Chapter 9: Druid Debuts, 2000–2007

Aidan Kelly and Derbhle Crotty, 2002.

other middle-class – who attempt to form a relationship when the woman becomes unexpectedly pregnant after a one-night stand. *The Good Father* was therefore one of the first plays to explore how social class worked in Ireland during the 'Celtic Tiger' period of rapid economic growth that had begun in the late 1990s – a period that had worsened inequalities in the country to such an extent that, by the beginning of the twenty-first century, only the United States had a wider gap between rich and poor. But O'Reilly's play was also simply a love story, an investigation of how people come together – and how (or whether) they stay together, especially when they encounter tragedy.

When she'd had a chance to read the script, Derbhle told Garry that she thought there were good things in it, but that it needed work – maybe lots of work. She paused and then asked Garry straight out – 'Are you saying you're going to do it?'

Garry was saying exactly that, and she wanted Derbhle to be in it, alongside Aidan Kelly – a contemporary of Derbhle's but not someone she'd acted with before. The play did need more work, Garry agreed – but it would get it, both before and during the rehearsal process. The plan was to open it in July 2002, at the Galway Arts Festival.

And so a few weeks later, Derbhle travelled to Galway on a Sunday evening, ready to begin rehearsals the next day. When she arrived, she found a new draft of the script waiting for her; she scanned it but didn't read it right through until the next morning, when there was a full table read with the company, including Christian himself. He'd been working in TV, he told everyone, and he was used to the idea of making changes to his writing as he went along – so he was ready to do the work that was needed to make *The Good Father* as good as it could be.

As Derbhle remembers it, Garry told everyone that she thought the first scene of the play was excellent. 'I love the setup and the characters, and really, this scene is the reason I want to do the play,' she'd told them. But then, after a pause, she went on: 'Scenes two and three … You know, they're going to need some work. For now, we'll just leave them as they are. For the moment.'

'I sat there,' Derbhle recalled, 'and I was thinking, *OK, so this is going to be interesting …*'

When the next day began, there were four people in the rehearsal room: Garry, Derbhle and Aidan – and also Tim Smith, a newly appointed Stage Manager (who would, over the next decade, work his way up to being the company's General Manager). Derbhle remembers Garry beginning the session with an invitation: 'Well, come on, come on. Talk to me. What do you think about this play?'

The two actors offered their views – they liked one passage because it offered a clue to their characters' motivations, they thought another might be slowing the action down, and so on.

'And then Christian came in later that day,' said Derbhle,

and Garry started giving a précis of what she felt about the play. But then she said, 'No, hold on. I'm talking a lot here. Come on, let's hear from you two. You had plenty to say this morning.' So we checked if it would be all right with everyone if we offered notes. And off we went. After that, we were all involved; our input was more than encouraged.

Derbhle was clear about what that meant:

> The play is entirely Christian's. But this was a collaboration in terms of feeding back and trying to work out on the floor the answer to the question: *what is this thing that we have here?*

No one is entirely sure how many drafts the play went through over the following four weeks – but there might have been as many as eighteen. 'It was a bit of a rollercoaster,' Derbhle recalled. 'A horrendous rollercoaster at times, and I do believe we went through something. But that first scene did always stand.'

The play was performed at the Druid Lane Theatre, and Francis O'Connor had designed the space in such a way that it resembled a nursery, with simple colours on the walls, and a mostly bare playing space – filled only by a cot which Aidan Kelly's character paints in expectation of their baby's arrival. The audience sat on all four sides of the performance area, watching the actors but also intimately aware of each other's reactions too.

Previews began, and the audience responded positively, even while the script continued to evolve. Opening night soon arrived – and the play got a standing ovation, which, in 2002, was a rare occurrence, usually reserved only for work that was truly exceptional. But the next morning, Garry gathered everyone together again. She told them that if they didn't feel up to it, that would be fine – but she thought that the play still had a little further to go. Would they agree to taking one more look at it?

It had always been apparent where the play was going to get to: that it would conclude with the couple achieving some sort of rapprochement – that, as Derbhle puts it, 'the door would be left open to hope', if only tenuously. But they needed to ensure that the last scene made complete sense based on everything that had come before. So they agreed to some further changes. And once those were made, the play remained as it was for the rest of the run.

Thereafter, the audience 'really became part of it,' said Derbhle:

> And so their response to it, we knew, was a very honest response. We knew that they'd come through this experience with us and that we'd all come out on the other side, together.

Audience reactions were often deeply emotional, whether from empathy, the personal memory of similar experiences or a combination of both. The apparent simplicity of the staging intensified those reactions. For example, the death of the baby was revealed to the audience not through expository dialogue but by Aidan Kelly standing wordlessly over the empty cot, holding its bars, and staring silently into it for an unbearably prolonged period – before dragging it abruptly off-stage. During the run, the front-of-house staff standing in the foyer could hear the audience crying out in shock when that scene was performed.

In the published edition of the script, Christian O'Reilly expressed his indebtedness to Garry, Aidan and Derbhle for 'challenging the play with such honesty and imagination in the rehearsal room, and for helping it to become the play it is today'. It returned to Druid in 2003 before touring nationally, including a month-long run in Dublin; it won the Stewart Parker New

Playwright Award, and since then has been produced many times in Ireland, in both professional and amateur productions.

The Good Father needed the intimacy of the Druid Lane space in order to thrive. Other new plays operated at a much larger scale, and therefore could only work at the Town Hall. A case in point was the premiere of Enda Walsh's *The Walworth Farce* at the Town Hall in 2006.

Originally from Dublin, Walsh had moved to Cork in the early 1990s and had begun making theatre there with Corcadorca, a theatre company that he co-directed with Pat Kiernan. Their first breakthrough was *Disco Pigs*, which premiered in 1996. Performed by Cillian Murphy and Eileen Walsh, it involved both actors directly narrating the story of their relationship. It was written with a fastidious inventiveness that was compared sometimes to the style of Beckett, and sometimes to the rap music of Eminem – but which was also admired for being very much its own thing. That production toured the world for three years and was made into a feature film in 2001, starring Cillian Murphy in one of his first screen roles (and, incidentally, also featuring Marie Mullen).

Walsh had followed up that success with *Misterman*, a one-man play that he acted in himself in a production in Cork in 1999, and then *bedbound* for the Dublin Theatre Festival in 2001. He was also commissioned by the London-based new writing company Paines Plough, for whom in 2005 he wrote *The Small Things*, which toured to the Galway Arts Festival in that same year. Again, those plays involved direct address of the audience; they were linguistically dense, and they presented stories that were both disturbing and oddly humorous. But they were also intimate – mostly premiered in small spaces, and all of them featuring only one or two actors.

The Walworth Farce was a significant advancement, both in terms of scale and form, and Walsh would later describe his first Druid production as a major turning point in his career, both artistically and in terms of his international reputation.

It is set in a London flat that's occupied by a father and his two adult sons, all of whom have emigrated to England from their home city of Cork. That set-up might initially have reminded audiences of Murphy's *A Whistle in the Dark*, another male-dominated Irish play about emigration and trauma (Walsh would later acknowledge that play as a significant influence on *The Walworth Farce*). But it is revealed that the trio have moved to London not to work but rather to hide from a terrible crime committed by the father back home. Perhaps in penance for that crime – or perhaps to avoid facing it – the father forces his sons to join him every day in retelling the story of his departure from Ireland in the form of a play, which is the farce of the title. And in that compulsive retelling of a traumatic story, *The Walworth Farce* resembles another Murphy play, *Bailegangaire*.

Walsh has spoken often of his admiration for Murphy, both personally and artistically, but *The Walworth Farce* was also doing something distinctive and original. The history of drama is full of nested narratives, from the play-within-a-play of Shakespeare's *Hamlet* to Michael Frayn's contemporary farce *Noises Off*. Walsh, however, was running at least four different stories simultaneously in *The Walworth Farce* – the story of the family's past in Ireland, their retelling of that story through performance in their London flat, the story of their everyday life in London when they're not performing (shopping for groceries, for example), and the stories of people from the outside world, both in Ireland and England.

He was also playing with and reinventing countless theatrical traditions, drawing on the cross-dressing conventions of pantomime (and indeed of Shakespeare), while also including a moment when a white actor uses make-up to perform as a black character, thus alluding to the place of blackface minstrels in Irish performance histories.

And he was also playing with some of the most famous tropes of the Irish dramatic tradition: the use of a single room to stand in for the whole nation, the creation of drama through the unexpected arrival of a 'stranger in the house', the presentation of father/son conflict as a metaphor for Ireland's history of political failure, the absence of a mother as a metaphor for male dysfunction – it was all there, as if Walsh's imagination was a mill for grinding old plays into something new.

Garry admired the play but she felt that she wasn't the right person to direct it, and instead she invited Mikel Murfi to take on the task. As an actor, he had trained at École Jacques Lecoq in Paris, and was therefore skilled in mime, clown and movement – all of which would be needed to manage the physicality of Walsh's play. And he had shown talent as a director when taking charge of the premiere of Mark Doherty's surreal comedy *Trad* for the Galway Arts Festival in 2004.

Joining him in the production were Denis Conway, who played the father, Dinny; Aaron Monaghan and Garrett Lombard, who played his sons; and Syan Blake as Hayley, a checkout operator from a local Tesco store.

Aaron Monaghan would later describe working on *The Walworth Farce* as a joyful experience, in large part because of how Murfi directed it. As with all Druid productions, there was a deep analysis of the text, but Murfi also offered a corresponding focus on movement and gesture. For example, he encouraged Aaron and Garrett to find a way for their characters to physically communicate with each other that Dinny would not notice – and those gestures entered the show's choreography, creating a kind of parallel script that was sometimes even more meaningful than the words being spoken aloud.

Enda Walsh was in the rehearsal room too, and Aaron recalls how he drew on the rest of the company's ideas to revise the script:

> One of the things Mikel wanted to do was to make the script feel personal to the character, so he suggested that each actor would bring in a personal object that could be left somewhere on the stage.

Denis Conway had won an Irish Times Theatre Award for his performance in *Richard III* a few years earlier – and during rehearsals the other actors had occasionally indulged in a bit of light-hearted joking about it (a joke, it must be said, that was borne from the younger actors' huge admiration for Conway). With Murfi's suggestion about bringing personal objects into the rehearsal room, Aaron saw another opportunity to make that joke:

> And I said, 'Oh, Dennis can bring in his theatre award.' But then Enda said, 'What do you mean?' I was explaining the joke, saying, 'Oh, Dennis is always, you know, being slagged for winning that award.'
> 'That's brilliant,' Enda said. 'That's great. Oh my God'.

A couple of weeks later, when the next draft of the play was brought into the rehearsal room, Enda had integrated that idea into the text. Each day, Dinny would encourage his sons with the promise that they might win an Acting Trophy if their performance was good enough – and each day, he would give the award to himself. It's one of the funniest features of the play – and it began with Aaron's good-natured joke during rehearsals.

When the play opened in Galway, on 20 March 2006, the audience seemed unsure of how to react. Some who were present

Winning the Acting Trophy – Denis Conway in *The Walworth Farce*.

thought that they'd just seen the first great Irish play of the twenty-first century, but others were simply confused. Druid had staged complicated plays before (*Bailegangaire*, most obviously), but *The Walworth Farce* was asking them to listen to the interplay of multiple stories while also following a style of visual storytelling that had been intricately choreographed. It was understandable if this produced cognitive overload for some.

For that reason, the actors had been prepared for the possibility that the audience might not like the show at all. 'I remember saying this very clearly to Mikel,' Aaron remembered:

> I said, 'I'm so proud of this. I'm so proud of the work.' I was proud of all that we'd done and all we'd achieved, and

The suitors in *Penelope*, 2010

I fully expected to go out there during the first previews and for no one to like it, for no one to get what we were doing, and for no one to appreciate it. But I told him: 'I couldn't be happier doing this.'

But over time, the play's reputation kept growing – especially as the company toured it internationally, to regular Druid destinations such as Edinburgh, New York and Sydney, but also to Berkeley in California, Wellington in New Zealand and Oxford in the UK. Tadhg Murphy replaced Aaron Monaghan for the Edinburgh Transfer in 2007 and acted in every Druid performance of the play thereafter; his interpretation of Sean came to be seen as a crucial part of the play's success, especially internationally.

Walsh would go on to write two more full-length plays for the company – *The New Electric Ballroom* in 2008 and *Penelope* in 2010, both in the Druid Lane Theatre rather than the Town Hall. They also staged a double bill of his one-act plays *Gentrification*, directed by Thomas Conway, and *Lynndie's Gotta Gun*, which was directed by Sarah Lynch, who, like Tim Smith, had started with the company in stage management and would eventually become General Manager. *New Electric Ballroom* and *Penelope* would also tour internationally, and did much to establish Walsh's international reputation, especially in the United States.

The Good Father launched Christian O'Reilly's career as a professional playwright, while the company also brought Marina Carr and Enda Walsh to greater levels of international prominence. But during this period Druid also premiered plays by people whose greatest successes would ultimately be in other genres – showing how their support of playwriting reverberated into other parts of the Irish cultural sector.

Those plays included the 2006 drama *Empress of India* by Stuart Carolan, who went on to write the unprecedentedly successful RTÉ crime drama *Love/Hate*; and, in 2007, *Leaves* by Lucy Caldwell, who is now best known as the author of several award-winning novels and short story collections.

Empress of India opened at the Town Hall in September 2006, ahead of a transfer to the Dublin Theatre Festival. It marked the return of Seán McGinley to a Druid production for the first time in over a decade; he was playing a washed-up actor whose vanity and selfishness had estranged him from his sons. There was also a subplot about a daughter who had gone missing, an absence that drives much of the play's narrative.

Also noticeable was a surprisingly strong emphasis on religion in the text, placing Carolan in a tradition that dates to Samuel Beckett's *Endgame*: he was creating characters who, like Beckett's, curse God for not existing, then curse him again for not punishing them for their blasphemy.

But even more surprising was the play's treatment of sexuality, which was presented with a bluntness that would have seemed unexceptional in a film but which provoked some discomfort when performed live. Carolan's approach to the theme was relatively explicit, in the sense that there was some mild nudity in the production – but it was not in any way exploitative. Rather, the apparent aim was to consider sex as one more manifestation of the messiness of the characters' lives, to present it in strictly human rather than abstractly moral or religious terms.

A kerfuffle ensued.

In Galway, a local Fine Gael politician publicly expressed outrage at the nudity in the production (letters to the *Galway Advertiser* suggested that a looming election might have been an explanation for his objections). When it transferred to Dublin, it became the subject of a heated debate on Joe Duffy's *Liveline* call-in radio programme – always a sign that an Irish artwork has touched a societal nerve.

Fergal McGrath, Druid's Managing Director at that time, defended the show, arguing that its bad language was no worse than anything that could be heard on any Irish street; he also mentioned that it had been billed as unsuitable for children in all the relevant marketing, and that it was simply addressing adult themes.

Another defender was Lelia Doolin, a former Artistic Director of the Abbey who had moved to Galway. It was 'an amazing, big, powerful tragedy' she said, one that articulated the 'very frenetic challenges and the despair of modern life'. She described Garry's direction as 'amazingly bold' and insisted that the play's ideas needed to be treated with respect. Lelia would be one of Garry's most ardent supporters during the years ahead.

All that outrage probably sold a few more tickets to the play, but it had the regrettable impact of distracting audiences from Carolan's ideas. Francis O'Connor had designed the set in such

Seán McGinley in *Empress of India*, on Francis O'Connor's mirrored set.

a way that an enormous mirrored surface loomed over the stage, reflecting distorted images of the characters back to themselves while also displaying shadowy images of the audience out into the auditorium. That design was in keeping with the play's themes (literalizing the narcissism of its central character) – but it was also an invitation for the audience to see themselves, literally and metaphorically, and thus to consider what place Catholicism might have in their lives, whether as a personal faith or as a faltering public institution.

By 2010, Carolan was being hailed nationally for his work on *Love/Hate*, which ran for five seasons – and which had, it must be said, a greater level of bad language, nudity and violence than anything in his stage play. *Love/Hate* would also occasionally fall victim to controversies that felt slightly manufactured, but the show's reputation has held up strongly since it concluded in 2014.

Caldwell's *Leaves* did not cause the same kind of stir, but was if anything even more intense than *Empress of India*.

Produced when Caldwell was only twenty-four, the play is set in contemporary Belfast and explores the aftermath of a teenage girl's attempt to take her life. Her parents' varying emotions – bewilderment, anxiety, denial – were dramatized by Caldwell with a finely wrought combination of sympathy and distance. The audience could understand what the parents were going through, but they could also judge them for their mistakes and missteps along the way.

Of even greater impact was the characterization of the girl's two younger sisters, who were played in the Druid premiere by real-life siblings, Daisy and Penelope Maguire. Their characters are of course worried for their sister, but Caldwell also shows that they are jealous of her, that they see her monopolization of their parents' attention as a threat to be overcome. Again, the writing allowed audiences to have conflicting reactions without needing to resolve them: of course the younger girls were wrong to feel as they did, and of course the younger girls were right to feel as they did.

As with *The Good Father*, the play was performed in the Druid Lane Theatre rather than the Town Hall – and, again, that smaller space produced an intimacy that was intense because it was inescapable. It then transferred to the Royal Court.

In both England and Ireland, it was praised as an impressive debut. In Galway especially there was a realization that Caldwell had just presented one of the first post-Troubles plays to be seen in the Republic. Her characters manage trauma, depression and the threat of violence, but they do so not as a response to political violence but in a way that could just as easily be happening in Galway, Dublin or London. Or indeed in Moscow – this is a play that (like Aron's *Donohue Sisters*) explores the interrelationships

Kathy Rose O'Brien in *Leaves* by Lucy Caldwell.

of three sisters (indeed, Caldwell would go on to adapt Chekhov's play of that name for the Lyric Theatre in Belfast in 2016).

Leaves won the George Devine and Susan Smith Blackburn prizes; it was subsequently translated into French and staged in Rennes in 2009 – demonstrating how it was addressing themes that resonated well beyond Ireland.

On Raftery's Hill, *My Brilliant Divorce*, *The Walworth Farce* and *Empress of India* had opened at the Town Hall Theatre, while *The Good Father* and *Leaves* were staged in Druid Lane – and that established a pattern of using the two spaces to achieve different goals.

There was obviously the matter of seating capacity – the Town Hall could fit almost four times as many ticket holders as the Druid Lane space, and from an economic point of view it could therefore generate the income that was needed to underwrite the large ensemble-based productions that were central to Druid's artistic mission.

But there were other artistic considerations to consider. The process of working and reworking *The Good Father* was undoubtedly enabled by the knowledge that it would open in a smaller and more intimate space, for example – but *On Raftery's Hill* would have been simply unbearable at such close quarters; that play needed the Town Hall's proscenium arch stage in order to create a buffer between the action and the audience. *The Walworth Farce* and *Leaves* were both about Irish families, but Walsh's play needed the large space of the Town Hall to fit those multiple narrative strands, while Caldwell's play needed an intensity of attention that only Druid Lane could have provided.

And the Druid Lane Theatre was, above all else, the company's home. Its uncertain future had at last been resolved in 1996, when, to celebrate Druid's twenty-first birthday, the McDonogh family donated the space to them. That was an act of exceptional generosity, especially given that a nationwide boom in property development was well underway at that stage. The Council had added to the celebratory occasion by formally renaming Chapel Lane as Druid Lane. Doing so was an acknowledgment of a simple fact – many Galwegians were by then using the 'Druid Lane' name anyway – but it was also important symbolically as a statement of the centrality of the company to Galway's life and identity.

While that new writing was being presented, Druid were also working on a plan to stage the complete works of Synge in a single day – and thus to produce some of the shortest Irish plays ever written in an event that would be one of the longest Irish theatre performances ever staged. Their concentration on new writing had allowed them to develop an ability to flex between the large and the small, the intimate and the overwhelming – and that was going to prove essential as they embarked upon their biggest project ever.

The *DruidSynge* ensemble in *The Well of the Saints*, 2005.

Chapter 10
John Millington Synge:
House Playwright, 2004–2010

AT SOME POINT in the mid-1980s, Garry had a surprising thought: 'Do you know what I'd love to do,' she had said, 'I'd love to leave Druid and go and found a company that did all of Synge's plays together.'

That idea stayed in her mind for a long time afterwards. She would occasionally allude to it in conversations and interviews – and although she directed none of Synge's plays during the 1990s, he remained an obvious presence in her imagination. *The Leenane Trilogy*, for instance, shows the influence of Synge in many ways, most obviously in the fact that McDonagh had taken the title of *The Lonesome West* directly from *The Playboy of the Western World*. And in the show programme for *The Beauty Queen* in 1996, Garry had indicated that her 'next' project would be the staging of a Synge cycle – some eight years before she actually had the opportunity to do so.

That biographical note showed that Garry had begun to perceive that she didn't need to leave Druid in order to achieve her ambition. 'It took a long time for that to percolate in,' she acknowledged:

> And then when it became a realistic thing that we were discussing [in the late 1990s], it took a long time to get the

resources for it – the resources to do six or seven hours of theatre at the time were huge. It took that amount of time, I suppose, for the company to grow sufficiently confident to be able to make this decision and carry it out and get the resources to do it.

Those plans were realized in *DruidSynge*, a day-long presentation of all of Synge's plays by a single ensemble of seventeen actors. It premiered in Galway in the summer of 2005, and the full cycle toured to Dublin, Edinburgh, Minneapolis and New York – while also playing for three days on Inis Meáin, the place that had done so much to inspire both Synge and Druid. There were also individual productions of some of the plays, especially *The Playboy of the Western World*, which travelled internationally from 2004 to 2009, the centenary of Synge's death.

DruidSynge would be exceptionally well received, both in Ireland and abroad – so much so that it now seems difficult to understand why Garry had once contemplated leaving Druid in order to produce it. But, as with all her most ambitious projects from *Bailegangaire* onwards, the seeming inevitability of the success was obvious only after the fact. When it was being planned, no one was sure that *DruidSynge* could actually be done – that it would work artistically, that it could be managed financially or that anyone would want to go to it.

The Leenane Trilogy had demonstrated that audiences were willing to dedicate an entire day to a theatrical marathon – but Synge's work was a harder sell than McDonagh's. By the year 2000, *The Playboy of the Western World* was still considered to be a world classic, a status that Druid had done much to reinforce, of course. But Synge had produced five other plays, some of which had fallen out of the Irish repertoire by the middle of the twentieth century. Staging a trilogy by an exciting young writer like McDonagh was one thing; reviving six century-old plays that (except for *The Playboy*) were rarely or never performed – well, that was a different proposition.

It didn't help that Synge was viewed by many as old-fashioned, especially in his use of an Irish speech that was so often imitated (and so often parodied) that it had come to feel stilted and inauthentic in many Irish productions. Druid's 1982 *Playboy* had done much to dispel that prejudice – but it had proven difficult to kill it off altogether. As Garry was all too aware, the derogatory term 'Synge-song' had often been used to criticise Martin McDonagh's dialogue when *The Leenane Trilogy* was being staged in Ireland in the 1990s, for example. That insult was founded upon a misunderstanding of both Synge and McDonagh, neither of whom was trying to compose ethnographically accurate reproductions of real Irish speech. But it was striking that, in the late 1990s, it was considered possible to attack McDonagh by comparing him to Synge.

All of that added up to uncertainty about whether Garry's plan was viable. Audiences might be able to listen to Synge's dialogue for a two-hour production of *The Playboy* – but would they tolerate it over a ten-hour period mostly made up of plays they didn't know? And what to do about the fact that the work was considered to be artistically uneven – ranging from established masterpieces such as *Riders to the Sea* to rarely staged curios such as *The Tinker's Wedding* before concluding with the unfinished (and lengthy) *Deirdre of the Sorrows*? How many actors would be needed to stage the whole cycle? Could a single actor be cast in several of Synge's plays and, if so, how could they possibly learn all those highly poeticized lines without confusing one role with another? How would the company manage set changes for six plays? And, above all else, how could they persuade anyone to go to such a production?

But Garry intuited that audiences would respond well to Synge if the plays were framed in the right way.

So she persisted.

By 2001, her plans were starting to feel more tangible. In an interview with Karen Fricker, she explained that she'd originally hoped to begin staging the cycle in 2000, but now thought it likely that it would begin in 2003. And she was ready to argue for the importance of the project, she said. 'Theatre should never be easy,' she affirmed:

> Nostalgia is easy, nostalgia is soft, and theatre should never be soft, ever. Which isn't to say that it shouldn't be incredibly entertaining ... but it's about taking something and transforming it into something else. It's not about authenticity. We have loads of modern tools for authenticity, but theatre can't be one of them.

She wasn't saying it explicitly but – when viewed from a post-*DruidSynge* vantage point – that interview showed that Garry was staking out a claim for how the production should be understood. The plays should be watched as if they were new works rather than vehicles for nostalgia. They would be 'incredibly entertaining' but wouldn't shirk from the difficulties that Synge posed, both to theatremakers and to audiences. And Druid were going to demonstrate that Synge was not trying to stage an 'authentic' version of Ireland: no, the company were going to do something different – they were going to show that there are some things that only the theatre can do.

The first *DruidSynge* production appeared in February 2004 – and it was one of the company's most keenly anticipated shows in years, selling out its run at the Town Hall Theatre before it even opened.

Chapter 10: John Millington Synge: House Playwright

The Playboy of the Western World, 2004, including Sonya Kelly (left) and Cillian Murphy (right).

For some, that anticipation arose because it had been almost twenty years since Garry's last production of *The Playboy*; there was now a whole generation of theatregoers who had heard about her work on the play but had never seen it.

For others, there was an awareness that this *Playboy* was a curtain-raiser: that it would be followed, over the subsequent eighteen months, with the full cycle of the plays.

But mostly the excitement was caused by Cillian Murphy's return to Druid, in the role of Christy Mahon.

Murphy was by then picking up regular roles in major feature films. He'd appeared in a supporting part in Anthony Minghella's *Cold Mountain* and alongside Scarlett Johannsen in *Girl with a Pearl Earring* in 2003; he'd also made a strong impact in the Irish films *On the Edge* in 2002 and *Intermission* in 2003 (the latter written by Mark O'Rowe and directed by John Crowley). But it was his performance in Danny Boyle's *28 Days Later* that marked him out as a lead actor – especially in a long opening

Anne-Marie Duff and Cillian Murphy, *The Playboy*, 2004.

sequence in which his character awakens from a coma to find himself in a completely deserted London. Holding the screen by himself for almost fifteen minutes, Murphy displayed uncommon presence and charisma. Those were the traits of a movie star – and although he'd worked with Druid before, his appearance as Christy was seen more as celebrity casting than a return visit.

Working with Maureen Hughes as casting director, Garry had assembled an exciting ensemble of other young actors, most of them new to the company. Appearing in the role of Pegeen was Anne-Marie Duff; like Cillian Murphy, she too was becoming well known for her work in film (including *The Magdelene Sisters* in 2002) and TV. Chris O'Dowd was included as Jimmy Farrell. Druid's *Playboy* was one of his first professional roles; a decade later, he was appearing regularly in movies like *Bridesmaids* and had been nominated for a Tony for his performance in *Of Mice and Men* on Broadway. Sonya Kelly was also in the cast, playing one of the village girls – and her experience of acting in a Druid production would later inform her work with the company as a playwright.

But perhaps the most important inclusions were of two actors who would play major roles in the Druid ensemble during the years to come: Eamon Morrissey and Aisling O'Sullivan.

By 2004, Morrissey had already had a long career in the Irish theatre. He'd been in the premiere of Friel's *Philadelphia, Here I Come!* for its Dublin opening in 1964 and its Broadway transfer two years later; and he'd also appeared in the premiere of Murphy's *Famine* in 1968. During the 1970s he'd begun to develop his own one-man shows, often derived from Irish literature; he also became well known throughout Ireland for his performances in the satirical TV show *Hall's Pictorial Weekly*. He was playing Pegeen's father in this production (but for later stagings of the play would be cast as Old Mahon), and he was able to bring his huge experience as an actor – his comic timing, his skills as a reader of plays, his physical dexterity – into the ensemble.

Aisling O'Sullivan's professional career had begun when she'd been brought into the Abbey during Garry's time there in the early 1990s. Her breakthrough role came in the premiere production of McDonagh's *The Cripple of Inishmaan* in London in 1997, when she played the protagonist's love interest with show-stealing gusto. Garry had then directed her in a new Mark O'Rowe play called *Crestfall* at the Gate Theatre in 2003; the play itself was controversial, but O'Sullivan's performance (alongside those of Marie Mullen and Eileen Walsh) was acclaimed.

For this *Playboy*, O'Sullivan played the Widow Quin and – as had happened with Marie in the 1980s – her performance was considered revelatory simply because she acted the role in the way that Synge had written it. Her Widow Quin had a sexual confidence that was assertive and also wryly disdainful of most of the men around her; and O'Sullivan delivered her lines with a considered rhythm that showed her character's thought processes happening in real time. This was a fully embodied performance in a play that is sometimes considered too wordy.

Alongside the casting, Garry was determined to stage a *Playboy* that looked different from everything that had come before. She'd reached the conclusion that the play had become too predictable. 'One thing that bothers me,' she explained, is that 'once you design a set for *The Playboy*, everyone in the auditorium knows what play is about to go on'. She wanted to get away from that:

> The Ireland of that time seems now to exist only in stage terms, in the sense of the báinín, and the rough clothes, and the fire and the bar, and the drinking, and all that. It doesn't seem to have a connection to anything any longer, other than a connection to itself.

She wanted to create a form of stage realism that would be rooted in Synge's own history. 'Synge was a Victorian,' she observed; he was also a European, which meant that 'this play belongs to the mainstream, the European historical mainstream'. That observation resulted in a style of costuming (designed by Kathy Strachan) that drew on models from the Edwardian period – Pegeen's father wore a top hat and tails, for instance.

And the heightening of the play's European roots provided an opportunity to emphasize just how theatrical it is. 'It is a play about play,' Garry explained, referring to how the characters change costumes again and again, how they keep making speeches, how they re-enact events that have already happened, embellishing them more with every telling – and so on. By the time she came out of rehearsals, she'd formed a new consciousness of

The Well of the Saints, 2004, Including Domhnall Gleeson (far left).

The Playboy 'as a piece of art'. In her earlier production she'd been focused on the drive and energy of the play; now she was more conscious of its 'extraordinary craft'.

The emphasis on theatricality was revealed in the decision – worked out with Francis O'Connor – to replace the bar in the script with a free-standing table. The table effectively became a second stage, and, with movement direction from David Bolger, it brought a new dynamism to the space, sometimes breaking up the interplay between the characters by creating a physical barrier between them, and sometimes heightening the action by giving a literal platform to demonstrate Christy's elevation in the eyes of the Mayo villagers. The design liberated Murphy's inherent athleticism – he leapt onto and around the table; his Christy felt like a spring that had at last uncoiled after years of being held in check.

Those who had seen Druid's 1982 *Playboy* thought the 2004 version was very different – just as good, but good in its own way.

But the most important thing was that audiences were now fully engaged by the *DruidSynge* idea – they were ready for more.

And so in the autumn of 2004, the company staged a double bill of *The Well of the Saints* and *The Tinker's Wedding*. The first of those plays brought Marie and Mick Lally back together in a Druid production for the first time in almost twenty years (and the Saint in that production was played, incidentally, by Domhnall Gleeson – another actor, unknown at the time of his *DruidSynge* debut, who would go on to be Tony-nominated). And the audiences turned out for it. Again the Galway run sold out, and it was also popular when it moved to the Dublin Theatre Festival in October 2004.

At that time, Garry still wasn't certain how the cycle would play out – maybe it would happen over two or three days; maybe each play would have a separate cast. But finally the idea of producing all of them in a single day with a shared ensemble, and opening in July 2005 (on Druid's thirtieth birthday) was settled upon.

The next step was to finalize her cast for the full cycle.

Shortly after the Cillian Murphy *Playboy* in 2004, Aaron Monaghan was hired for his first job with Druid – and he felt sure that he was going to get fired on his first day working with them.

He had graduated from the acting programme at Trinity College Dublin a couple of years previously, where he'd been spotted in his final year performance by Maureen Hughes. She thought he was exceptional – like 'an Irish Mark Rylance', she thought. He'd been picking up roles at the Abbey but Maureen felt that he could be ideally suited to the *DruidSynge* ensemble that she was working with Garry to assemble. An audition was arranged.

Chapter 10: John Millington Synge: House Playwright

As a first step, Aaron had been asked to appear in a rehearsed reading of *The Walworth Farce*, with Mikel Murfi directing; it would involve two and a half days rehearsing and then a performed reading for the company. But on one of the evenings, he would also audition for Garry to play a role in *The Playboy*. Aaron went to Heuston Station in Dublin and, as he recalls it:

> I missed the train to Galway literally by one minute. And so I ended up being a couple of hours late and I thought *this is just awful, this is terrible*, you know? And I thought I was going to be sacked. But I ended up doing the reading anyway.

The first day of *The Walworth Farce* ultimately went well – Seán McGinley read the role of Dinny, giving Aaron the opportunity to perform for the first time with one of Druid's longest-standing members. And then he was told that it was time to meet Garry.

> And so we were in the theatre in Druid Lane and she read opposite me. We read a scene of *Playboy* and I read it terribly. And then she kinda went, 'Okay …' So we read another scene; she read as the Widow. And then she got me to read *another* scene. I'd read the play a couple of times and I'd seen it. But it wasn't going well.

It was normal for a young actor like Aaron to be nervous, and he was probably still a little flustered from arriving late to Galway. But he thought that the audition was getting worse by the minute:

> And then she said, 'Look, let's go to *The Tinker's Wedding*'. So she started getting me to read these other plays that I hadn't known. I hadn't a clue what I was doing. And then she got me to read a bit of *Riders to the Sea*. So I was thinking, *I've messed this up so badly. This woman needs*

> *to give me so many chances with so many different plays, and I just keep messing them up.*

What Aaron didn't know at that time was that Garry was casting not just for *The Playboy* but for the entire cycle; the reason she was trying him out in multiple roles *wasn't* because he kept 'messing up'. It was because she'd decided she wanted to cast him as Christy and was seeing how she could fit him in across a variety of the other plays too.

A few weeks later, the offer came in. Aaron was being asked to play Christy Mahon in a production of *The Playboy* that would open at the Perth Festival in February 2005, and he would then reprise that role, and appear in three other plays in the *DruidSynge* cycle, in July.

Of course he was delighted, and of course he accepted – but there was just one problem. He was appearing in an Abbey Theatre revival of *The Shaughraun*, and the final week of its run coincided with the start of rehearsals for *The Playboy* in Perth. Could Druid and the Abbey find a way to make it work?

They tried. The idea was to replace Aaron with another actor for the final week of *The Shaughraun* at the Abbey, and although there were plenty of people who could have played Aaron's role, it just wasn't possible to find a way to make it work. 'So for a couple of days, maybe a week,' Aaron explained, 'the offer from Druid had to be rescinded.' But then Garry phoned Aaron, telling him that she'd been looking at flights. The entire company was due to fly out to Australia on a Thursday. They would have a day off and then go straight into technical rehearsals the following Monday. 'Are you willing,' Garry asked him, 'when you finish the show on Saturday night, to go straight to the airport?' She had determined that, if Aaron flew from Ireland a few hours after *The Shaughraun's* last performance on the Saturday night, he could get off the plane in Perth and go straight into tech.

Chapter 10: John Millington Synge: House Playwright

Aaron Monaghan and Ruth Negga rehearsing *The Playboy*, 2005.

'So at that point I did of course jump at it,' said Aaron:

> I didn't sleep on the plane. I was afraid to miss the connection or something like that. So I got off the plane in Australia, had a shower, got a sandwich and went to theatre. And literally just arrived in time. They had finished the bits of the tech that Christy Mahon isn't involved in, so then we did the rest of it. And I'm pretty sure we performed the show that night.

Aaron was playing Christy alongside Ruth Negga as Pegeen – marking the first time that a black Irish actor had played that part. And there were other changes to the cast: Marie was playing the Widow Quin, and also featured were several actors who would go on to appear in the full *DruidSynge* cycle, including Nick Lee, Louise Lewis and Gemma Reeves.

After the run in Perth, Aaron returned to Ireland – and rehearsals for *DruidSynge* got underway. The initial offer of four roles had increased to five. Did he ever find himself daunted by that prospect?

'Yeah, privately I was,' Aaron admitted. 'But I was usually too busy to be scared':

> When we weren't doing the plays, we were learning lines, and there was very little time for anything else. So when you're so consumed with preparing like that, you don't have time to be afraid. But yeah, it was terrifying. And it was exhausting as well.

Aaron particularly appreciated the opportunity to learn from actors like Eamon Morrissey and Marie.

> There was a lot of rough and tumble with the plays; they were very physical. And the thing was, no matter how tired I got during the rehearsals, I could see Eamon rolling around the stage. And he was in his sixties; I think he was sixty-five or sixty-seven at the time. And I just thought, *Jesus, I'm twenty-four. No excuses here.*

He also found Marie an exceptionally supportive presence in the rehearsal room:

> I'd watched Marie in many plays. And I realized – she's able to stay in the corner of the room, and whenever I had a problem with a scene she always took on the problem as if she was the one who was having the difficulty. And she would do it in the most beautifully polite way possible.

Chapter 10: John Millington Synge: House Playwright 277

> So she was saying that *she* had a problem but what she's actually doing is she's diagnosing *your* problem. And she just unlocks something for you. She eases things – not the tension necessarily, because 'tension' sounds like a combative thing. But you find you can suddenly start to work again in a very peaceful and exciting way. She's incredible.

Mick had also rejoined Druid for the production, so Aaron enjoyed having the opportunity to work with him as well:

> Obviously, I was aware that Mick had co-founded the company. Beforehand I thought, *God, he's going to be very active.* But he wasn't. He was kind of like a goalkeeper: he was quietly supporting from the back and looking after us. So Mick was an authority figure but in a quiet way. He spoke beautifully and he'd give you tiny little notes as well.

And of course there was the experience of working closely with Garry for the first time:

> I clearly remember, we were in the rehearsal room and I was on a table and Garry was directing and I was listening to her. And I was thinking that she's done this play dozens of times, and she's giving me these notes, and it's like she's rediscovering it – like it's her first time to work on it. And I realized: that's what it's like to work with Garry: she's working with fresh ingredients every time. She wasn't trying to get me to do what Maelíosa had done in the 1980s, or what Cillian had done the previous year. She was thinking, *This is the Christy Mahon I'm working with now.*

As rehearsals continued, the actors started to notice patterns; they started to see how the plays were speaking to each other – with

The Playboy of the Western World, 2005.

a phrase in one appearing in similar form in another, a character in one being reimagined in another. The production was starting to come together.

———

Aaron had already had a chance to perform as Christy in Perth – but Garry needed to find a new Pegeen (Ruth Negga's performance in Perth was considered beautiful by everyone who saw it, but she wasn't available for the full cycle). Garry turned to Catherine Walsh.

Catherine was then in her thirties, and thus a little older than most actors are when they first play Pegeen – but she was of course keen to play the role. 'I had originally auditioned for Pegeen when

Chapter 10: John Millington Synge: House Playwright

Catherine Walsh, *In the Shadow of the Glen*, 2005.

Cillian was doing it,' she explained. She had been performing in a Druid production of John B. Keane's *Sharon's Grave*, which had transferred to the Gaiety in Dublin in late 2003 – and on the opening night Garry asked her if she'd ever read *The Playboy*, because she was going to be doing auditions for it in the Gaiety Bar the next morning:

> I said I'd read it about ten years ago, and I was mad spending the opening night of *Sharon's Grave* looking for a copy of the script. Garry said that you don't need to read it, just come in and do it. Well, Anne-Marie Duff got the part, and then Ruth Negga got it when it went to Australia. So when it came back around again I couldn't believe it. It was quite earth-shattering to get it; it was a great gift.

That gift extended to playing a second role in the cycle, that of Nora Burke in *In the Shadow of the Glen*.

Pegeen and Nora: those are two big roles, but because she wasn't in the other four plays there were times during the rehearsal period when Catherine would find herself being free for a couple of days while the actors rehearsed the rest of the cycle. That free time might have created space for anxiety but, as she explained:

> Garry had a great thing of saying that we should feel free to call in to rehearsals. So even if you weren't in a play, you were able to watch it, and always feel you were part of it. So when they were doing another play, I always felt, *I'm in a novel, I'm just not in this chapter.*

Galway, July 2005. *DruidSynge* began at one o'clock in the afternoon with a performance of *Riders to the Sea*, with Marie playing the role of Maurya, the elderly Aran Islander who learns that her last surviving son has just died.

That play famously concludes with a keen – Synge's attempt to reproduce accurately a mourning practice that he had observed on the islands, which involved local women lamenting a death through a series of cries that were simultaneously a sincere expression of grief and also a highly stylized performance.

The combination of Maurya's final speech with the inarticulate moans of the other women gives the play a kind of sonic intensity that can make it feel operatic; for *DruidSynge* the vocal delivery was accompanied by movements that had been choreographed by David Bolger. He directed the young women in the cast to move their arms along the cabin floor, rhythmically bowing as if in alignment with the Atlantic waves beyond the cabin walls. And then Marie delivered the play's last words: 'No man at all can be living for ever, and we must be satisfied.'

Only about thirty minutes had passed, but it already felt as if *DruidSynge* had reached a peak of intensity.

Rather than staying with that intensity, Garry instead decided to create a contrast with it. So, instead of staging the

Chapter 10: John Millington Synge: House Playwright

The Tinker's Wedding, 2005.

plays in their order of composition, she moved next to *The Tinker's Wedding*.

Marie had quickly changed her costume to take on the role of Mary Byrne, one of the eponymous 'tinkers'. Her character's role in the play is to subvert the attempts of a younger woman to marry her son, but she and the putative daughter-in-law (played by Simone Kirby) eventually forge an alliance when they're insulted by the priest who's supposed to be performing the wedding ceremony. That play concluded with Marie sitting on Eamon Morrissey (as the priest), whom she'd tied in a sack and threatened with violence. The laughter couldn't have been louder.

The first interval came.

Next up was another pairing that brought out unexpected contrasts: *The Well of the Saints* and *In the Shadow of the Glen*.

For the first of those plays, Eamon Morrissey and Marie Mullen played a blind man and woman whose sight is miraculously restored by the wandering saint of the title. That production brought the whole ensemble on the stage for the first time, in a crowd scene when the villagers are so shocked by

the beggars' refusal to show gratitude that they threaten them with violence.

That portrayal of a large community uniting against a pair of outsiders made *Well* feel expansive; *In the Shadow of the Glen* was contrastingly intimate, with all the action happening within the walls of a country cabin. Eamon was playing Dan Burke, an old farmer who fakes his own death in order to expose his wife's infidelity. Mick was the tramp who saves the wife from a beating, persuading her to join him as a vagrant because he has 'a fine bit of talk', and Catherine Walsh played Nora. With his shock of white hair and his pale skin, Eamon looked like he'd been imported from a horror movie – but what stood out was the lyricism of Mick's delivery when he encourages Nora to join him on the open road.

Then a longer interval came. A series of long tables had been set up in the cobbled square in front of the theatre, allowing the whole audience of 400 people to share a meal together under an unusually sunny Galway sky.

Mick Lally and Eamon Morrissey in *In the Shadow of the Glen*

Chapter 10: John Millington Synge: House Playwright

Catherine Walsh, Aaron Monaghan and Marie Mullen in *The Playboy*, 2005.

As people ate, there was a lot of laughter. *Riders to the Sea* and *In the Shadow of the Glen* are often described in theatre histories as great plays; now the audience had seen for themselves why that was the case. And there was also a sense of surprise – many of those present had seen Druid's double bill of *The Well of the Saints* and *The Tinker's Wedding* during the previous year, and had expected to see a remounting of those productions, perhaps only with a few changes in the casting. But what they got were two wholly reimagined productions – with noticeable differences in tone, line delivery, lighting and costumes.

After dinner, the next play in the cycle was going to be *The Playboy of the Western World*, they knew – would it also be different from the version they'd all seen a year before?

Again, there was a surprise. As Aaron had intuited during rehearsals, the *DruidSynge Playboy* was a thoroughly reimagined production. One of the major differences from the 2004 staging was the interplay between the three main characters. In 2005,

Aaron Monaghan and Catherine Walsh in *The Playboy of the Western World*, 2005.

Aaron was in his twenties, Catherine in her thirties, and Marie (as the Widow Quin) in her fifties. The relative maturity of the two women shifted the dynamic: there were times when they seemed more like co-conspirators than rivals.

Yet the second-act love scene was joyously stirring in its portrayal of the two characters' dawning excitement in each other – a mood that was heightened by David Bolger's choreography of Aaron and Catherine's movements, which were tentative, awkward and distant at first – and then passionate.

As nine o'clock approached, it was time to watch the final play, *Deirdre of the Sorrows*. The reaction to *The Playboy* had been so positive that it felt like the natural conclusion to the day – so there was a little apprehension in the audience that *Deirdre* might prove anticlimactic.

Synge had written that play in the aftermath of *The Playboy* controversy, at a time when his health was rapidly declining – and when he died on 24 March 1909, it was left unfinished.

Yeats, Gregory and Molly Allgood worked together to complete a stageworthy version of script, premiering it in 1910. But since then it had been viewed as a flawed work, partly (the received wisdom went) because it was not based on Synge's observations of rural life but was taken from Irish myth. Was there a risk that *Deirdre* could deflate the energy that had been built up in the preceding five *DruidSynge* plays?

As the audience began to watch *Deirdre* they certainly saw that it was different from what had come before. The previous plays had been about peasants; *Deirdre* is about a king (played by Mick Lally) whose desire to marry Deirdre is thwarted when she elopes with a handsome young soldier. Yes, there were resemblances too – the story of an old man's sexual jealousy is found both in *Deirdre* and *In the Shadow of the Glen*, and Deirdre's defiance has its antecedents in Pegeen and Nora Burke. But this play was pervaded by a sense of fatalism that was probably caused by Synge's knowledge of his own impending death; that mood was present in the other plays but not with this kind of intensity.

Garry had needed to find a way of making *Deirdre* feel like it was part of a single body of work – to ensure that, as Catherine Walsh had put it, it would feel like one chapter in a single novel. That effect would be achieved in many ways, but Francis O'Connor's design was a major contributor to making *Deirdre* feel integral to the production overall.

The action for all the plays was performed on a single stage that had been covered with soil. Most of the plays are set indoors, so Francis was creating a theatrical metaphor rather than recreating real landscapes; he was conveying a sense of the six plays sharing the same roots, the same source.

That feeling of rootedness only grew in *Deirdre of the Sorrows* when two young children appeared on stage in its third and final act, and began to dig into the soil – making graves for

Gemma Reeves, Deirdre of the Sorrows.

the characters while Gemma Reeves as Deirdre delivered her final speeches beside the corpses of her lover and his brothers.

When the play (and therefore *DruidSynge* in its entirety) concluded, all the actors returned to the stage; one of the children who'd been digging in the soil was now holding a framed photograph, which was turned around towards the audience to reveal the face of Synge. And that was the production's final image.

Given his importance to the Irish tradition, it's striking how short Synge's career as a dramatist was: his first play was produced in 1903, and he died six years later – and for most of that period he knew that he was unlikely to live for very long. The consciousness of his own death hovers over the plays. It's in *Riders*, when Maurya loses one of her sons while lamenting the loss of another. It's detectable in the joke shared by *Shadow* and *Playboy* about an old man who seems dead – but isn't. And it's certainly in *Deirdre*, the only one of Synge's plays that actually does feature a death on stage.

Chapter 10: John Millington Synge: House Playwright

In the Shadow of the Glen, with the two white boards on the right.

Garry connected all those features together with the simple device of leaving two white boards on stage for all six plays. They appear first in *Riders* as timber for the construction of a coffin – and they stay in place for the others, acting as a discreet *memento mori* that is actualized at the end, when the two boards collapse, following which the child reveals Synge's portrait.

For the audience, the impact of those stage images was to produce a sense of loss at Synge's early death, encouraging the question of what more he might have done if he'd lived for longer. But there was also the realization that his work's greatness lies in the fact that he knew his career would be short. 'There is a vision that is at the centre of his work that tracks through each piece,' Garry explained – and *DruidSynge* had presented that vision in a unified form that had elevated the plays from their individual parts, allowing them to stand as a metaphor for a single artistic lifetime.

Reviews of the full cycle were uniformly enthusiastic, in Ireland, Britain and the United States. Most suggested that three of the actors were operating as 'golden threads' that pulled the works together – Aaron and Marie (who appeared in five of the six plays) and Eamon (who appeared in four of them). Marie in particular was celebrated for her work across the cycle, with *The New York Times* stating that 'Ms Mullen's achievement may well come to rank among the legendary acting accomplishments of the era.'

But it was also understood that this was the achievement of an ensemble: that the actors, designers and crew had been marshalled behind a single vision. The production therefore cemented Garry's reputation as one of the leading directors in the world, and again *The New York Times* theatre critic offered the kind of praise that most theatremakers never get, stating that *DruidSynge* was 'a highlight not just of my theatregoing year but of my theatregoing life'.

Further international tours followed. *The Playboy* was brought to Tokyo in 2007, with Aaron, Marie and Eamon all staying in the production, being joined by Cathy Belton in the role of Pegeen. Druid then returned to the United States with *Playboy* in 2008 – and on that occasion Catherine Walsh came back to the ensemble, but, like Marie before her, moved from playing Pegeen to playing the Widow Quin.

And there would be one final production of the *DruidSynge* version of *Playboy* on a tour of the UK in 2009, when Clare Dunne played Pegeen, Derbhle Crotty the Widow Quin, and Aaron once more played Christy. It came back to Galway for a short final run at the Town Hall.

The *DruidSynge* project was brought to a conclusion on 26 July 2009, at St Nicholas Cathedral in Galway, when Garry curated a series of readings of Synge's prose, poetry and plays to mark the centenary of his death. Aaron and Eamon participated, and so did Catherine Walsh – who was joined by her sister Eileen,

Chapter 10: *John Millington Synge: House Playwright* 289

Mick Lally in *DruidSynge*, 2005.

herself performing in a Druid production during that summer (Tom Murphy's *The Gigli Concert*). Gemma Reeves, Denis Conway, Mikel Murfi and Mick Lally completed the cast.

Sadly, that *DruidSynge* finale represented the last time that Mick would perform with Druid. He had been suffering from emphysema for a number of years – and although he'd continued to act as often as possible, his difficulty breathing meant that he had to limit his time on stage. Nevertheless, it was a shock to everyone when it was announced that he had passed away on 31 August 2010. He was just sixty-four years old.

There were tributes to him from across the Irish political spectrum. The Taoiseach Brian Cowen praised Mick's contributions to television and theatre in both the English and Irish languages; and the Minister for Arts Mary Hanafin spoke about Mick's unparalleled ability to connect with audiences. Michael D. Higgins, who had a more direct personal connection with Druid than most other Irish politicians, expressed his 'great sorrow and shock', while also praising Mick as a 'consistent supporter of causes where rights were at stake' – as for example when he had joined striking Dunnes Stores workers on a picket line in 1985 to share in their protest against handling goods from South Africa while the apartheid system continued. Ireland's trade unions also issued statements of regret for Mick's loss, highlighting how much he'd done to campaign for people's rights during his career.

Druid also issued a statement. 'The mood in Druid is one of total shock and disbelief,' Garry wrote:

> Mick Lally was a man without measure. He was my hero and I looked up to him. Druid owes everything to him. If he hadn't agreed to join Marie and I in the summer of 1975 then Druid would not have existed. Everyone at Druid has lost a colleague and dear friend.

A few days later, at his funeral, she told the gathered mourners that, 'among the people I most loved to have rows with, the one I most loved to row with was Mick', and that he always 'had the gift of making you feel you were the very person he was hoping to meet'. She also remembered him as someone who 'always had a new book, poem, music or something he had read in the paper to share with you'. (That intellectual generosity was mentioned by many of the people who had known him.) 'He was a good and cultured man,' Garry concluded. 'I'll miss him to the end of my days.'

Chapter 10: John Millington Synge: House Playwright 291

Peige Lally with Marie and Garry at the Mick Lally Window Seat, 2011.

Druid would take many steps to ensure that Mick would be remembered. The Druid Lane Theatre had been fully redesigned by DePaor architects while *DruidSynge* was touring the world, and it had reopened after a major refurbishment in 2009. In 2011, to mark the first anniversary of Mick's death, Garry and Marie invited Peige Lally to join them at the theatre, where they unveiled a new window seat in his memory.

And in 2014, they went a step further – renaming the venue the Mick Lally Theatre.

Chapter 11
Cycles, 2010–2015

JEROME HYNES once asked Tom Murphy a question: 'What is happiness to you?' 'When he asked me,' Murphy later recalled, 'I said, "Happiness is when I look at the clock and it's ten past seven, and when I look at the clock the next time, it's ten till two." It's stepping out of time.'

Murphy was thinking about how it's possible to lose yourself in a play, or in any work of art – or simply in a good conversation. In expressing that idea, he was also capturing something essential about Druid's approach to making theatre: the company seemed happiest in itself when it was moving forward rather than fixating on the present moment or (worse) looking backwards.

Thus, to the many people who asked Druid what they could possibly do to repeat the success of *DruidSynge*, their answer was always the same: Druid doesn't do encores – it was just going to keep doing what it had always done: it would make theatre.

But as the company advanced further into its third decade, there was also an inevitable need to come to terms with the fact that time is finite – that productions, no matter how successful, eventually finish their run; that collaborators, no matter how essential, eventually move on to other things; that reputations, no matter how secure, can someday be lost. And also, of course, there was a deeper understanding of how life itself is finite: that the people who had contributed to making the company would someday be lost to it.

Everyone in Druid knew that of course: they had seen it in the early 2000s when Ray McBride had been forced to retire prematurely due to illness, and they would see it again when Mick passed away in 2010.

Nevertheless, nothing could have been prepared them for the painfully shocking news, just three months after the *DruidSynge* premiere, that Jerome Hynes had died suddenly. He was a couple of weeks shy of his forty-sixth birthday.

He had been with Garry and the rest of the company on Inis Meáin just a week before his death, watching them perform *DruidSynge*. He had then returned to Wexford to get ready for that year's opera festival – but, while addressing staff and visiting artists at the Theatre Royal, he had collapsed suddenly. He died soon afterwards, of a brain aneurysm, it was later announced.

At the Druid offices in Galway, Fergal McGrath said that the phone had been ringing all through the day from people who remembered Jerome from his time at Druid. 'He was an extraordinary man,' said Fergal, emphasizing how Jerome had almost single-handedly shaped the profession of arts management in Ireland. Fergal said that it was incredible how many organizations he had been part of. But, he added, also incredible was 'the number of people Jerome was supportive of'.

At his funeral in Wexford, Garry and Marie both eulogized him from the altar. Marie remembered being with him a few weeks earlier on Inis Meáin: he had been there, she said, 'to witness the sun setting on the plays of John Millington Synge', another Irishman who had died far too young.

Garry offered a kind of prayer: 'We are human and we must cry out, storming the doors of heaven in protest. Why Lord did you take such a good man from us?' she asked. She said that her loss as Jerome's sister was nothing when compared to that of his wife Alma and his three sons. 'We are bereft of you, Jerome, and will struggle with our lives without you. For me, nothing will ever be the same again.'

As the company matured – but also as it faced the losses of Jerome and Mick – it began to exhibit evidence of a more reflective attitude. There was still that restless creativity, but it was accompanied by a newer impulse to assert the value of all that the company had achieved – and then to use those achievements as the foundation for new things: new cycles, new writing, a new ensemble.

Most other Irish theatre companies had actively controlled the shaping of their own histories. Yeats and Gregory wrote obsessively about the Abbey's early years; Hilton Edwards and Micheál MacLiammóir published several books about the Gate; Mary O'Malley wrote a memoir about the Lyric in Belfast; and Field Day published pamphlets to contextualize their stage productions.

Druid were different. They had published a short book to celebrate their tenth anniversary, and they had collaborated with the university in Galway on a 2004 conference about *The Playboy of the Western World* that resulted in a collection of essays edited by Adrian Frazier. But they had otherwise generally avoided telling people what their work meant, or how it should be understood.

After *DruidSynge*, though, more people than ever before were interested in writing about them – and that produced a persistent demand from students and academics for interviews and access to archival materials. The resulting experience – of seeing in print how they were being seen by others – necessarily nudged Druid into thinking more about their place in history. With that in mind, in 2009 they formally donated their archive to their old university, which was by then going by the name of NUI Galway.

And another factor, as always, was the uncertainty of access to state supports. In the early 2000s, Druid received more funding from the Arts Council than almost any other theatre company in Ireland (only the Abbey and the Gate received more). But that money was usually provided from one year to the next – which meant that there was an ever-present risk that a sudden change of policy could shutter the company with only a few months' notice.

The consequent feeling of precarity worsened after a banking crash in 2008 – a worldwide problem that was experienced with acute severity in Ireland, bringing the Celtic Tiger period to an abrupt and painful halt. Irish arts funding was drastically cut (from an already low base), and over the course of five years a huge number of Irish theatre companies were forced either to suspend operations or close altogether – including Island in Limerick, Red Kettle in Waterford, Galloglass in Tipperary, and the Dublin-based companies Ouroboros, Corn Exchange, Calypso, Barabbas, the Focus and Storytellers, among others.

Druid survived that cull, but the dismantling of the entire ecosystem of theatre companies showed that brutal decisions could be made very quickly. After the crash, it wasn't enough for Druid to assume that their importance would always be recognized by funders, government and the wider public. They had to keep emphasizing it, directly and often.

In the spring of 2010, Druid's more considered approach to balancing past and future was made evident when they announced that, for their thirty-fifth birthday, they were going to stage a performance made up of excerpts from their most memorable productions – and that their audiences would be invited to vote

Rebecca Bartlett and Jane Brennan, *Same Old Moon*, 2010.

for the one they wanted to see most. The result was a weekend event at the Town Hall, called 'From Galway to Broadway and Back Again', in May 2011.

And lest anyone think Druid were resting on past successes, they emphasized that the box office takings would be used to fund their Educational Outreach and New Writing programmes.

That title provided a neat encapsulation of the importance of both New York and the west of Ireland to Druid's identity – while also signalling the increased importance of US tours to Druid's annual activities since *DruidSynge*. But also present in that title was a subtle repudiation of the idea – common in theatre biographies – that the actor or director always dreams of leaving behind their small town in order to get to the big city. Druid's

Mikel Murfi and Cillian Murphy, *At the Black Pig's Dyke*.

members had seen their names in lights on Broadway – but they had gone 'there and back again'. The route from Galway to New York went in both directions, they showed: it rotated like a carousel rather than ascending like a stairway to heaven.

The Galway/Broadway performance included reprises of recent successes, with scenes from *The Cripple of Inishmaan*, *The Walworth Farce*, John B. Keane's *Year of the Hiker*, and *My Brilliant Divorce*, all of them featuring actors who had appeared in full productions of those plays during the preceding two or three years.

There was space for a little nostalgia too, as when Jane Brennan and Rebecca Bartlett performed a scene from Aron's *Same Old Moon* – which they had both acted in back in 1984.

But there were also fresh investigations of several plays, as when Cillian Murphy and Mikel Murfi performed one of the mumming scenes from *At the Black Pig's Dyke*, or when Clare Dunne and Ray Scannell played a short excerpt from D'Alton's

Seán McGinley and Marie Mullen, *The Playboy of the Western World*.

Lovers' Meeting – in both cases leaving the audience with the conviction that new productions of those plays would be well worth seeing.

Also surprising was a scene from *The Playboy*, featuring Marie and Seán McGinley. They were much older than their characters by that time and, though they were married to each other, they had not shared a Druid stage for many years – so the scene could have felt gimmicky or sentimental. But it was more than convincing, both emotionally and theatrically: a *Playboy* with older actors might just be worth exploring, it seemed.

Then there were moments that pointed towards the future. Enda Walsh read from his new play *Penelope*, which was about to go into rehearsals ahead of its premiere in Druid Lane for that year's Arts Festival. And Marie returned to *Bailegangaire*, but rather than reprising her original role, she now took on the part of Mommo – a first step towards playing that character in a full production three years later.

Finally, there was that question to answer – which of the plays had audiences voted for? By a considerable margin, the 'winner' was Tom Murphy's *Conversations on a Homecoming*.

Showing the renewed strength of his relationship with the company, Murphy had gone to Galway that weekend to watch the performances. He had a great time there (he and Enda Walsh found themselves hurtling around the city in a rickshaw late at night, in search of one last pint). But he'd also had a chance to see his work bring performed by a new generation of Druid actors – and thus to form a sense of new artistic possibilities.

Soon he and Druid were talking about doing *Conversations* again – but as part of a much bigger project: one that would attempt to push Irish theatre forward by going deeply into the country's past.

When Tom Murphy told Jerome that he found happiness by stepping out of time, he was leaving something unsaid: that stepping *into* time – by digging into a history, personal or public – can lead to unhappiness. That doesn't mean that retrospection should be avoided. But it does mean that it can be painful.

That worldview might in turn explain why time – and the question of how we step into and out of it – is one of the central themes of *DruidMurphy*, a day-long performance of three of Murphy's plays that premiered in 2012. The first play in the cycle was *Conversations on a Homecoming*, which is set in the 1970s; it was followed by *A Whistle in the Dark*, which is set in 1960; and the cycle concluded with *Famine*, which takes place in 1846.

Because the plays went back in time, the movement from one play to the next was like a stripping away of layers in an archaeological dig: Druid were going back in time in a theatrical production that also was moving forward in time, and thus they

DruidMurphy promotional poster.

were showing how Ireland's present had been produced by its past. In the 1960s, Murphy had expressed the idea that he himself was a victim of the Irish Famine from 120 years earlier: for Irish audiences in 2012, there was the uncomfortable suggestion that they too might be victims of that event.

Before the production had even opened, audiences were primed to think about the tension between history and the present by the vivid promotional posters that started appearing online and around Galway. They show a young man standing on a boat, with the twin images of a ruined cottage (perhaps representing the past) and a lighthouse (perhaps indicating a future) on the shore behind him. That image is evocative of the histories of Irish emigration: the only home in the picture is falling down, and the light is directed outwards (and seemingly westwards) rather than into the landscape, perhaps suggesting that Ireland is a place of darkness and decay but that America offers hope.

But the man's pose creates ambiguity. He is slouched and pensive and he doesn't seem hopeful; he doesn't look like someone who's just been liberated. And that produces a question. Is his boat leaving Ireland – or returning to it?

That ambiguity gives visual form to an ambivalence that pervades Murphy's theatrical treatment of emigration: his plays often seem to suggest that the only thing worse than leaving Ireland is staying in Ireland. Murphy often said that his own times of 'greatest despair' were at the railway station in Tuam, watching his family members leaving home:

> I come from a very big family, and eventually there was just my mother and myself left – everyone else had emigrated. It was just the beginning of the Second World War. I remember my eldest brother leaving – we didn't see him for twenty years, and so he became a mythic figure in my imagination. But nearly everybody's family in the west of Ireland was decimated by emigration.

Murphy didn't want the three plays to be seen as a trilogy, but 'there is a thread to do with emigration' that he wanted to bring to the fore. There were also tiny echoes from one work to the next, such as the repeated use of names: two of the three plays feature a character called Liam, for example, and two of the three feature a character called Michael (and both Michaels were played in *DruidMurphy* by the same actor, Marty Rea – a newcomer who would go on to play a major role in the development of the company). Those are common Irish names, but their recurrence reveals Murphy's long-term preoccupation with characters who are trapped in time, forced into seemingly endless cycles of repetition.

For *DruidMurphy*, Garry again decided to collaborate with Francis O'Connor and David Bolger, who were listed in the show credits as Associate Directors, with responsibility for design and movement respectively.

By describing them in that new way, Garry was acknowledging how important their contribution to her work had become. But she was also indicating that she was adopting a new approach to directing Murphy. In past productions of his plays, she'd been preoccupied with his use of the spoken word, by the musicality of his language. Of course she was going to continue concentrating carefully on that feature of the work, but she was also revealing an ambition to develop a visual language for the plays, one that would be just as rigorous and eloquent as the text. That involved developing a design concept that would allow the three plays to exist in their separate environments but which would also bring cohesion to the *DruidMurphy* experience as a whole.

Francis was excited by the challenge of creating a single environment that would contain three very distinctive plays. 'We knew we wanted to create a world,' he said:

> We knew what was really successful about *DruidSynge* was that we were creating one space that could re-articulate itself from one play to the next. So we were trying to do that again.

That would be tricky for Murphy, because the plays are set in such different places: *Whistle* takes place in a house in Coventry, *Conversations* in a pub in north Galway, and then there is the 'epic, sprawling landscape and interiors in *Famine*'. As Francis and Garry discussed that challenge, they agreed that they wanted to create one overall environment, and then place the sets for the individual plays inside the environment, gradually revealing it as the action moved from one play to the next.

Conversations on a Homecoming, 2012. The corrugated iron design is visible upper-left.

For the first two plays, then, the floor of the set would be covered in boards – accurately representing their real indoor environments. But then sections of the floor would gradually be removed until, in *Famine*, all that remained would be the bare soil in which the potatoes are growing (and in which of course they ultimately fail to grow).

That idea worked for the surface of the set, but Francis was still struggling to find a way to evoke the overall world that would contain the space. One idea was to embed coffin lids into the walls of the set, but as he sketched Francis realized that the image was too literal, too 'on the nose'. Finally, he had a breakthrough. 'I was with Garry,' he recalled:

> We were banging our heads against a wall because we knew what the individual spaces would be, but we couldn't get our heads around what the holding space would be around it. We had all sorts of ideas but none of it was firing.

And so they went for a break. Francis grabbed a coffee and was browsing online. By chance he came across an image of a township in South Africa:

Niall Buggy and Eileen Walsh in *A Whistle in the Dark*.

Marie Mullen in *Famine*.

> And it was a building that was made of corrugated sheeting and banana boxes. And I thought, those sheets look sort of like tilled fields. You know, in a kind of weird way. So I got really excited about that and I showed it to Garry, suggesting that the world that contained the three plays could be made of corrugated rusty sheets. And so I sketched it, but decided that we wouldn't present the sheets vertically; we'll put them at an angle so that it looks like driving rain and tilled fields.

Once they had agreed on that aesthetic, Francis worked to extend it subtly into other visual features, such as the costumes and furniture, picking up on the rust-like colour of the sheets.

In recognition that the plays were about the theme of emigration, it was decided that *DruidMurphy* would open not in Galway but in London, at the Hampstead Theatre. Michael D. Higgins, who had been elected President of Ireland in 2011, was the guest of honour. From there it returned to Galway for the Arts Festival, and toured to the Lincoln Center in New York and to the Kennedy Center in Washington DC – while also playing in the Aran Islands, and for a single night in Murphy's home town of Tuam.

That tour also presented an opportunity to integrate actors who were new to the company, including Rory Nolan and Marty Rea. Garrett Lombard would later remember their tour together as 'tough work' that was made manageable by the 'family atmosphere' created by the new ensemble.

And then shortly after the *DruidMurphy* tour finished, the conversation returned to a revival of *Bailegangaire*.

DruidMurphy opening: Francis O'Connor, Bobby McDonagh, Garry, David Bolger, President Michael D. Higgins, Sabina Higgins and Tom Murphy.

Garry had been saying for a while that she would be ready to direct another production of *Bailegangaire* as soon as Marie was ready to play Mommo. Murphy helped to move things along by revealing that he had written a kind of prequel, called *Brigit*, which would show Mommo's life with her husband and three grandchildren before the tragic events that are described in *Bailegangaire*.

Garry realized that it would be possible to produce the two plays back to back, so that they could be watched an alternating nights or in a single day's performance. And Marie could be at the heart of both productions, playing Mommo as a middle-aged woman in *Brigit* and then as the old woman who tries to finish the story of her earlier life in *Bailegangaire*. At first with trepidation but then with determination, Marie agreed to do them both together.

Marie's initial reluctance to play the part was a result of the strength of her memory of Siobhán McKenna in the role. How

Tom Murphy and Garry Hynes in rehearsal, 2014.

could she make the role her own, she wondered; how could she make it feel like she was doing something new rather than staging an encore of McKenna's performance? In an interview with Kernan Andrews in *The Galway Advertiser* she recalled the impact that McKenna had on her:

> To meet with a star the calibre of Siobhán McKenna was extraordinary. She took us under her wing. There was a great generosity about her. We were young, inexperienced actors, trying to get to grips with parts that were beautifully written and of great maturity, and she held us through that.

But with the arrival of *Brigit*, Marie had a chance to come at Mommo from a new perspective. 'When I heard that Tom was writing a new play I couldn't wait to read it … The lives of Mommo and the children came back to me.' She found herself being drawn once again to Murphy's portrayal of the women:

Chapter 11: Cycles, 2010–2015 309

Aisling O'Sullivan, Marie Mullen and Catherine Walsh in *Bailegangaire*, 2014.

He understands the humanity and compassion of women [and] of women as carers – which Mommo was [in *Brigit*] and Mary is [in *Bailegangaire*]. He understands women's extraordinary capacity to love and he celebrates it. He doesn't make his women saints; he exposes their dark sides.

As the plays finished rehearsals and were ready to open at the Town Hall, Marie declared that playing Mommo was 'a great privilege': 'For me, to do two Tom Murphy plays is the culmination of everything I have ever done,' she said.

Druid's re-engagement with Murphy coincided with another long-running investigation of an Irish playwright's work – that of John B. Keane.

In the late 1990s, when Irish drama was all the rage in London, a theatre in that city had staged a revival of Keane's 1959 play *Sive*. The reviews were generally good, but one critic had a complaint: thinking it was a new play, he felt that Keane might be guilty of a lack of originality – *Sive*, he thought, was too derivative of the plays of Martin McDonagh.

In theatrical terms, that was like saying that the Beatles had plagiarized Oasis.

But McDonagh's success had brought renewed attention to Keane, who for many years had been one of Ireland's most popular dramatists – but who also for many years had been one of its most underrated dramatists. He was a mainstay of the amateur sector (indeed, *Sive* had premiered as an amateur performance when it was rejected by the Abbey), but from the 1980s onwards he was often dismissed as a populist playwright: the kind of dramatist you stage when you want to sell a lot of tickets but not if you want to make serious art.

Garry had never shared those sentiments – so it felt somewhat inevitable when, in 2001, the Abbey Theatre decided to make the connection between Keane and McDonagh more visible by inviting her to direct a revival of his 1969 play *Big Maggie*, with Marie playing the title role. That production was seen as innovative simply because it took Keane seriously – maybe too seriously, Garry later thought, suspecting that, by trying to emphasize the play's artistic elements, she might have neglected how funny it is.

Garry decided to return to Keane at the earliest opportunity, though – and programmed *Sive* for Druid for the following year, 2002. For that production, Derbhle Crotty played the role of Mena – a woman who drives her young niece to suicide by insisting that she marry a farmer who is much older than her. On the page, that set-up can seem melodramatic – and in production, it is often performed that way. But because Druid had developed that style of heightened naturalism through playing McDonagh, audiences were better able to identify the artistry of *Sive* – to see it not as naturalism but more as a folk drama with roots in the real world.

Further Druid productions of Keane's plays followed: of *Sharon's Grave* in 2003, *The Year of the Hiker* in 2007, and then *Big Maggie* in 2011. The last of those productions received enormous pre-publicity as a result of the casting of Keith Duffy – a former member of the Irish boy-band Boyzone – as Teddy Heelin, a commercial traveller who comes between Maggie and her daughter. But it was the performance of Aisling O'Sullivan, returning to Druid for the first time since her Widow Quin blew everyone away in 2004, that made the production feel so suggestive.

Aisling is, like Keane himself, from Kerry, but she had only ever seen a production of one of his plays (*The Field*, directed by Joe Dowling) before taking on the role of Maggie. Speaking to Eithne Shortall before the production opened, she explained how she had instantly seen that her character was not the pantomime villain that she had been portrayed as in the past:

> She was a young woman when she got married, and for twenty-five years she was married to a roaring alcoholic, and a violent man to boot. She was with this man come hell or high water. Her relief, her emancipation, was his death.

That characterization might have felt old-fashioned in Ireland in 2011, some fifteen years after the legalization of divorce – as if the story of Maggie was closer to the fate of the Widow Quin than to the lives of anyone in present-day Ireland. But Aisling was convinced of Maggie's relevance; she felt that the character was her own ancestor – that 'she's all of our ancestors, where we've all come from'.

Keith Duffy and Aisling O'Sullivan, *Big Maggie*, 2011.

Irish women had gained equality, Aisling said – but it had been hard won: when *Big Maggie* premiered, women were still forced to quit their jobs upon marriage; they were still considered by many to be 'property of their fellas'. Things might have changed but the after-effects were still being felt: 'I imagine we're still slightly reeling as Irish women,' said Aisling. 'We're not that far away from it – when women didn't have a voice.' Like Tom Murphy suggesting that he had been a victim of the Irish Famine, Aisling was implying that the oppression of Irish women was a source of ongoing trauma.

Reinforcing Aisling's interpretation of the role, the show programme included an excerpt from the manifesto of the Irish Women's Liberation Movement, 'Chains or Change: the Civil

Wrongs of Irish Women', which had been published in 1971, just two years after *Big Maggie* premiered. They weren't suggesting that *Big Maggie* was a feminist play – but it certainly seemed like they were staging it as a feminist production. Druid had often shown how the revival of plays written by Irish men could be a powerful vehicle for revealing and addressing the status of Irish women – but in their production of *Big Maggie*, they were making that connection much clearer than they had before.

And Irish audiences responded with massive enthusiasm. By the time it finished its national tour, it had been seen by more than 32,500 people in ten venues around the country.

When *Big Maggie* was wrapping up its run, in October 2013, Garry announced that Druid were going to establish a new ensemble: 'a core group of freelance actors who work closely with Druid to shape the future direction of the company's work,' she stated.

That move was partly a response to the continued instability of the Irish arts sector. The crash of 2008 had been followed by the humiliation of an €85 billion bailout from the IMF, the European Central Bank and the European Commission in December 2010. It was followed by a devastating period of fiscal austerity: taxes increased, public services deteriorated, emigration resumed. The idea of having a career in the arts felt almost fantastical in such an environment; Druid's formation of an ensemble was a necessary attempt to push against that tide.

But they were also acknowledging that the quality of Druid's acting had become one of the definitive elements of their international reputation. There had been many awards and plaudits to recognize that – but a particularly nice one had come in 2011, when they were touring *The Cripple of Inishmaan* across the United States. One stop along their tour route was the Kirk Douglas Theatre in Los Angeles – and after their performance there, Douglas himself wrote to the company, stating that:

> I must tell you I have never seen such a balanced performance. Each character seems to be perfect in their part. It is a wonderful production and I am proud that it is playing in the Kirk Douglas Theater.

Coming from a man who had acted with Laurence Olivier, Anthony Quinn, Burt Lancaster, Doris Day and Jean Simmons (among many others), that was some compliment.

But Douglas was also saying something that the company might have said (quietly) about themselves – they always wanted their ensembles to feel carefully balanced; they always wanted audiences to feel that each actor was perfect for their role. Formally establishing a permanent company gave visibility to what they were already doing anyway.

The ensemble would of course include Marie, said Garry, and Maelíosa would also become a member (though only for a short period). And they would be joined by many of the younger actors who'd been working with them during the preceding decade: Derbhle Crotty, Garrett Lombard, Aaron Monaghan, Rory Nolan, Aisling O'Sullivan and Marty Rea. Druid weren't saying that they would *only* work with those actors, or that they would *always* work with those actors, but they were committing to the ideal that acting is not just a job but a career, and that it therefore needs to be nurtured over the long term.

Thus, as actors grew older, they could move into and out of each other's roles. They had already seen how Aaron could act in a role that Maelíosa had played (Christy Mahon), how Aisling could step into a role that Marie had played (Big Maggie), and how Marie in her turn could take on parts that had been played

Martin McDonagh and Garry, *Cripple of Inishmaan* rehearsals, 2008.

by Siobhán McKenna and Anna Manahan (in *Bailegangaire* and *The Beauty Queen of Leenane*). This wasn't about the older actors passing on one 'correct' way of performing a role – Garry's style of direction would mitigate against that risk anyway. But the actors could suddenly see themselves 'in time', imagining the roles that they might be play thirty or forty years hence.

The establishment of an ensemble was also a reflection of Garry's remarkable ability to know the right people to work with at the right time. Over the years, company members often heard her quoting Tyrone Guthrie's axiom that directing is nine-tenths casting – though in her case, that skill extended to her ability to choose designers (as shown when she changed her mind about including Francis O'Connor in her production team for *The Beauty Queen of Leenane*), composers, movement directors (David Bolger especially), and countless other collaborators.

Aaron Monaghan and Kerry Condon in *The Cripple of Inishmaan*, 2008.

The new ensemble also allowed Druid to find new echoes between seemingly disparate plays – which was another long-standing feature of the company's work that hadn't often been named explicitly. Thus, the casting of Aaron Monaghan as Christy Mahon in 2005, as Billy in *The Cripple of Inishmaan* in 2008, as Liam in *Conversations on a Homecoming*, Harry in *A Whistle in the Dark* and Micheleen in *Famine* in *DruidMurphy* in 2012, and as Estragon in Beckett's *Godot* in 2018 made visible the ways in which Synge had influenced Murphy and Beckett – and how McDonagh in his turn was drawing on the achievements of all three.

A similar kind of echoing was evident in several of Aisling O'Sullivan's Druid roles during the same period – in *The Colleen Bawn* and *Big Maggie* in 2013, followed by her performances as Dolly in *Bailegangaire* in 2014 and Maureen in a revival of *The Beauty Queen of Leenane* in 2016. In Boucicault's *Colleen*, premiered in 1860, she plays Anne Chute – a confident and witty Anglo-Irish heiress. Her Maggie also had a kind of power,

Aisling O'Sullivan and Marie Mullen in *The Beauty Queen of Leenane*, 2016

albeit one founded on a resistance to oppression by men. But Dolly and Maureen are isolated figures – in Maureen's case tragically so. When viewed in linear time, starting with a play that premiered in 1860 and ending with one that premiered in 1996, the status of those women seems to have deteriorated severely. Aisling's remarks in her *Big Maggie* press interviews, that 'we're still reeling as Irish women', can be tracked through those performances.

With the announcement of the new ensemble, Garry also revealed exciting plans that would again involve an investigation of the past. One of the new ensemble's first productions, she revealed, was tentatively called 'the Irish Shakespeare project', and it was going to be written by Mark O'Rowe.

During 2014, a banner appeared in the Mick Lally Theatre. Running from one wall of the foyer to the other, it repeated a single phrase: 'What Is My Nation?'

That's one of the most famous phrases in the history of Irish theatre – spoken by Captain Macmorris, Shakespeare's only Irish character, who appears in the play *Henry V*. In the original text, Shakespeare deliberately misspelled Macmorris's dialogue: the word 'is' is rendered as 'ish', which was Shakespeare's attempt to imitate the way in which English was spoken by Irish people.

'What ish my nation?': those words have haunted Irish literature and drama ever since. Macmorris's question captures the sense of national yearning that Irish people experienced in the face of English colonization – before, during and after Shakespeare's time. But that 'ish' also feels like a bad joke, an attempt to ridicule the Irish by highlighting their inability to 'speak properly'. Irish writers from James Joyce to Seamus Heaney have felt the need to respond to Macmorris's question – and it says much that, in the almost 400-year history of Shakespearean performance in Ireland, there is no record of Macmorris being included when *Henry V* was staged there.

But on their banner, Druid had changed 'ish' back to 'is'. They weren't saying it directly – not yet, anyway – but with the 400th anniversary of Shakespeare's death coming up in 2016, it seemed like a reckoning was about to get underway.

The idea of Druid returning to Shakespeare had been in the air for a few years. After Garry had brought *DruidMurphy* to the Lincoln Center Festival in New York in 2012, its director Nigel Redden had asked what she wanted to do next. 'This may sound rather crazy,' Garry replied, 'but there are thoughts of doing a Shakespeare history cycle.'

'Sounds good to me,' said Nigel – and very much to Garry's surprise, he offered funding for some workshops.

One of the first questions those workshops tried to resolve was how to come at Shakespeare from an Irish point of view. Thomas Conway recalls that one of the first ideas was to pair Shakespeare's work with that of an Irish dramatist. The company quickly realized that approach wouldn't work, and that 'there was a kind of process where we had to face up to the idea that we could do Shakespeare without the crutch of an Irish writer' to accompany him. That realization led to an approach to Mark O'Rowe, who was asked to produce an edited version of four of the history plays, *Richard II*, the two parts of *Henry IV*, and *Henry V*: it would still be Shakespeare, but shaped by O'Rowe.

The workshops also presented Garry with an opportunity to think practically about how to make Shakespeare work in an Irish theatrical context. His plays were regularly being produced in Ireland at that time – and there had been significant breakthroughs in Irish approaches to the comedies by the directors Gerry Stembridge (who staged *The Comedy of Errors* at the Abbey in 1993, when Garry was AD), and Lynne Parker, whose 2006 *Taming of the Shrew* was in conversation with Garry's *Playboy of the Western World* from the previous year's *DruidSynge* production

But the history plays had been left almost completely untouched by Irish directors, aside from an important Jimmy Fay production of *I Henry IV* at the Abbey in 2002, with a script edited by O'Rowe. Understandably, then, Garry had been troubled by the relationship between those plays, their language and Anglo-Irish history. 'When it comes to Shakespeare, I've always envied the French and the Germans and Romanians and so on,' she explained, 'because they can distance themselves from the narrative of English history through the act of translation.'

But that act of distancing wasn't possible in Ireland – not just because of the shared language but also because the history that is being celebrated in Shakespeare's plays overlaps so much with the history of England's subjugation of Ireland. To give just one example: as imagined by Shakespeare, Richard II's downfall is caused partly because he is distracted from court politics by his desire to defeat rebellion in Ireland, an impulse that he expresses with genocidal contempt. Garry knew that she would be asking an Irish actor in an Irish theatre to deliver Richard's statement that the Irish are a race of vermin that should be exterminated. How could an Irish company take ownership of scenes like that one? That needed to be thought through quite carefully.

That led to an early decision that the cycle would be performed by an ensemble who would deliver the lines in their own Irish accents. Those accents wouldn't be uniform: Aisling O'Sullivan is from Kerry, Derbhle Crotty is from Cavan, and Marty Rea is from Belfast – so they would deliver their lines as Henry V, Henry IV and Richard II, respectively, with their own individually varying tones, intonations and rhythms.

By making that choice, Druid were thinking about how Shakespeare could be presented for an audience attuned to Irish rhythms and sounds. But, paradoxically, they were also being faithful to Shakespeare. Much of the English that is spoken in Ireland had come to the country during the Tudor plantations. Consequently, a lot of supposedly 'Irish-English' is drawn from the English that Shakespeare himself would have spoken. Thus, when the actors pronounced the word 'devil' as 'divil' in *DruidShakespeare*, they might have been accused of translation, of putting a layer of Synge-song topsoil over the Shakespearean base. But in fact they were saying the word in something close to the original pronunciation.

So for the actors, saying the lines in their own accents could be a kind of reclamation – a mischievous contention that, if there is a 'right' way to say Shakespeare, it was more likely to be found in Galway (or Kerry, Cavan or Belfast) than in Stratford-upon-Avon.

―――――

A second major decision was that two of the three kings would be played by women rather than men. Having recently completed the male-dominated *DruidMurphy*, Garry wanted to direct a more balanced cast. But she also knew that if she did the histories as Shakespeare wrote them she would have almost no roles for the women she wanted to work with. 'Politically I could not make that decision,' she said. But she also felt that there were artistic benefits as well: 'a gender-blind production would help to make it ours,' she said.

And so it did. Derbhle had played Bolingbroke (later Henry IV) during the workshops, so when she was formally cast in that role she had already given a great deal of thought to how she could play it:

> I had a very strong feeling, and it was borne out very early in rehearsals, that we weren't going to be pretending to be male or presenting as male. My voice is fairly low pitched anyway so I was never consciously dropping the tone, and I wasn't deliberately adopting a male form.

Those technical decisions informed her discussion of how Bolingbroke should be dressed:

Derbhle Crotty and Aisling O'Sullivan in *Druid-Shakespeare*.

From quite early on, when we were talking about costuming with Francis and Garry, the feeling was that we should possibly even emphasize the feminine in terms of how the character appeared. I don't mean emphasizing them in terms of using Madonna-like breasts or something like that, but rather acknowledging the fact that this is a woman, that we wouldn't be trying to flatten or bind or disguise the women's bodies in any way.

There had been many gender-blind and cross-gender stagings of Shakespeare before – but doing it in an Irish context produced new meanings, they soon realized.

In the history of Anglo-Irish cultural representation, Ireland had repeatedly been represented as feminine, both by Irish and English writers. For those who were in favour of union between the countries, Ireland was often symbolized as a meek but beautiful heroine: she might need occasionally to be rescued or disciplined by her manly English lover, but in return she would provide humanity, humour and domestic warmth. And for those who opposed English dominance, Ireland was often an abused or ravaged maiden (usually the victim of a dastardly English solder), or, as in Yeats and Gregory's *Kathleen Ni Houlihan*, a noblewoman whose four green fields had been stolen from her.

With Derbhle as Henry IV and Aisling as Henry V, Druid were subverting that trope, showing that English kings could be performed by women from rural Ireland, with no effort to disguise their Irishness, their accents or their gender. As with *Big Maggie*, Druid had found that exploring a classic play by a male author could crack open a new way of thinking about the history of Irish women – and, in this case, the intersection of Irish women's history with English colonization.

Alongside those determinations about casting and costumes, there was also the need to design the set – and Francis and Garry quickly agreed that they would use the soil-based floor that had been present throughout *DruidSynge* and which had been gradually exposed through *DruidMurphy*.

When the play opened at the Mick Lally Theatre (MLT), audiences had to gather outside the building, waiting in Druid Lane rather than the foyer. The foyer space itself had been turned into a kind of graveyard; as the audience were led in, they saw Aaron Monaghan in costume, standing over an open grave, digging – a visual echo of the final image from *DruidSynge*, of Deirdre beside her lover's grave, but perhaps also an allusion to the gravedigging scene in McDonagh's *Skull in Connemara*, which had been acted out by the man whose name had recently been given to the theatre where the performance was happening.

The *Druid-Shakespeare* company in rehearsals at the MLT.

The seating plan of the MLT usually places the audience on three sides of the playing area – straight on and left and right of the centre. For *DruidShakespeare*, Francis had also designed a raised platform that ran around the walls of the auditorium. That set-up was partly based on the practical need to fit an enormous production into a small playing area – but (as had happened with the language) it was also an inadvertent recreation of the original, since the MLT playing area looked like the kind of thrust stage that would have been used in the original Globe Theatre.

And at the centre of the playing area was that floor of Irish soil. 'It was decided that we would play on a surface that we are used to and that we are connected to – a surface that made sense to us,' Garry explained. Francis elaborated further:

> It was about being able to bring an Irish terrain with us on tour, no matter where we went – essentially, being able to play on an Irish landscape on any stage.

Raining in the MLT: Aisling O'Sullivan in *Druid-Shakespeare*

The final play in the cycle, *Henry V*, would conclude with rainfall, Garry and Francis decided – meaning the soil would turn to mud each night. There is plenty of rain in Shakespeare, of course, but the introduction of the Irish weather into the indoor space felt apt for Galway, a city that experiences 230 days of rain on average each year (more than twice as much as London). *DruidShakespeare* would be a deliberately messy production – audience members in the front rows at the MLT often left the theatre wet and mud-splattered. That messiness arose from a need to root the plays in a landscape and a climate, but it was also making something visible: staging Shakespeare in Ireland *is* messy. Rather than disguising, ironizing or fleeing that fact, Druid wanted to make use of it.

Amongst its first audiences, there was some apprehension about the *DruidShakespeare* running time – almost seven hours in total. There was also the fact that the history plays are not well known in Ireland: *Henry IV* had been a mainstay on the Irish stage before independence in 1922, but was rarely performed afterwards (the only major exception being when Orson Welles presented a stage version of his *Chimes at Midnight* in Dublin and Belfast in the late 1950s); and *Richard II* and *Henry V* had almost never been staged there at any time (there are records of only thirteen performances of the former and twenty-three of the latter between 1660 and 1904, far fewer than most of Shakespeare's other plays during the same period). *DruidShakespeare* was a strange hybrid: a collection of 'classic' works that, for most Irish audience members, felt like new plays.

But the resultant freedom from expectation gave the actors permission to build their characters out of nothing more than their own work in the rehearsal room. Marty Rea developed Richard II as an unearthly figure. Completely bald and covered in white make-up, he was compared by some audience members to a Japanese kabuki performer and by others to Michael Jackson – but undeniable was the fact that such a performance would have been unlikely in England, where it would have been criticized as historically inaccurate.

In contrast, Rory Nolan was praised for playing Falstaff so expertly: he had already developed a reputation in Ireland as an excellent comic actor; donning an enormous fat suit for the part, he played the role with a well-judged balance of gusto and restraint.

And finally, although audiences didn't necessarily know the performance history of Bolingbroke and Prince Hal, they understood right away that Derbhle and Aisling were doing something with those characters that just hadn't been done before.

After its MLT premiere *DruidShakespeare* took off on a tour of Ireland. That included an outdoor performance in Kilkenny, a city that has one of the longest traditions of Shakespearean performance, going back to at least the eighteenth century. There

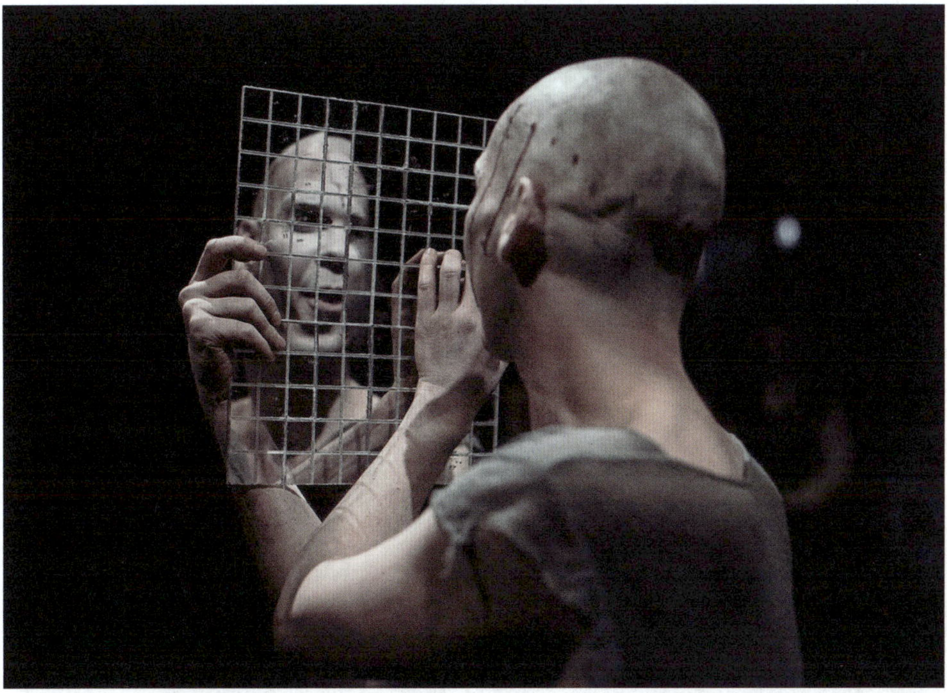

Marty Rea as Richard II, 2015.

Rory Nolan (centre) as Falstaff in *DruidShakespeare*, 2015.

Derbhle Crotty and Aisling O'Sullivan in rehearsal, 2015.

was also a fit-up production in Skibbereen, a tiny town in west Cork of about 2,500 people – which meant that the arrival of the *DruidShakespeare* cast and crew temporarily increased the population by more than 1 per cent. And – acknowledging the role that Nigel Redden had played in making the whole thing shift from crazy idea to achieved reality – they also brought it to New York, playing for two weeks at the Gerald W. Lynch Theater.

Chapter 11: Cycles, 2010–2015

By premiering *DruidShakespeare* in 2015, Druid were marking their own fortieth anniversary. It was noticed by many that they were also *not* marking a major date for Shakespeare: 2016 would be the 400th anniversary of his death, and most companies around the world that had plans to stage Shakespeare were holding off from doing so in order to mark that important date. But Druid would be finished with their Shakespeare cycle by then, ready to move on to other things.

The company's decisions about what to produce were always influenced by different factors – Garry's own process as a director, the availability of actors, the need to get the funding in place and so on.

But although it wasn't deliberate, there was something pleasingly cheeky about the company's suggestion that Druid's fortieth birthday trumped Shakespeare's 400th anniversary.

Chapter 12
On the Outside/On the Inside, 2016–2024

IN 1983, Garry, Marie and Mick got together to do a joint interview with *Theatre Ireland*. Mostly, they discussed their shared love of Synge, and the value of performing in rural venues. But then, towards the end of the interview, Garry made a surprising declaration: 'Druid has become an institution,' she said.

Marie reacted with horror. 'Not at all, we are not!' she said. 'It depends on your attitude!'

Garry chose to respond diplomatically: 'It's a question for each individual to answer,' she replied. And that brought the discussion to a close.

So: was Druid an institution?

Over the years, that question would be left in a state of unanswered tension – and for good reason.

Druid's evolution since 1975 had coincided with a collapse in the authority of many major Irish institutions. The Catholic Church was the most prominent of those – and maybe the guiltiest of them too – but there had been numerous other examples of people in power displaying corruption, moral cowardice, abusive behaviour or ineptitude. Who would want to be counted amongst such company?

Even within the Irish theatre sector, institutions had not fared well. The Abbey had been in a state of crisis for much of its history, due to a lack of funding, structural and governance problems, disagreements about artistic policy – and sometimes all three at the same time. The status of being *the* national theatre seemed to bring with it so many competing expectations that it was often difficult for the Abbey's leaders to just put on plays without somebody somewhere reacting negatively.

So Marie's resistance to the suggestion that Druid had become an institution was completely understandable.

But Garry's claim was equally warranted. Whatever word they used to describe themselves, by 1983 Druid had become leaders in the Irish arts sector: their decisions and achievements had symbolic as well as material consequences. When they started going on Unusual Rural Tours, they were stating that the small towns of Ireland had an intrinsic value – but the reason that statement was meaningful was because a visit from Druid was regarded as significant. And when Garry and Marie won awards on Broadway a decade later, their successes were celebrated as achievements not just for Druid or the Irish theatre, but for Ireland in its entirety. As a company, they had become iconic.

So in that *Theatre Ireland* interview, Garry had simply been acknowledging the reality that Druid had social and cultural capital – and that they could do things with it.

Of course, they would continue to show resistance when they felt they were being told what they should do during the years ahead. But, especially once their fortieth birthday was behind them after 2015, there was no getting away from the fact that Druid had acquired a monumental status – in Galway, in Ireland and in world theatre.

Chapter 12: On the Outside/On the Inside

But gradually the company had become more at peace with that reality, and they began to use it more actively in order to bring about positive change: for their home city, for the art and craft of theatremaking and for Irish society generally.

That ambivalence about being seen as an institution had its roots in Garry and Marie's determination, from the time they founded the company onwards, that they would stand out. Until their reputation was more firmly established, they therefore tended to hold themselves apart from other Galway-based organizations – especially the university.

'It was so important when we started off to tell everybody that we were not part of the university, that we weren't a bunch of students doing plays,' Garry explained:

> We wanted to be seen as 'proper grown-up people doing plays' … We worked really, really hard for two or three years to completely distance ourselves from the university in order to establish that we stood on our own.

And, for its own part, the university – as a naturally conservative entity – was slow enough to take pride in Druid's success, at least at an official level.

But, over time, the two drifted back towards each other, beginning in the late 1980s, when Colm Ó hEocha was the university's president. It awarded Garry an honorary doctorate in 1998 and, when it initiated its first postgraduate programme in Drama and Theatre Studies in 2000, its interactions with Druid began to multiply.

An important turning point, albeit as a result of tragic circumstances, happened in 2006, when the university sought to honour Jerome's memory by launching a One-Act Play festival and award on the first anniversary of his death. Every year, students would be invited to write original plays which would then be staged over a week in the spring semester by the Drama Society; the play judged to be best would be given the Jerome Hynes Award. The university commissioned John Coll to produce a sculpture in Jerome's memory; since then, it has been presented to the festival's winner every year.

By 2010, the university and Druid had decided to work more formally together, and they signed a partnership agreement that would bring Druid artists into the university's classrooms for masterclasses, while allowing both organizations to collaborate on joint projects. Alongside that agreement, Garry was appointed an adjunct professor and began teaching masterclasses in directing.

In a public interview at that time, Thomas Conway asked her if she had found the prospect of teaching daunting. 'Absolutely,' she said – because she felt that she herself was still learning. But she also saw the importance of sharing her experiences:

> I do remember when it became clear that Druid was going to go on for a while – I remember thinking, maybe around the late 1970s, 'sometimes I wish I could go and become an assistant director and go and sit in somebody else's rehearsal'. Sometimes I used to feel a bit starved of other influences on me. I remember that when we have young people in the room, and I think, 'Actually, this is what I wanted when I was young'. So I began to think that I needed to give something back.

Over the following years, other members of the company gave masterclasses too, teaching into a new undergraduate degree in Drama that the university launched in 2012. Thomas Conway became the first Druid Director-in-Residence at the university, also

Marie Mullen at the University of Galway quadrangle in *DruidGregory*, 2020.

in 2012. Combining that role with his work as Druid's new writing manager, he provided a conduit between the two organizations. And in 2020, showing that the relationship had come full circle, Druid returned to the campus, staging *DruidGregory* in the university quadrangle, responding to the prohibition against indoor performances due to COVID-19 by doing something that felt epochal both for Druid and for the university.

That impulse to 'give something back' extended to mentoring young theatremakers, people who had already begun their careers but needed help with taking their next steps. That led in 2014 to the development of a new annual programme called FUEL. Initially developed by Craig Flaherty, it provided a week's residency at the MLT to young companies based in the west of Ireland – offering them mentorship, space and of course the simple benefit of having a link with Druid. Marty Rea, who had taken on the role of New Writing Associate after Thomas Conway left the company, was also very involved in the scheme during its first couple of years.

And then in 2018, the company launched a bursary for women who were 'working on the island of Ireland in the areas of design, directing and dramaturgy'. It was intended to redress a 'historic imbalance' in the career progression of women in the Irish theatre.

That award was named the Marie Mullen Bursary – a designation that might have come as a surprise to some of Marie's friends and colleagues, who knew her to be a very modest person – 'too modest' sometimes, Garry would say. Marie might initially have felt some discomfort at the idea of having a bursary in her name, but she ultimately described it as a 'privilege'.

She remembered how she too had been 'nourished and inspired by the work of so many artists in my long career in Irish theatre' and saw the bursary as an opportunity to do something similar. She was looking forward to 'supporting and working with the women who benefit from it,' she said.

The bursary had a speedy impact on the careers of several theatre artists. For example, Sarah Baxter was awarded it in 2020, and has since returned to the company, first as an Assistant and then as an Associate Director. Clíodhna Hallissey, the 2019 recipient, had taken Druid masterclasses while a student of Drama at the University of Galway, where she became interested in the company's approach to costume. That led her to becoming a bursary recipient, and from there she became Druid's Costume Supervisor, then an Assistant Costumer Designer and then Co-Costume Designer (with Francis O'Connor).

The use of Marie and Jerome's names in those awards was intended to honour both people – but it was also proof of the strength of their reputations: the awards were prestigious precisely because of who they were named after.

For Garry too there was a deepening awareness that her own public reputation could have an impact on causes and organizations that were important to her. She therefore began to speak more publicly about her private life – for example, by contributing to Charlie Bird's book *A Day in May*, which recorded the impact of the 2015 marriage equality referendum on more than fifty members of Ireland's LGBTQ community.

Personal testimonies like those gathered by Bird had been critically important to the successful Yes campaign, which had foregrounded the stories of ordinary gay people in Ireland as a way of showing how inequality and discrimination had affected them. The referendum passed with almost two-thirds of the votes in favour, making Ireland the first country to legalize same-sex marriage by popular vote. The telling of real stories by real people was one of the major contributors to that result.

The marriage referendum had been profoundly important for Garry, she told Bird. She had married her long-time partner, the film producer Martha O'Neill, in a civil partnership ceremony at the Mick Lally Theatre in December 2014. They had known that the referendum was imminent and hoped it would pass, but had decided to go ahead with the civil partnership anyway, 'because I don't want to wait for an election,' Garry explained.

She told Bird how she'd made a conscious decision in her thirties to come out. 'Looking back on it, I wish I'd done it earlier,' she said, while acknowledging that it was a hard thing to do in Ireland in the 1980s. Garry's siblings were supportive of her: her sister Aedhmar reacted by saying, 'I thought you were going to say you were pregnant. Oh, Christ. Thank God.' Nevertheless, Garry often wondered if things might have been different for her if she'd gone to college ten years later than she did.

But maybe it wasn't just the times she'd been living in, she told Bird:

> I am a private person. And making my sexuality the subject of a public journey didn't feel right to me. But it was a pity … You can't have regrets, but if I did have a regret it would be that.

Overall, Garry concluded, 'I've gone from secrecy and exclusion to openness and embrace.'

Another form of power that institutions wield is the ability to provide stability to people who might otherwise leave theatre in search of security elsewhere.

Druid's foundation of an ensemble of freelancers in 2014 had been an attempt to provide both security *and* freedom: for the actors, Druid had made a long-term commitment to them, but they could still work for other theatres. But the company had also built up a broad workforce of carpenters, scenic painters, electricians and costume-makers. Could anything be done to improve their situation as well?

It should go without saying that theatremaking is not just an art but a craft: it might be very hard to stage a play without actors, but it's also very difficult to stage one without carpenters, technicians and costume cutters. But there had been a worsening problem since the Celtic Tiger crash: Irish theatres, struggling just to stay in business, were increasingly inclined to outsource those kinds of jobs, placing the long-term sustainability of practical theatremaking in a precarious position on the island.

That problem had come to a head in 2009, when the Abbey announced that it needed to implement a redundancy process that was likely to result in thirty jobs being lost. As part of that process, management determined that they could make substantial savings by procuring sets externally rather than

Druid's Ballybane set construction facility.

building them in-house – resulting in a decision to close the Abbey workshop in April 2010. That proposal did not go down well, either in the theatre industry or with the wider public, in part because of an assumption that the externally-procured sets would mostly be coming from the UK: no one wanted to see Abbey staff losing their jobs, of course, but there was also just a cognitive dissonance in an Irish national theatre cutting its staff so that their work could be done by people in Britain instead (though over the years the theatre would indeed procure sets from Ireland, north and south, and from the EU and Britain).

As the impact of that decision reverberated during the following years, Druid realized they had to face a decision of their own: either to follow the example of the Abbey and outsource – or to go it alone, as the only theatre in Ireland with its own set construction facility. That led to the decision in 2016 to establish their own workshop in Ballybane (a suburb in the east of Galway City), while also transforming their costume store in Nun's Island into a formal costume workshop.

Led by Barry O'Brien, who had been working with the company since the mid-1990s, they put together a team of craftspeople who had the specialized skills needed to build sets and to make props and costumes. That initiative created and maintained jobs in Galway, but it was also an investment in the future of theatre craft in Ireland, ensuring that the skills would not die out.

The Ballybane facility brought together many people who'd been working with Druid for a long time. Gus Dewar had been making sets for the company since 1999, for example; he now became their Master Carpenter. He loved his job's variety, he said; every day, he was 'building something that's never been built before'. Over the years, he'd had amazing experiences:

> Among them, I'd pick out dragging the makings of a set and stage for *DruidSynge* up to the top of Dún Chonchúir on Inis Meáin, a job I'd count as both the hardest work and the most fulfilling task of my career; and building our two outdoor productions in Coole Park in order to help keep theatre alive during the pandemic. These are experiences I'll never forget.

The centralization of such expertise allowed Druid's designers to push their ideas further than before, knowing they would be able to go back and forth with Galway-based craftspeople before a show opened.

An immediate example of the benefit of doing so came in Francis O'Connor's design for a production of *Waiting for Godot* that had been programmed when four members of the ensemble – Garrett Lombard, Aaron Monaghan, Rory Nolan and Marty Rea – had approached Garry to propose doing that play. 'I was just thinking the same thing' was her response; the production was thus scheduled for the summer of 2016.

Chapter 12: On the Outside/On the Inside   341

Rory Nolan in *Waiting for Godot*: beside the tree and rock.

Beckett's stage directions for *Godot* are famously – maybe even infamously – specific: an empty road, a rock and a tree. But rather than feeling limited by the text, Francis designed two highly distinctive stage objects: a tree with tiny nails sticking out of it, and a rock that seemed smoothly egg-like.

The prop-maker and artist Gillian Christie was given responsibility for realizing the rock design. Working from Francis's model box, she had to come up with something that would be made of durable material but would also be waterproof (because the play was going to be staged both in the MLT and outdoors, including on Inis Meáin). The rock would need to be heavy enough to bear the actors' weight, robust enough to last for the duration of the production, and light enough to be portable. And it needed an outer shell that would appear to be 'smooth as marble' without actually being made from anything so heavy and expensive.

As she worked, she noticed that the surface colours of the materials were not so much being imposed by her as being disclosed by the materials themselves:

> Surface colour and tonal characteristics revealed themselves organically, as flowing water washes over rock [and] many hours of sanding revealed that the peculiarities and properties of material layers built up now resembled a natural stone surface. Working closely together at every stage of the process, Francis recognized the beauty in the surface qualities emerging and chose to maintain the polished surface rather than apply a final coat of paint.

That kind of collaborative approach simply wouldn't have been possible if the design materials had just been emailed to a supplier in another country.

Another prop-maker, Bill Wright, had a similar experience when building the tree. It was made from nails that are used in the construction of the traditional Galway hooker (the boat that had appeared in Mairead Noone's illustration on the cover of Druid's first show programme).

Bill had to source those nails from a hardware shop in Connemara: 'they are made by a small factory in the UK and this is the only place in Europe that produces these nails,' he explained. Francis's design required that the nails should have a rusted appearance, so they needed to be weathered – and quickly. 'I did this by dumping the nails into an oil drum filled with wood and coal and setting fire to it,' said Bill:

> The heat melted off the zinc. The nails were then put in a vinegar and salt solution for a couple of days, then laid outside to weather for a week. After welding them to form the tree it was again put out to weather for a few days to rust off the weld spots.

The result was an extraordinary object – one that was true to Beckett's script (and with its use of nails, it was also nodding to the crucifixion imagery in the play), but which was also beautiful in its own right. It was made in Galway but also, by using the hooker nails, it was rooted in Galway: it just couldn't have been made anyplace else.

Being an institution also means being held accountable – and in 2015 Druid, alongside the rest of the Irish theatre sector, needed to ask itself some difficult questions about its programming of work by women.

The immediate cause was a popular campaign called #WakingtheFeminists, which had arisen in protest against the announcement by the Abbey Theatre in October 2015 of its programme for the following year, which was to be called 'Waking the Nation', and which planned to commemorate the centenary of the Easter Rising. The theatre had provoked a furious reaction when it revealed that, of the ten productions planned in 2016, only one was written by a woman, and only two would be directed by women.

That announcement led to a series of protests that began on social media and which, under the leadership of Lian Bell and Sarah Durcan, resulted in a public meeting at the Abbey on Thursday 12 November 2015, in which hundreds gathered to listen to the testimonies of Irish women theatre-makers about the many forms of discrimination they had faced.

By that time, the Abbey had apologised, but the campaign had outgrown its initial focus on the national theatre anyway: there was a widespread understanding that the 'Waking the Nation' programme was a symptom of a much deeper problem.

Garry wrote to *The Irish Times* to address that fact directly. Acknowledging that the Abbey certainly had questions to answer, she nevertheless admitted that 'we are all at fault here':

> We must have the conversation internally within our own organizations and more broadly between us as an industry and we must do this as a matter of priority. This is a significant moment and what Irish theatre looks like a hundred years from now will in large part be determined by how we respond to it.

Over the following months, Druid engaged with the #WTF campaign group, which was led by the designer Lian Bell. But they also discussed the problem internally, looking at their own history, and looking at examples of good practices in other international theatres.

But then they had to face some online protests at their own programming, for the year 2017. They had intended to stage three plays that year – *The King of the Castle* by Eugene McCabe, *Crestfall* by Mark O'Rowe and a revival of the *Godot* production that had featured Marty, Aaron, Garrett and Rory. Two of those three plays foregrounded women's experiences, and one of them – *Crestfall* – had an entirely female cast and was to be directed by Annabelle Comyn. But, coming just a year after the Abbey controversy, the exclusively male line-up of playwrights stood out in a way it might not have a few years previously.

Garry pushed back against some of the ensuing criticism, pointing out that programming happens years in advance, and that change takes time. She also rejected the idea that 'any one programme at any one time can have exact gender parity':

> Real change will not be immediate nor can it be a simple matter of ticking individual boxes; it is not simple statistics. What matters is our commitment to real and sustainable change and the work we put in to making that change happen.

She then went on to define how Druid was trying to produce that change, highlighting three specific practices:

- commissioning new plays by women
- achieving gender balance across our panels
- producing plays which, although written by men, address honestly the situation of women in our society and present strong, interesting roles for women

That third bullet point was a valuable encapsulation of Druid's long-term attitude to staging the classical repertoire. As they had recently shown with *Big Maggie* and *DruidShakespeare*, plays written by men could be used to highlight challenges faced by women. Those plays also created work for women: *Big Maggie*, for example, calls for a cast of eleven actors, six of whom are women; *Bailegangaire* has roles for three women only, and *Beauty Queen of Leenane* is evenly split between male and female roles.

Garry had been adopting that attitude to the work of male writers since the start of her career – she'd even been doing it when she was still a student, as shown with her DramSoc production of *Elizabeth I* in 1975. The 'box-ticking' approach of only looking at the gender of the playwright risked making that kind of theatremaking invisible.

So on that basis, it seemed fair for Garry to argue that a purely statistical analysis was too simplistic.

Nevertheless, those raw statistics did highlight patterns that Druid needed to do something about. Between 2000 and 2015, the company had given full productions to ten new plays – and of those, only three were written by women. That put Druid slightly ahead of the national average (for the Irish theatre sector overall at that time, only 20 per cent of new plays were written by women). And those three plays had been given particularly high-profile productions, with *On Raftery's Hill* going to the Kennedy Center, *My Brilliant Divorce* to the West End and *Leaves* to the Royal Court.

But three out of ten is not an equal proportion, and that was an irrefutable fact that needed to be faced.

So in the post-WTF period, Druid would try to show that they were serious about tackling the problem. From 2016 to 2024, they produced seven new plays. One, Brian Watkins's *Epiphany*, was by a man, but all the others were by women. They included *Helen and I* by Meadhbh McHugh in 2016, *Shelter* by Cristín Kehoe in 2018 and *The Beacon* by Nancy Harris in 2019. There was also a theatricalized performance of the poetry of Eavan Boland, recited and acted by Siobhán Cullen as a live-streamed production during the COVID-19 pandemic, in 2021. And there were also three new plays by Sonya Kelly: a writer who would emerge as one of the most exciting that Druid had yet worked with.

Sonya Kelly had been inspired to write her first Druid play, *Furniture*, by a visit to the Irish embassy in Paris. While she was there, she spotted a chair by Eileen Gray, a major designer and architect who had been born in Ireland and died in France. Sonya had leaned in to look more closely at it – but was scolded by a member of the embassy staff that she mustn't touch it. That got her thinking about the strangeness of owning a chair that was too precious for anyone to sit in it. 'I went home that night and wrote the first act' of the play that would eventually become *Furniture*, Sonya said.

Having worked with Druid as part of the cast of the 2004 *Playboy*, she had continued performing with other Irish companies for a number of years, and had also moved into performing stand-up comedy. The latter experience fed into the composition of her first play, *The Wheelchair on My Face*, in 2011. It was developed as part of a Fishamble, Dublin Fringe and Irish Theatre Institute 'Show in a Bag' scheme, which had been devised in the wake of the 2008 crash to support actors by guiding them in the creation of shows that they could perform in themselves, taking their work on tour with nothing more than the 'bag' of the scheme's title.

The Wheelchair on My Face worked exactly as planned: Sonya would appear on an empty stage, telling the story of her childhood, and of how she went for many years with undiagnosed problems with her eyesight. Opening at the Dublin Fringe, it was received warmly as it toured in Ireland, and in 2012 it won a Fringe First Award in Edinburgh.

She followed that up with *How to Keep an Alien*, for Rough Magic in 2014. Again it was an autobiographical play, performed by Sonya herself – but she also showed her growing theatrical adventurousness by writing her own stage manager into the script, giving him lines to deliver while he also worked on the show in full sight of the audience.

Although the title seemed redolent of a 1950s American B-movie, the 'alien' she was writing about was not a little green man but her Australian partner, Kate Ferris – and the drama was about Sonya's attempts to keep Kate in Ireland by ensuring that she could secure a visa to live there. It was a comedy and a love story – and, appearing just a year before the Marriage Equality referendum, it was also a timely intervention into Irish life. But in addition it revealed a problem that continues to exist: for non-EU citizens, navigating the Irish immigration system was like – well, like being trapped in a 1950s American B-movie.

Furniture would be a step forward from those two plays. Rather than writing for herself, Sonya decided that she now wanted to create roles for other actors – whom she placed in a triptych of short works that individually explored how her characters use furniture not just as a practical tool for living but as an expression of who they really are. Each play features two actors, and each play could have been staged independently of the others – but cumulatively they add up to a single work that examines the theme from different perspectives.

The Druid Debut call for play submissions was announced while Sonya was finishing up her draft. She sent *Furniture* in – and soon got the call she'd been hoping for: Druid wanted to workshop and then stage a reading of the play during the 2017 Arts Festival. Her reaction? 'Game on!' she said:

> It's a call I always wanted to get; the company get over 200 scripts a year and only two are chosen for the Debuts. Once I got the call I went straight back to the script and worked and worked at it, especially the last section, which I knew wasn't right.

She engaged intensively with the actors to prepare for the reading: 'and there were questions, questions, questions being asked of the script and my brain felt so frazzled!' But that openness to interrogation paid off: the reading was exceptionally well received, and she began to discuss the possibility of staging a full production for 2018, directed by Cathal Cleary. Doing that would mean rewrites, she knew.

Earlier in her career, Sonya had got good advice from a script editor. Writing a play, the editor said, was like redecorating a house – 'everyone wants to paint, but no one wants to do the sanding'. Sonya had taken that advice to heart:

> Sanding is starting a play over again because you just realized that you're telling the wrong story. Sanding is opting not to defend your decisions just because you are the writer, or refusing to cut because they sound pretty. Sanding

Chapter 12: On the Outside/On the Inside 349

Garrett Lombard and Niall Buggy in *Furniture*, 2018. Set by Francis O'Connor.

is about hearing a note from someone you respect and returning with an answer, even if it means months of work go in the bin. Sanding is admitting it's not right because that's the only way you're ever going to fix it. Sanding is cutting twenty pages you spent a month on and replacing it with a line, or a look, or nothing. Sanding is doing two years of research before you write a word. Sanding is your play telling you, 'You are done when I say you are done.'

Her openness to 'sanding' her way through *Furniture* meant that, by the time it premiered, it had gone through eighteen drafts. But it was worth it: 'with each draft came sharper jokes, bigger payoffs and a deepening of the play's overall message that *Furniture* is not about furniture. *Furniture* is about people.'

Furniture was widely acclaimed, and Druid revived it for a thirteen-venue national tour in 2019.

Garry knew that she wanted the company to keep working with Sonya, so in May 2020 they commissioned another new play from her – which would be called *Once Upon a Bridge*.

Sonya had come across a news story a few years earlier about an incident in which a woman on Putney Bridge in London had been accidentally pushed into the path of an oncoming bus by a passing jogger – who just kept on running, causing the woman to shout after him, 'Why me?' Inspired by that scenario, Sonya imagined three interlinking monologues that would come at a loosely reimagined version of that story from different points of view: that of the man responsible for the accident, of the woman he'd crashed into, and of the bus driver whose speedy reactions prevented a more serious incident.

Once she'd worked out how to tell the story, she started sanding:

> After the first draft was submitted and approved, I did a further nine drafts, going back and forth, back and forth with director Sara Joyce. We rigorously worked on the arc of the story, the politics, the subtext, setting up the dramatic highpoints, passing the baton of logic from one moment to the next until it was as lumpless and bumpless as we could possibly make it for rehearsal.

The next stage was to get the play into a room with the three actors – Siobhán Cullen, Adetomiwa Edun and Aaron Monaghan – and the script changed to take on board the performers' perspectives. Garry also offered notes, and Sonya took advice from the costume designer Clíodhna Hallissey and many other members of the company.

When the play had been commissioned, Ireland was in the first lockdown of the COVID-19 pandemic. No one knew for sure

Chapter 12: On the Outside/On the Inside   351

Adetomiwa Edun being filmed for *Once Upon a Bridge*, February 2021.

when (or if) live theatre would resume – but Sonya had written it in such a way that it would be suited to the pandemic-era restrictions: the actors would speak out to the audiences in separate areas of the stage, and they wouldn't need to touch or otherwise interact with each other. In theory, it could be performed live.

But then in early 2021 Ireland was placed under a second lockdown – and the restrictions imposed upon people (and upon theatre companies) were among the most severe in the world.

Druid made the decision that they would perform the play live over four nights in the Mick Lally Theatre – but they would livestream it rather than letting audiences into the building. The company had been experimenting with live filming of their productions just before the pandemic (their 2019 staging of Tom Murphy's adaptation of *The Cherry Orchard* was the first Irish production to be broadcast to cinemas), so they felt ready to use that technology.

> **Druid Theatre**
> @DruidTheatre
>
> Thank you everyone for your patience. We are now in a three minute countdown - if you don't see it refresh your page. And off we go again ...
>
> 8:14 PM · Feb 13, 2021

The show goes on – a tweet about Once Upon a Bridge.

That decision pushed them towards imagining ways to foster a sense of connection with the audiences at home, to convey a feeling of liveness that would be true to the theatricality of the play that Sonya had written, and which would remind everyone of what it was like to see a Druid show in person. Each evening's performance was therefore introduced by the venue manager Síomha Nee, and the company also used social media to enhance their audience's feeling of participation.

Inevitably, however, one of the performances fell afoul of technical issues: about fifteen minutes into that night's run, the company realized to their horror that the images and sound were out of synch with each other. Hoping that the problem might resolve itself – but quickly realizing that it wasn't going to – they had to decide in the moment to stop the performance, and get technical support. That all took about half an hour – and then they resumed.

It felt like a disaster – would the audiences be furious?

But far from being annoyed by those tech problems, viewers seemed instead to be delighted by them. Social media was full of messages of support: 'we are all with you,' wrote one person on Twitter, adding that they had 'missed that excitement and adrenalin of live theatre'. Druid's audience members had all had plenty of their own experiences of tech going wrong during the preceding year, but what really seemed meaningful to them was the reminder that, in the live moment, anything can happen – which sometimes means that things can go wrong.

Sonya followed that experience with a third play for Druid, *The Last Return*, in 2023. Set in a theatre foyer where a disparate group of theatregoers queue in the hope of getting a returned ticket to a sold-out show, it was a drama that, similarly to *Furniture*, seemed to be about theatre tickets but was really just about people.

Even so, its central set-up might have made for uncomfortable viewing at times. Especially in Galway, Druid shows in the post-COVID period often sold out before they'd even opened. Which meant that, yes, there was a literal queue for returns to some of the performances of *The Last Return*.

In May 2024, the book *Sonya Kelly's Druid Plays* was published in London, with an introduction by Garry. 'I don't know any other writer like Sonya Kelly,' Garry wrote, 'and I don't think I ever will ... I'm so proud that Druid has played a role in her rise to success.'

The livestreaming of *Once Upon a Bridge* and *The Cherry Orchard* were new developments for Druid, but – perhaps paradoxically – the company found that their history of having to improvise venues out of nothing meant that they were well-prepared to keep making theatre when COVID-19 hit.

The legal restrictions imposed by the Irish government had resulted in a situation where, for much of 2020 and 2021, theatre could only be performed outdoors. But Druid had been staging work outside for years, most recently when their 2016 *Godot* had been performed on Inis Meáin, at the Céide Fields in Mayo and at Glencar in Wicklow. And so in 2020 and 2021, they staged major works in Coole Park, with a cycle of Lady Gregory's plays in the first year and Thomas Kilroy's adaptation of *The Seagull*

DruidGregory at Kylemore Abbey, 2020.

during the second. Both productions were designed to comply with COVID restrictions – but neither of them did anything that Druid hadn't done many times already.

Putting on work at Gregory's home estate represented a literal homecoming – bringing professional productions of her plays back to the place where many of them had been written. Making theatre in the woods of Coole also allowed Druid to explore the environmental features of their work in new ways – to consider how their live performances could interplay with natural features such as birdsong, the passage of the sun into nightfall, and the presence of trees and flowers. Thus, for *The Seagull* Francis designed a set that had timber planks along the wall, and which was dwarfed by the trees nearby (Francis even included those trees in his model box – showing that they were part of the set).

The pandemic was certainly challenging for Druid, as it had been for everyone in the creative arts worldwide. But where other

Francis O'Connor's model for *The Seagull*.

companies had to 'pivot', Druid found themselves continuing with practices that they had already developed. That ability to adapt quickly contrasted with the problems faced by the building-based companies around Ireland and elsewhere, many of which struggled to adapt to ways of working that they had little prior experience of. Again, it seemed like being an institution could be disadvantageous in some contexts.

Much of the responsibility for getting Druid through the pandemic fell to the person who'd been appointed Executive Director in 2015 – and that was Feargal Hynes, Garry's nephew and Jerome's son.

At the time of his appointment, Feargal had just graduated from University College Dublin, where he had studied Commerce and been President of the Students Union. There had been only six other Managing or Executive Directors between father and son: Jane Daly, Louise Donlon, Ciarán Walsh, Fergal McGrath, Tim Smith and Sarah Lynch. But Feargal would quickly establish

Maelíosa in *The Colleen Bawn*, 2013

a reputation in his own right: he showed a lot of his father's dynamism, but he also got things done in his own way.

Even so, for long-term observers of the company, there was something both poignant and positive about seeing the next generation coming into the company.

That sense of the passing of time was intensified with the sad news in 2021 that Ray McBride had died, after a long illness that had confined him to a wheelchair for almost two decades. In a note of condolence, President Higgins remembered him first as a 'unique and exceptional' artist but also 'for the dignity and courage with which he faced his long illness'.

And then two years later, on Easter Sunday in 2023, Maelíosa died suddenly at his home in Sydney. He had last appeared with

Druid ten years earlier, as Dada in *A Whistle in the Dark* and as the unctuous Mr Corrigan in Boucicault's *The Colleen Bawn*. But he had kept in touch with the company, and continued to meet up with Galway friends on his trips back to Ireland. In 2018 he had even directed in the city again, taking charge of a production for An Taibhdhearc to celebrate its ninetieth anniversary.

His loss was felt keenly in Ireland, and also of course in Australia, where he was celebrated for setting up O'Punkskys, and as an inspiring and supportive teacher.

Reeling from the shock, Garry and Marie both issued statements of sympathy for his family and friends. 'He was such a positive force,' Marie said; Garry described him as 'an essential part of the Druid story, gone way too soon and we will miss him very much'.

As Druid were mourning Maelíosa's loss in 2023, they were also getting ready to begin rehearsals on another cycle, this time of three of Seán O'Casey's plays.

The idea of an O'Casey production had been mooted shortly after *DruidSynge*, the original idea being to stage the three plays traditionally known as O'Casey's *Dublin Trilogy* – the *Shadow of a Gunman* (about the Irish War of Independence), *Juno and the Paycock* (set during the Civil War) and *The Plough and the Stars* (about the Easter Rising) – together with a fourth play, *The Silver Tassie*, which is about the participation of Irish soldiers in the First World War.

Garry had already directed two of those plays: *The Plough* at the Abbey in 1991 and *Juno* for a 1999 outing, at Dublin's Gaiety Theatre, that starred Michael Gambon, and which featured a young Cillian Murphy in one of the supporting roles. She admired the plays greatly but felt that their scale was so huge that Druid would need to collaborate with another theatre to do all four of them – and, given its Dublin setting, it also seemed appropriate to work with the Abbey in bringing the project to fruition. She approached Fiach Mac Conghail to discuss possibilities, and towards the end of 2007 Druid announced that work on the cycle would soon get underway.

What followed was a very public disagreement between the two theatres. Druid announced that the performances could not go ahead because the Abbey had tied up performance rights for some of O'Casey plays, while the Abbey countered that it had always planned on producing O'Casey, and had done nothing wrong. The theatre did express an interest in inviting Garry to direct there, but stated explicitly that a co-production with Druid was not something that interested them.

Ultimately, everyone lost out. The proposed cycle didn't happen, though Druid did stage *The Silver Tassie* in 2010; and Garry didn't direct at the Abbey again until after Fiach Mac Conghail's departure as the theatre's Director in 2016. The Abbey did stage some of O'Casey's plays during Mac Conghail's tenure, but those productions had met with a mixed reaction; and it was quite revealing that, when Mac Conghail's successors Graham MacLaren and Neil Murray were asked what they intended to do shortly before they started at the Abbey, one of their few specific commitments was that they definitely would *not* be staging *The Plough and the Stars*.

Garry moved on from that disappointment, and when asked over the subsequent years if she was thinking about doing O'Casey she usually replied that she was busy with other ideas.

Things eventually began to shift as a result of the Irish government's 'Decade of Centenaries' programme, which

Rehearsing *DruidO'Casey*, 2023.

aimed to commemorate the many events between 1912 and 1922 that had brought about Irish independence and the partition of the island.

When presented in that context, staging the O'Casey plays might *look* like an act of commemoration, as if Druid was helping the Irish state to congratulate itself on its own durability. But Garry knew that O'Casey's work could provide an opportunity to ask questions about how far Ireland had really come. Despite the *Trilogy*'s status as an Irish classic, O'Casey was himself quite ambivalent about Ireland: he was a nationalist but his larger commitment was to socialism – and he just wasn't convinced that the achievement of Irish independence had made life any better for the most vulnerable people in the country. O'Casey's plays, Garry noted, were deeply concerned with matters such as housing, health care and equality. And each of those themes was just as topical in the post-pandemic period as it had been in the 1920s.

Initially, her plan was to stage the cycle in 2022, coinciding exactly with the centenary of the Irish state. But with COVID-19 still flaring up intermittently, the company ultimately decided that it would be too risky to stage it that year. Garry had imagined a cast of about nineteen actors and would need a crew of thirty or more people backstage – and she knew that if one of those people became ill, the whole thing could be shut down for days at a time. They would just have to wait.

So the cycle began instead in 2023 – opening in Galway at that year's Arts Festival (where one performance of the cycle was indeed disrupted by COVID), before going to the Lyric in Belfast. And then it played for two weeks at the Abbey Theatre, which had just appointed two new directors, Caitríona McLaughlin and Mark O'Brien. They were delighted to welcome Druid there, they said.

When *DruidO'Casey* began, the first thing that audiences saw was not the Dublin tenement that they might have been expecting, but a large timber-framed box that impeded their view into the set. Garrett Lombard then walked on stage, dressed in the uniform of an Irish Citizen Army volunteer, and he knocked upon that wall. It was then raised to reveal the home of Jack and Nora Clitheroe, thus beginning the day with *The Plough and the Stars*.

The Plough was the last of the three plays to be written, premiering in 1926, but it comes first chronologically, being set in 1916. Garry had been toying with the idea of staging the plays in their order of composition, moving back in time just as she'd done with *DruidMurphy*; that approach could also allow her to track the evolution of O'Casey's playwriting, she thought.

But that idea was quickly discounted: the final scene in *The Plough and the Stars* shows a group of British soldiers sitting in a Dublin attic, and that really wasn't the image that Garry wanted to leave her audiences with.

Aaron Monaghan as Fluther Good in *The Plough and the Stars*, 2023.

Instead, she'd finish with *Juno* – which ends with two Irish women on an empty stage together, thinking about how best to build a future for themselves.

As ever, Garry was keen to avoid any suggestion that she was directing a documentary – a risk of misinterpretation that was heightened by the presentation of the plays in chronological order, as if Druid's aim was to faithfully recount the birth of a nation. The presentation of the three plays within the box was one way of avoiding that risk by heightening the audiences' sense of the theatricality of the experience. Garry and Francis also ensured that a deliberate sense of the artificiality of the action would frame the experience overall, as was revealed when the production moved towards the final scene of *Juno and the Paycock*.

That's a moment in the play in which hopelessness almost completely replaces the humour that had dominated the action until that point. Juno knows that her son has been murdered, that her daughter Mary is pregnant by a man who has just run off, and that her own husband Captain Boyle – who thought he had inherited a fortune – is in fact broke and spending the last of his pennies getting drunk in a snug somewhere with his friend Joxer Daly.

To underscore that mood of bleakness, they decided that the set pieces should not just be removed (mirroring the fact that the family's possessions have been repossessed by debt collectors) but that they should be flipped around, revealing the backstage view to audiences in the auditorium. Thus, instead of walls, the audience saw the back of the theatrical flats, their wheels on casters visible, with weights holding them in place.

Far from commemorating the past, that image emphasized the artificiality of Druid's reconstruction of history – and by doing so it showed how Ireland, Irishness and the Irish state were (like all national entities) just an invention: things that are created, just as a play is a thing that is created. And, like plays, nations can be edited, revived, revised or replaced by something better.

———

DruidO'Casey would be one of the company's biggest successes – and it was certainly *not* seen as offering any kind of institutionally sanitized version of Ireland's past. Far from telling audiences *this is what happened then*, *DruidO'Casey* left a literal empty space for the audiences to look at.

And that empty space seemed to invite a question:

What now?

Riders to the Sea, 2025.

Post-Script
Opening Night, 2025

IT WAS 15 July 2025, shortly before seven in the evening, and Marie Mullen was standing off-stage in the Mick Lally Theatre in Galway, waiting for a play to begin.

To mark the company's fiftieth anniversary, Druid were producing a double bill of Synge's *Riders to the Sea* and *Macbeth*, which would run for a fortnight as part of the Galway International Arts Festival. Tickets had sold out instantly when they were released; a waiting list for return tickets had almost two thousand names on it. Across the city, there was huge excitement about the company's birthday. Around the corner from Druid Lane, Charlie Byrne's Bookshop had created an enormous window display of posters, scripts, and programmes from Druid's history – while Kenny's had dedicated its gallery space to a month-long exhibition of photos of the company from the late 1970s to the present by Joe O'Shaughnessy. There was a sense everywhere that this was an occasion of significance not just for the Irish theatre but for Galway too.

The combination of plays by Synge and Shakespeare had come as a surprise to many. Both are tragedies, but they differ in length, language, reputation and many other features. But throughout their fifty-year history, Druid had kept putting seemingly different works into conversation with each other – and thus were marking their anniversary by again collapsing the boundaries between plays that were normally held apart from each other.

Their first season, back in 1975, had been a staging not of one play but of three (which is a magical number, as *Macbeth* makes clear). To their first audiences, Synge's *Playboy of the Western World*, Brian Friel's *The Loves of Cass Maguire* and Kevin Laffan's *It's a Two Foot Six Inches Above the Ground World* had also seemed distinctly different from one another – in form, tone and setting. But when the plays were staged together, audiences had seen surprising patterns, overlaps and shared concerns.

Those three plays in 1975 had shown in their individual ways that you can never really leave home – that, even if you emigrate, you still have to take yourself with you. That theme would persist throughout Druid's history, from its celebrated reinvention of Molloy's *The Wood of the Whispering* in 1983, to Murphy's *Conversations on a Homecoming* in 1985, to McDonagh's *The Beauty Queen of Leenane* in 1996, to Enda Walsh's *The Walworth Farce* in 2006, to *DruidMurphy* in 2012, to Nancy Harris's *The Beacon* in 2019. Neither *Riders to the Sea* nor *Macbeth* is about emigration – but both would show that you can never escape yourself.

All three plays in that first season also focused on women who had been forced into narrow roles by the men in their lives – whether in the hostility and judgment experienced by Pegeen and the Widow Quin in *Playboy*, or in the presentation of the mother in Laffan's play, whose insistence that her husband should use birth control is overruled by her priest. During the years ahead, Druid would many times insist on centring the lives and experiences of women, as in the many great Druid plays by Geraldine Aron, such as *Same Old Moon* or *My Brilliant Divorce* – and in Tom Murphy's *Bailegangaire*, Marina Carr's *On Raftery's Hill* and Lucy Caldwell's *Leaves*, among many others.

Post-Script: Opening Night, 2025

Marty Rea in *Macbeth*.

The company had also committed itself to examining the classic repertoire as a way of rethinking how women are remembered, in both theatrical and political history. They had done so by staging *Playboy* in 1975, and in their fiftieth-anniversary production they did do so once again. Marie was performing first as Maurya in *Riders to the Sea* and then as Lady Macbeth; Marty Rea was playing her son in the first play and her husband in the second. The casting of Marie and Marty in those overlapping roles highlighted intriguingly how both plays are tragedies that turn on a moment when a man refuses to listen to a woman.

And finally, those three plays in Druid's first season dramatized the fate of a generation of young people whose hopes had been stunted and thwarted by their elders. That too had been a major Druid theme, as seen in Vincent Woods's *At the Black Pig's Dyke*, Druid's productions of *Sive* and *Big Maggie* and in the *DruidO'Casey* cycle of 2023. *Macbeth* and *Riders* added texture to that pattern: both are plays in which parents outlive their children.

Druid had always sought to allow those kinds of echoes to resound between the plays they produced. Sometimes, they do that by creating cycles such as *DruidSynge* or by producing works like Sonya Kelly's *Furniture*, in which distinctive stories are placed together.

And often those ripples from one production to another had been emphasized by the casting of actors in distinctive roles that, upon investigation, had subtle affinities. Thus, when Marty Rea stepped onto the stage as Macbeth later on that opening night, audiences might have been able to detect traces of the monstrous ambition he had displayed in the lead role in Druid's production of Tom Murphy's *The House* during the previous year. And when Macbeth sees the finite span of human life as a 'tale told by an idiot', those same audiences might find themselves thinking of Rea playing Vladimir in Druid's 2016 *Godot*, in which he mused on how the gap between birth and death is so absurdly short that gravediggers should be equipped with a forceps.

In her first programme note for a Druid production, Garry had explained that the company's aim was simply to 'make voyages'. That ambition had continued into 2025. They had never set out with a manifesto that they wanted audiences to agree with: a Druid production might echo an event in Irish society or the wider world, but it never tried to be a direct allegory for it. Their approach had been investigative and diagnostic rather than accusatory or polemical.

And that approach in turn had led to the evolution of an acting style that in its own way blurs distinctions. During the company's first two decades, their performances were often described as 'naturalistic'; they were admired especially for their ensemble-based approach to the authentic realization of west of Ireland life. That feeling of naturalism was often intensified by the company's history of bringing plays to the places that had inspired them, as with their celebrated visit to Inis Meáin with Synge's *Playboy* in 1982, their tour of McDonagh's *Beauty Queen* to Leenane itself and their presentation of Lady Gregory's plays in Coole Park.

But, gradually, audiences had come to realize that Druid's style of acting was heightened, that it went beyond naturalism without becoming melodramatic or operatic. Sometimes that heightened approach could attain a mythic power (as in Murphy's *Bailegangaire*); sometimes it could be transcendent (as in the love scene between Christy and Pegeen in *Playboy*); sometimes it could be ironizing or distancing (as in Kelly's *Furniture* and *The Last Return*). And sometimes it would shift imperceptibly into and out of the supernatural, as was about to happen in *Riders to the Sea* and *Macbeth*.

That approach to acting had been evident across Druid's body of work – both in the productions that were directed by Garry and in those that were directed by Maelíosa Stafford, Enda Walsh, Mikel Murfi, Sara Joyce and many others.

That acting style had been founded upon an understanding that audiences share the responsibility for creating theatrical meaning – that theatre gives everyone licence to look past surface appearances. Thus, in 1975, the 22-year-old Marie Mullen played a woman in her seventies in *Cass Maguire*, just as she would now, in her seventies, play Lady Macbeth. Druid's approach to acting had sought to empower audiences, asking them to perceive things that they cannot literally see. Lady Macbeth sees bloodstains that are not there; Macbeth sees a dagger that is not there; and in *Riders to the Sea* Maurya sees a vision of her son who is, tragically, not literally 'there'. That is what theatre does; this is how theatre works.

A fiftieth birthday is a big occasion, but Druid's impulse had always been to look forwards rather than backwards. They were a company, after all, that had opened their own theatre in Chapel Lane in 1979 not by producing a new Irish play but by staging Brecht's *Threepenny Opera*. When they were invited to open the Hawk's Well Theatre in Sligo three years later, they again were expected to do an Irish play – but had instead staged Shakespeare's *Much Ado About Nothing*. For their tenth birthday, in the summer of 1985, they produced *'Tis Pity She's a Whore* by John Ford. And they celebrated their fortieth birthday with *DruidShakespeare*. Thus, one of Druid's most consistent practices had been to surprise their audiences by staging writers like Shakespeare when they were instead expected to stage writers like Synge. And so at the age of fifty they were doing both at the same time.

And finally, the night's performance would mark a half-century-long professional relationship between Garry and Marie. Not every Druid show was directed by Garry; not every Druid show featured Marie. But the fifty-year history of the company was also the history of the evolution of a friendship that was, quite simply, unique in the story of Irish theatre.

And so on that night in Galway, the auditorium grew silent, and the actors took their positions. Marie was dressed in the long black hooded cloak of an Irish peasant woman; she would enter the performance space by walking from the foyer of the Mick Lally Theatre onto the clay-filled floor on the set that Francis O'Connor had designed.

Other members of the ensemble were also ready to begin – Marty Rea was there; Garrett Lombard and Rory Nolan were standing by for their performances in *Macbeth*; and also present were many younger actors, some of whom were making their debut with the company.

Garry, as was her usual opening-night practice, had slipped away quietly beforehand, planning to rejoin everyone when the performance had concluded.

And over to Marie's right, hanging on the wall of the foyer, there was a photo of Mick, unloading props on the beach in Inis Meáin back in 1982.

Marie stepped forward.

The play began.

Druid Productions
1975–2025

1975
- *The Playboy of the Western World* by J. M. Synge
- *It's a Two Foot Six Inches Above the Ground World* by Kevin Laffan
- *The Loves of Cass McGuire* by Brian Friel
- *Act Without Words II* by Samuel Beckett
- *Orison* by Fernando Arrabel
- *The Glass Menagerie* by Tennessee Williams
- *An Entertainment on a Marriage* by David Campion & James Saunders
- *Children of the Wolf* by John Peacock

1976
- *Countdown* by Alan Ayckbourn
- *It Should Happen to a Dog* by Wolf Mankowitz
- *Who's Afraid of Virginia Woolf?* by Edward Albee
- *Treats* by Christopher Hampton
- *The Pongo Plays* by Henry Livings
- *In the Glens of Rathvanna* by J. M. Synge
- *The Pot of Broth & Purgatory* by W. B. Yeats
- *Off Obie*, a trilogy of American one-act plays by various authors
- *Happy Days* by Samuel Beckett
- *Mother Adam* by Charles Dyer

1977
- *S.W.A.L.K.* by various authors
- *Tom Paine* by Paul Foster
- *Birdbath* by Leonard Melfi
- *There Are Tragedies and Tragedies* by George Fitzmaurice
- *The Playboy of the Western World* by J. M. Synge

- *The Pursuit of Pleasure* by Garry Hynes
- *The Promise* by Aleksei Arbuzov
- *Aladineen O'Druideen* by Druid Theatre Company

1978
- *The Enchanted Trousers* by Oliver St. John Gogarty
- *After Magritte* by Tom Stoppard
- *Sean, the Fool, the Devil, and the Cats* by Ted Hughes
- *The Proposal* by Anton Chekov
- *The Tinker's Wedding* by J. M. Synge
- *The Colleen Bawn* by Dion Boucicault
- *Bar and Ger* by Geraldine Aron
- *Woyzeck* by George Buchner

1979
- *Eternal Triangle* by Frank O'Connor
- *The Threepenny Opera* by Bertolt Brecht
- *A Village Wooing* by George Bernard Shaw
- *An Evening at Coole* by Lady Gregory
- *A Galway Girl* by Geraldine Aron
- *The Importance of Being Earnest* by Oscar Wilde

1980
- *Thirst* by Myles na gCopaleen
- *The Real Inspector Hound* by Tom Stoppard
- *Island Protected by a Bridge of Glass* by Garry Hynes
- *Fascinating Foundling* by George Bernard Shaw
- *Sundance* by Meir Ribalow
- *A Doll's House* by Henrik Ibsen

1981
- *I Do Not Like Thee, Doctor Fell* by Bernard Farrell
- *Master of Two Servants* by Carlo Goldoni (adapted by George Mully)
- *Dial M for Murder* by Frederik Knott
- *The Nightingale and Not the Lark* by Jennifer Johnston
- *Geography of a Horse Dreamer* by Sam Shepard
- *Endgame* by Samuel Beckett
- *Hancock's Last Half Hour* by Heathcote Williams
- *Much Ado about Nothing* by William Shakespeare

1982
- *Private Dick* by Richard Maher & Roger Mitchell
- *Accidental Death of an Anarchist* by Dario Fo

- *The Shaughraun* by Dion Boucicault
- *The Playboy of the Western World* by J. M. Synge
- *In the Shadow of the Glen* by J. M. Synge

1983
- *The Rising of the Moon* by Lady Gregory
- *Action* by Sam Shepard
- *Mother Courage and Her Children* by Bertolt Brecht
- *The Rivals* by Richard B. Sheridan
- *Bedtime Story* by Sean O'Casey
- *The Wood of the Whispering* by M. J. Molloy

1984
- *Famine* by Tom Murphy
- *Same Old Moon* by Geraldine Aron
- *The Beggar's Opera* by John Gay
- *On the Outside* by Tom Murphy & Noel O'Donoghue
- *The Glass Menagerie* by Tennessee Williams

1985
- *The Playboy of the Western World* by J. M. Synge
- *Conversations on a Homecoming* by Tom Murphy
- *'Tis Pity She's a Whore* by John Ford
- *The Importance of Being Earnest* by Oscar Wilde
- *Bailegangaire* by Tom Murphy

1986
- *Dracula* adapted by Frank McGuinness
- *Loot* by Joe Orton
- *Conversations on a Homecoming* by Tom Murphy (New York)
- *The Playboy of the Western World* by J. M. Synge (New York)

1987
- *Waiting for Godot* by Samuel Beckett
- *A Touch of the Poet* by Eugene O'Neill
- *A Whistle in the Dark* by Tom Murphy (in association with the Abbey Theatre)
- *Oedipus by Sophocles* (in a version by W. B. Yeats)
- *The Hostage* by Brendan Behan

1988
- *The Factory Girls* by Frank McGuinness
- *Trumpets and Raspberries* by Dario Fo
- *Little City* by Seamus Byrne
- *I Do Not Like Thee, Doctor Fell* by Bernard Farrell

1989
- *A Little Like Drowning* by Anthony Minghella
- *Wild Harvest* by Ken Bourke
- *Lovers* by Brian Friel

1990
- *St Patrick's Day* by Richard B. Sheridan
- *Antigone* by Jean Anouilh (translated by Lewis Galantière)
- *The Donahue Sisters* & *The Stanley Parkers* by Geraldine Aron
- *Lovers' Meeting* by Louis D'Alton

1991
- *The Increased Difficulty of Concentration* by Václav Havel
- *Look Back in Anger* by John Osborne
- *John Hughdy* & *Tom John* by Vincent Woods
- *Cheapside* by David Allen
- *Shadow and Substance* by Paul Vincent Carroll

1992
- *Carthaginians* by Frank McGuinness
- *Werewolves* by Teresa Lubkiewicz (translated by Helena Kaut-Howson)
- *Odd Habits* by Marianne Fahy & Deirdre O'Kane (from the works of Mary Lavin and Francis Molloy)
- *Gaslight* by Patrick Hamilton
- *The Midnight Court* by Brian Merriman (adapted by Seán Tyrell from a translation by David Marcus)
- *At The Black Pig's Dyke* by Vincent Woods

1993
- *Private Dick* by Richard Maher & Roger Mitchell
- *There Are Tragedies and Tragedies* by George Fitzmaurice
- *The Ointment Blue* by George Fitzmaurice
- *Belfry* by Billy Roche

1994
- *The Playboy of the West Indies* by Mustapha Matura (in association with Tricycle Theatre)
- *Summerhouse* by Robin Glendinning
- *Silverlands* by Antoine Ó Flatharta
- *Song of the Yellow Bittern* by Vincent Woods

1995
- *Poor Beast in the Rain* by Billy Roche
- *The Blue Macushla* by Tom Murphy

Druid Productions 1975–2025

1996
- *The Beauty Queen of Leenane* by Martin McDonagh
- *The Loves of Cass McGuire* by Brian Friel
- *The Singular life of Albert Nobbs* by Simone Benmussa (from a story by George Moore)

1997
- *Shoot the Crow* by Owen McCafferty
- *The Leenane Trilogy: The Beauty Queen of Leenane, A Skull in Connemara, The Lonesome West* by Martin McDonagh

1998
- *Philadelphia, Here I Come!* by Brian Friel
- *The Way You Look Tonight* by Niall Williams

1999
- *As You Like It* by William Shakespeare
- *The Country Boy* by John Murphy

2000
- *On Raftery's Hill* by Marina Carr
- *The Hackney Office* by Michael Collins

2001
- *The Spirit of Annie Ross* by Bernard Farrell
- *My Brilliant Divorce* by Geraldine Aron

2002
- *The Good Father* by Christian O'Reilly
- *Sive* by John B. Keane

2003
- *My Brilliant Divorce* by Geraldine Aron (West End)
- *Sharon's Grave* by John B. Keane

2004
- *The Playboy of the Western World* by J. M. Synge
- *The Well of the Saints* by J. M. Synge
- *The Tinker's Wedding* by J. M. Synge

2005
- *DruidSynge: Riders to the Sea, The Tinker's Wedding, The Well of the Saints, In the Shadow of the Glen, The Playboy of the Western World, Deirdre of the Sorrows* by J. M. Synge

2006
- *The Walworth Farce* by Enda Walsh
- *The Year of the Hiker* by John B. Keane
- *Empress of India* by Stuart Carolan

2007
- *Leaves* by Lucy Caldwell
- *Long Day's Journey into Night* by Eugene O'Neill
- *My Brilliant Divorce* by Geraldine Aron

2008
- *The New Electric Ballroom* by Enda Walsh
- One-Act Plays (*Gentrification, Lynndie's Gotta Gun*) by Enda Walsh
- *The Cripple of Inishmaan* by Martin McDonagh

2009
- *The Gigli Concert* by Tom Murphy

2010
- *From Galway to Broadway and Back Again* (Druid's thirty-fifth anniversary celebrations)
- *Penelope* by Enda Walsh
- *The Silver Tassie* by Sean O'Casey

2011
- *The Cripple of Inishmaan* by Martin McDonagh
- *Give Me Your Hand* by Paul Durcan
- *Big Maggie* by John B. Keane

2012
- *DruidMurphy: Conversations on a Homecoming, A Whistle in the Dark, Famine* by Tom Murphy

2013
- *The Colleen Bawn* by Dion Boucicault

2014
- *Be Infants in Evil* by Brian Martin
- *Brigit* by Tom Murphy
- *Bailegangaire* by Tom Murphy

2015
- *DruidShakespeare: Richard II, Henry IV (Pts 1&2), Henry V* by William Shakespeare, adapted by Mark O'Rowe

2016
- *Big Maggie* by John B. Keane
- *Waiting for Godot* by Samuel Beckett
- *Helen and I* by Meadhbh McHugh
- *The Beauty Queen of Leenane* by Martin McDonagh (twentieth anniversary production)

2017
- *Crestfall* by Mark O'Rowe
- *King of the Castle* by Eugene McCabe

Druid Productions 1975–2025

- 2018
  - *Sive* by John B. Keane
  - *Furniture* by Sonya Kelly
  - *Shelter* by Cristín Kehoe
  - *DruidShakespeare: Richard III* by William Shakespeare

- 2019
  - *Epiphany* by Brian Watkins
  - *The Beacon* by Nancy Harris

- 2020
  - *The Cherry Orchard* by Anton Chekhov, in a version by Tom Murphy
  - *DruidGregory: The Gaol Gate, Hyacinth Halvey, McDonough's Wife, The Rising of the Moon* by Lady Gregory; *Cathleen Ní Houlihan* by Lady Gregory and W. B. Yeats.
  - *On the Outside* by Tom Murphy & Noel O' Donoghue

- 2021
  - *Once Upon a Bridge* by Sonya Kelly
  - *Boland: Journey of a Poet* by Eavan Boland, edited by Colm Tóibín
  - *The Seagull* by Thomas Kilroy (after Chekhov)
  - Three Short Comedies: *A Pound on Demand, Bedtime Story, The End of the Beginning* by Sean O'Casey

- 2022
  - *The Cavalcaders* by Billy Roche
  - *The Last Return* by Sonya Kelly

- 2023
  - *DruidO'Casey: The Plough and the Stars, The Shadow of a Gunman, Juno and the Paycock* by Sean O'Casey

- 2024
  - *Endgame* by Samuel Beckett
  - *The House* by Tom Murphy

- 2025
  - Three Short Comedies: *A Pound on Demand, Bedtime Story, The End of the Beginning* by Sean O'Casey
  - *Riders to the Sea* by J. M. Synge
  - *Macbeth* by William Shakespeare

Druid Timeline

1975	Druid is established, initially known as Druid: The Repertory Theatre of Galway
1978	Druid participates in the inaugural Galway Arts Festival
1978	Druid's first collaboration with the playwright Geraldine Aron
1979	Druid moves into its new home on Chapel Lane
1980	Druid's first international tour, they bring four plays to Edinburgh Festival Fringe and take home a Fringe First award
1982	Druid is invited to open the newly built Hawk's Well Theatre in Sligo with a production of Shakespeare's *Much Ado About Nothing* with President Patrick Hillery as guest of honour
1982	Druid's first tour to the Aran Islands where they perform Synge's *The Playboy of the Western World*
1983	Druid's production of M. J. Molloy's *The Wood of the Whispering*
1984	Druid's first production of a Tom Murphy play, *Famine* at the Seapoint Ballroom in Salthill
1985	World premieres of two Tom Murphy plays, written for Druid: *Conversations on a Homecoming* and *Bailegangaire*

1986	Druid's first transatlantic tour with performances of *The Playboy of the Western World* and *Conversations on a Homecoming* in New York
1991	Maelíosa Stafford becomes Artistic Director of Druid following Garry Hynes's appointment to the Abbey Theatre
1992	Druid's 100th production, *At the Black Pig's Dyke* by Vincent Woods, directed by Maelíosa Stafford and designed by Monica Frawley
1996	The world premiere of *The Beauty Queen of Leenane* by Martin McDonagh, the inaugural production at Galway's new Town Hall Theatre
1996	Druid celebrates its twenty-first birthday with a gala performance of Brian Friel's *The Loves of Cass Maguire*, President Mary Robinson attends as the guest of honour. Druid Lane is renamed by Galway City Council to mark the milestone birthday.
1997	Druid's first play cycle, *The Leenane Trilogy* by Martin McDonagh, comprises a revival of *The Beauty Queen of Leenane* and the world premieres of *A Skull in Connemara* and *The Lonesome West*
1998	Following multiple runs in Ireland and a West End run, *The Beauty Queen of Leenane* opens on Broadway and wins four Tony Awards including Best Director for Garry Hynes who becomes the first woman in history to win that award
1999	*The Lonesome West* opens on Broadway and is nominated for four Tony Awards
2000	The company's play reading series Druid Debuts begins
2000	The world premiere of *On Raftery's Hill* by Marina Carr
2002	A major new production of John B. Keane's *Sive*, marking the beginning of the company's exploration of the playwright's canon
2004	A major new production of Synge's *The Playboy of the Western World* starring Cillian Murphy and Anne-Marie Duff

2005	Druid's next play cycle is the staging of all six of Synge's plays, *DruidSynge*
2006	The world premieres of *The Walworth Farce* by Enda Walsh and *Empress of India* by Stuart Carolan
2008	Druid returns to the work of Martin McDonagh for a major new production of *The Cripple of Inishmaan*
2009	Following extensive renovations, Druid's home theatre on Druid Lane is reopened
2010	Druid celebrates its thirty-fifth anniversary with a special event at the Town Hall Theatre featuring excerpts from productions over the years, performed by a large cast of returning Druid actors
2010	A major new production of Sean O'Casey's *The Silver Tassie*
2010	Druid's co-founder Mick Lally passes away after a short illness.
2010	The formalization of the longstanding partnership between Druid and the University of Galway
2012	*DruidMurphy*, Druid's next cycle, combines three plays from Tom Murphy's canon: *Conversations on a Homecoming*, *A Whistle in the Dark* and *Famine*
2014	Druid's home theatre on Druid Lane in Galway is renamed the Mick Lally Theatre
2014	Druid introduces a new artist development programme, the annual FUEL Artist Residency
2014	Druid presents a Tom Murphy double bill: a revival of *Bailegangaire* thirty years after its world premiere, and the world premiere of a new play, *Brigit*
2015	A play cycle of epic proportions, centuries in the making, *DruidShakespeare* condenses four action-packed plays – *Richard*

	II, *Henry IV (Parts 1 & 2)*, and *Henry V* – into one thrilling drama played out over six hours, produced to celebrate Druid's fortieth anniversary
2016	Druid's production of Beckett's *Waiting for Godot* earns major critical acclaim and tours around the world for three years
2016	To mark its twentieth anniversary, Druid presents a new production of Martin McDonagh's *The Beauty Queen of Leenane*
2018	Druid's newest artist development programme, the annual Marie Mullen Bursary, is an award for women working in Irish theatre
2018	The world premieres of *Furniture* by Sonya Kelly and *Shelter* by Cristín Kehoe
2018	Druid return to Shakespeare with a new production of *Richard III* which tours Galway, Dublin and New York
2019	The world premieres of *Epiphany* by Brian Watkins and *The Beacon* by Nancy Harris
2020	In a first for Irish theatre, Druid broadcasts its new production of Tom Murphy's version of Anton Chekhov's *The Cherry Orchard* live from Galway to cinemas across Ireland and the UK
2020	With the country in lockdown, Druid travel to Lady Gregory's home, Coole Park, for *DruidGregory*, a new play cycle production of her one-act plays, followed by a fourteen-venue, four-week tour of Gregory's beloved County Galway
2021	Druid ventures into live online theatre with the world premiere of Sonya Kelly's *Once Upon a Bridge*, viewed by audiences in thirty-five countries around the world
2022	Building on an existing partnership first formalised in 2010, Druid and the University of Galway announce a new 10-year partnership to focus on expanding academic links, student engagement, local and global events and the creative sector in the West

2022	The world premiere of *The Last Return* by Sonya Kelly which plays Galway, Edinburgh and Dublin, earning a Fringe First award and two Irish Times Theatre awards
2023	Druid's latest play cycle, *DruidO'Casey*, tackles the great works of Sean O'Casey, his Dublin Trilogy of plays: *The Plough and the Stars*, *The Shadow of a Gunman* and *Juno and the Paycock*
2025	Druid celebrates its fiftieth anniversary with a programme of events centred around a double bill in Galway of Synge's *Riders to the Sea* and Shakespeare's *Macbeth*

Sources

This book makes extensive use of the Druid Theatre archives, which are held at the Hardiman Library at the University of Galway. The full catalogue is available to view online at https://library.universityofgalway.ie/collections/archives/
The information in the timeline and production history was prepared by Druid Theatre and, together with extensive production information, can also be viewed on the Druid website www.druid.ie

DRUID ORAL HISTORY

The Druid Oral History project was funded by the University of Galway from 2014 to 2016 and was carried out by Thomas Conway and Ciara O'Dowd. Transcriptions have been lightly edited for clarity and length. Quotations from the following recordings appear in the text:

- Aaron Monaghan
- Anne Butler
- Catherine Walsh and Eileen Walsh
- Derbhle Crotty
- Donagh O'Donoghue
- Eamon Morrissey
- Francis O'Connor
- Garry Hynes and Derbhle Corty, public interview, Fordham University 2015

- Garry Hynes on *Bailegangaire* and *Brigit*
- Garry Hynes, Marie Mullen and Maelíosa Stafford
- Jane Daly
- Maelíosa Stafford
- Mairead Noone
- Marie Mullen
- Maureen Hughes
- Nigel Redden
- Peige Lally
- Rebecca Bartlett
- Tom Murphy and Jane Brennan
- Vincent Woods

NEWSPAPERS AND OTHER MEDIA SOURCES

Many of the quotations from newspapers, especially for the period from 1975 to 1990, are taken from the Druid archive. Sources that are available online include:

Kernan Andrews, 'It's the culmination of everything I have ever done', *Galway Advertiser* https://www.advertiser.ie/galway/article/71904/its-the-culmination-of-everything-i-have-ever-done

Jane Brennan and Amelia Stein https://www.ameliastein.com/theatre/women-in-history-women-in-irish-theatre/jane-brennan/

Peter Crawley, 'The Crystal Heard of Druid', *The Irish Times*, 2006 https://www.irishtimes.com/news/the-crystal-heart-of-druid-1.1027085

Peter Crawley, 'Getting the dirt on DruidShakespeare; Druid theatre company is giving the playwright's Henriad an Irish flavour by tweaking the text and the terrain', *The Irish Times*, 9 May 2015 https://www.irishtimes.com/culture/can-we-treat-shakespeare-as-one-of-our-own-getting-the-dirt-on-druidshakespeare-1.2205304

Garry Hynes, Letter to *The Irish Times*, 'Women and the Abbey Theatre' https://www.irishtimes.com/opinion/letters/women-and-the-abbey-theatre-1.2417289

Sonya Kelly, 'Doing the Sanding' https://www.druid.ie/about/news/sonya-kelly-on-the-craft-of-playwriting

Tom Murphy, interview with Belinda McKeon https://www.theparisreview.org/blog/2012/07/09/home-to-darkness-an-interview-with-playwright-tom-murphy/

Jeff O'Connell, 'Remembering John Arden', *Galway Advertiser* 5 April 2012. https://www.advertiser.ie/galway/article/50939/remembering-john-arden

RTÉ, 'Playboy On Aran Island' https://www.rte.ie/archives/2019/0108/1021919-druid-on-inis-meain/

RTÉ, 'Famine' https://www.rte.ie/archives/2024/0117/1427110-famine-druid-theatre/

Eithne Shortall, 'A woman of strong heart; Aisling O'Sullivan is often asked to play tough characters. Eithne Shortall pins her down on why exactly this is', *The Sunday Times* (London) https://advance.lexis.com/api/document?collection=news&id=urn:contentItem:544S-2X11-JCC9-V02S-00000-00&context=1519360 .

ACADEMIC BOOKS

Burke, Mary, *Tinkers* (Oxford: Oxford University Press, 2009).

Caulfield, Mary, and Ian Walsh, *The Theatre of Enda Walsh* (Dublin: Carysfort Press, 2015).

Chambers, Lilian, Ger Fitzgibbon and Eamonn Jordan, eds, *Theatre Talk: View of Irish Theatre Practitioners* (Dublin: Carysfort Press, 2001).

Donohue, Brenda et al., *Gender Counts* (Dublin: Wakingthefeminists, 2017).

Frazier, Adrian, ed. *Playboys of the Westerns World* (Dublin: Carysfort Press, 2005).

Grene, Nicholas, *The Politics of Irish Drama* (Cambridge: Cambridge University Press, 1999).

Grene, Nicholas, ed., *Talking About Tom Murphy* (Dublin: Carysfort Press, 2002).

Grene, Nicholas, *The Theatre of Tom Murphy: Playwright Adventurer* (London: Bloomsbury Publishing, 2017).

Hill, Shonagh. *Women and embodied mythmaking in Irish theatre* (Cambridge: Cambridge University Press, 2019).

Lonergan, Patrick, *The Theatre and Films of Martin McDonagh* (London: Methuen, 2012).

Lonergan, Patrick, *Irish Drama and Theatre Since 1950* (London: Bloomsbury, 2019).

McIvor, Charlotte, and Ian R. Walsh, *Contemporary Irish Theatre: Histories and Theories* (Berlin: Springer Nature, 2024).

McTighe, Trish and David Tucker, *Staging Beckett in Ireland and Northern Ireland* (London: Bloomsbury, 2016).

Morash, Christopher, *A History of Irish Theatre, 1601–2000* (Cambridge: Cambridge University Press, 2002).

Ó hAodha, Micheál, *Siobhán: A Memoir of an Actress* (Dingle: Brandon, 1994).

O'Gorman, Siobhán and Charlotte McIvor, eds, *Devised Performance in Irish Theatre: Histories and Contemporary Practice* (Dublin: Carysfort Press, 2015).

O'Toole, Fintan, *Tom Murphy: The Politics of Magic* (Dublin: New Island, 1994).

Pine, Emilie, *The Politics of Irish Memory* (Basingstoke: Palgrave, 2010).

Richtarik, Marilyn, *Acting Between the Lines* (Washington DC: CUA Press, 2001).

Roche, Anthony, *Contemporary Irish Drama* (Basingstoke: Palgrave, 2009).

Sihra, Melissa, *Women in Irish Drama* (Basingstoke: Palgrave, 2007).

Sihra, Melissa, *Marina Carr: Pastures of the Unknown* (Chaim: Springer, 2021).

Smith, Gus, and Des Hickey, *John B.: The Real Keane* (Cork: Mercier Press, 1992).

Acknowledgments

This book draws extensively from material at the Hardiman library at the University of Galway, and thanks are due to Catriona Cannon, John Cox, Monica Crump, and Kieran Hoare for everything they have done and continue to do to support the development of the Druid Archive. I must particularly acknowledge the help of Barry Houlihan, who provided access to archival files and was a constant source of advice. It's hard to imagine what Irish theatre scholarship would be like without Barry's support, but there would certainly be much less of it in print without him.

Much of the information in this book is drawn from the Druid Oral History project, which was conducted by Thomas Conway and Ciara O'Dowd in 2015 and 2016. Funding for that project was provided by Mike Kavanagh, who was then Academic Secretary of NUI Galway.

I am grateful to Paul Fahy of Galway International Arts Festival for permission to reproduce images from the festival's archive. Thanks also to the Abbey Theatre archivist Mairéad Delaney for permission to reproduce the image from the show programme of *A Crucial Week in the Life of a Grocer's Assistant*, and for being an essential and generous source of information and advice.

The relationship between the University of Galway and Druid has deepened since the formalization of a partnership between them in 2010. A list of university personnel who have supported that partnership would run to several pages, but it is essential to mention the crucial roles played by Jim Browne, John Concannon, Adrian Frazier, Tom Joyce, Caroline Loughnane, Liz McConnell, Ciarán Ó hÓgartaigh, and Sean Ryder. In that context, I particularly want to thank Máiréad Ní Chróinín, the Druid Theatre Artist in Residence at the university since 2019. She did a huge amount to imagine and then realize plans for the celebration of Druid's fiftieth birthday within the university.

I must thank all my colleagues and students in Drama and Theatre Studies and English at the university, especially three people who provided moral support, practical help and advice (or went to meetings so that I didn't have to) during the first half of 2025 when this book was being finished – Marianne Kennedy, Charlotte McIvor, and Ian Walsh. I also want to express how my understanding of Druid has been deepened and expanded by supervising PhD researchers who wrote about the company's work: Nelson Barre, Clara Mallon, Emer McHugh, Finian O'Gorman, and Shelley Troupe. I'm also grateful to my fellow members of the Theatre Historiography Working Group of the International Federation for Theatre Research, from whom I've learned a huge amount about documenting the theatrical past.

The development of the Druid/university partnership was also a result of the enthusiasm of many people who work or have worked at the company, including Fergal McGrath, Felicity O'Brien, Tim Smith, Sarah Lynch, Craig Flaherty, Síomha Nee, Brian Fenton, and Feargal Hynes. I must also acknowledge the many Druid actors, writers, designers and producers who have come to the university to give masterclasses or talks over the years. Thomas Conway was the first Druid Director in Residence at the University of Galway, and I learned an enormous amount from him during our years as colleagues – about Druid and much else besides. Thomas also kindly read an earlier draft of this manuscript, offering invaluable notes and corrections (though of course any remaining errors or omissions are entirely my responsibility). I am also grateful to David Mullane and, especially, Anneliese Davidsen for all their support with this book. Anneliese drove the project forward with great enthusiasm, and her advice and encouragement all the way through was exceptionally helpful.

I am very grateful to everyone at Lilliput Press, especially Stephen Reid and Antony Farrell.

Thanks as always to my family – to Thérèse, Saoirse and Cónall. I have been going to Druid shows with Thérèse for almost thirty years, and it means a great deal that writing this history has given me an opportunity to remember much of our own history together.

And finally, huge thanks to Marie Mullen and Garry Hynes.

Druid Theatre Acknowledgments

As we celebrate 50 years of memorable Irish performances, Druid gratefully acknowledges the support of its friends and partners in Galway, throughout Ireland, and around the world.

In particular, we extend deep appreciation to our Funding Partners – the Arts Council, Smurfit Westrock, University of Galway, and Galway City Council.

We give special thanks to McDonogh Capital Investments, our 50th Anniversary sponsor, whose generosity today continues a relationship that began with the gift of our permanent home in 1979, ensuring Druid's survival and helping shape Galway's cultural life.

We are grateful for the following friends and partners supporting Druid in our fiftieth year:

Community & Education Partner
Adrian Brinkerhoff Poetry Foundation

Programme Partners
Culture Ireland
Department of Culture, Communications and Sport
Jerome L. Greene Foundation

Corporate Patrons
Corrib Oil
The Ireland Funds

Corporate Guardians

An Post
Claddagh Credit Union
Connacht Hospitality Group

Galway Culture Company
Irish American Partnership
Tigh Neachtain

Business Leaders

Ashford Castle
Ferrys Solicitors
Galway Advertiser

The Kings Head
MKO Ireland
Sheridans Cheesemongers

Business Partners

Aniar
Arachas
Ballynahinch Castle
Cava Bodega
Cliffs of Moher Hotel
Connacht Tribune
Ecclesiastical Insurance
iSupply
Kilfeather & Company Solicitors
MacSweeney & Company Solicitors

Old Ground Hotel Ennis
OnePageCRM
Penn Engineering
Platform94
Stillwater Communications
TG4
T J Hyland & Co. Accountants
Travelodge Plus Galway City
Tri Everest Wealth Management

Transformational Partners

Anne Anderson & Franklin Lowe
Mary & Donal Boylan
Michael & Margaret Brewster
The Cielinski Family
Anthony Cullen
Jeffrey Davis
John Fitzpatrick
Simon Freakley
Loretta Brennan Glucksman
Joseph Hassett & Carol Melton
Aedhmar Hynes & Kelvin Thompson
Thomas Campbell Jackson & Penny Jackson
Kevin Jennings
Adrian & Christina Jones
Paul & Melissa Keary
Mark Kennedy & Eilín de Paor

Kumi & Bill Martin
Matthew McBride
The McCann Family
Dermot McDonogh & Joan Moroney
Geraldine McGinty & John Grealy
Christina McInerney
Tom McInerney & Jessica Leonard
Grainne McNamara
Maureen Mitchell
Colleen Murphy
Nigel Redden
Frank Ryan
Ann Shannon
Matthew Patrick Smyth
Lori & Jim Steinberg
Carol & Tom Wheeler

Druid Theatre Acknowledgements

Platinum Friends

Mairéad & Frank Cashman
Eoghan & Grainne Curtin
David Eden
Louise Furey-Burke
Cathal Goan & Maighread
Ni Dhomhnaill

Joe Gormley
Tom & Eilis Joyce
Nora Murphy
Debra & Alan Rosenberg
Helen Ryan
Denise & Bill Whelan

Golden Ticket Friends

Mary Apied
Rebecca & Tom Bartlett
Michael J Burke
William Cabin
Mary Finan
Garry Hynes & Martha O'Neill
Hannah Kiely
Laura Laub
Séamus Mac Mathúna
Darren Manelski
John & Anne Marshall

Lorna Martyn
Marvoy Ltd.
Elizabeth McConnell
Mary Raftery Mitchell RIP
Donncha O'Connell
Michael O'Siadhill & Christina Weltz
Catherine Santoro
Guillermo Suescum & Melanie Hughes
Jack & Linda Viertel
Lawrence Walsh

Silver Spoon Friends

H Gerald Caldwell
Paula Carroll
Valerie Cole
Liam Cronin
Laura Crowley
Brendan Daly
Anneliese & Matt
Muredach Fergus & Irene O'Dea
Dorothea Finan
Maurice Foley
Mary Hawkes-Greene
Brega Howley
Sean & Ailbhe Hughes
Alma Hynes
Feargal Hynes
Ronan Kavanagh

Joan King
Patrick Lonergan
Niamh Lynagh
Sandra Mathews
Úna McKeever
Michael McMullin & Lys Browne
Sighle Meehan
Joe Murphy & Nicola O'Brien
Murtagh and Co. Accountants
Robert Neill
Niamh Nestor
Sinéad Ní Ghuidhir
David Niland
Micheál O'Cinneide
Brigid O'Connell
John & Mary O'Conor

Silver Spoon Friends continued

Riana O'Dwyer
Cliona O'Farrelly
Roisin O'Loughlin
David & Gobnait O'Shaughnessy
Jay Perry
Dorothy & Seamus Robinson

Maeve Robinson & Gary Mathews
Margaret Ruttledge & Seán Doyle
Sinéad Ryan
Mary & John Scanlan
Karl & Mary Verbruggen
Wildfire Films

Garry Hynes would especially like to thank Martha O'Neill RIP and all her colleagues at Wildfire Films for their extraordinary work in creating a series of documentary films about Druid productions in recent years, from *DruidSynge* to *DruidShakespeare* and beyond.

We extend heartfelt thanks to all our friends, supporters, and partners – past and present, named and unnamed – whose generosity has sustained Druid for 50 years and continues to inspire our vision of Irish performance for the world.

Picture Credits

Most of the images published in the book are taken from the Druid archive at the University of Galway or from Druid's own files and archives, and remain copyright of Druid Theatre unless otherwise specified. Where relevant, archival catalogue details are given using the acronym UGDA (University of Galway Druid Archive), as well as photographers' details where these are available. The information below also includes additional details about the content of some of the photographs or images, where appropriate.

INTRODUCTION. p. ix: Photo by Colm Hogan.

CHAPTER 1. p. 2 – UGDA T2/9/1/692; p. 3 – UGDA T2/9/1/692; p. 5 – UGDA T2/5/672; p. 9 – UGDA T2/9/1/692; p. 10 – T2/3/653. Cover drawing by Mairead Noone; p. 13 – T2/9/1/693; p. 17 – UGDA T2/9/1/69; p. 19 – T2/9/1/695.

CHAPTER 2. p. 20 – UGDA T2/1/2; p. 23 – UGDA T2/3/655; p. 25 – UGDA T2/1/2/9; p. 27 – UGDA T2/9/2/698; p. 28 – UGDA T2/9/1; p. 29 – UGDA T2/9/1/694; p. 31 – UGDA T2/12/923; p. 32 – UGDA T2/1/3/17; p. 33 – UGDA T2/1/2/13; p. 35 – UGDA T2/9/1/692; p. 39 – UGDA T2/3/654; p. 41 – UGDA T2/9/3/704; p. 43 – UGDA T2/3/654; p. 45 – UGDA T2/3/654; p. 46 – UGDA T2/12/923; p. 47 – UGDA T2/9/4/709; p. 48 – T2/9/3/702, photo by Joe O'Shaughnessy; p. 49 – UGDA T2/3/657.

CHAPTER 3. p. 53 – UGDA T2/3/656; p. 55, photo by Joe O'Shaughnessy; p. 58 – UGDA T2/9/4/707; p. 59 – UGDA T2/1/4/38–39; p. 61 – Published on https://www.druid.ie/about/the-mick-lally-theatre/about-the-theatre; p. 63 – UGDA T2/1/5/40-41, photo by Joe O'Shaughnessy; p. 65 – UGDA T2/1/5/40-41, photo by Joe O'Shaughnessy; p. 66 – UGDA T2/1/5/40-41; p. 68 – UGDA T2/1/5/40-41, photo by Joe O'Shaughnessy. Includes Paul O'Neill, Máire Stafford, Maelíosa Stafford, Seán Stafford, Ray McBride, Adrian Taheny, Joyce McGreevy, Marie Mullen and Seán McGinley; p. 69 – UGDA T2/1/6/53-54; p. 70 – UGDA T2/1/6/53-54; p. 71 – UGDA T2/1/6/53-54; p. 73 – UGDA T2/3/659; p. 76 – UGDA T2/9/7/722; p. 79 – UGDA T2/3/659.

CHAPTER 4. p. 80 – UGDA T2/9/8/729; p. 83 – Photo by Joe O'Shaughnessy; p. 87 – UGDA T2/9/8/729; p. 88 – UGDA T2/9/8/729; p. 89 – UGDA T2/84 (1-2); p. 91 – UGDA T2/9/8/728; p. 93 – UGDA T2/9/8/728; p. 97 – UGDA T2/1/7/75-78; p. 101 – T2/9/9/733, features Maelíosa Stafford and Máirtín Jaimsie; p. 103 – T2/9/9/733; p. 104 – T2/9/9/733, p. 105 T2/1/9/93-94; p. 108 – UGDA T2/1/10/99-101.

CHAPTER 5. p. 111 – published on http://archive.druid.ie/websites/20092017/productions/conversations-on-a-homecoming-1985#photos; p. 114 – UGDA T2/9/9/732. Features Maelíosa Stafford and David Calvert; p. 115 – UGDA T2/1/10/102-103; p. 116 – UGDA, T2/9/10/736; p. 117, photo by Joe O'Shaughnessy. Garry Hynes stands in the centre of the photo beside the cake, and is joined by the cast of *'Tis Pity She's a Whore,* including Ciarán Hinds, top right. Also seated around the cake are Maelíosa Stafford (left). Ray McBride (top right), and Jerome Hynes (bottom right); p. 118 – T2/1/11/121-125;

p. 119 – UGDA, T2/1/10/111-113; p. 122 – UGDA T2/1/10/99-101; p. 125 – UGDA T2/9/10/735; p. 127 – UGDA T2/1/11/116; p. 129 – UGDA T2/9/11/742; p. 131 – UGDA T2/9/11/742; p. 132 – UGDA T2/9/11/742; p. 134 – UGDA T2/9/12/748, photo by Amelia Stein; p. 135 – UGDA T2/9/12/748, photo by Amelia Stein; p. 138 – UGDA T2/1/12/130; p. 140 – UGDA T2/1/11/116; p. 141 – UGDA T2/9/13/755A. Image includes Seán McGinley, Peter Gowen, Maelíosa Stafford, Godfrey Quigley, Johnny Murphy, Mick Lally and David Herlihy

CHAPTER 6. p. 147 – UGDA T2/9/9/734; p. 151 – Show programme, *A Crucial Week in the life of a Grocer's Assistant*. Courtesy of the Abbey Theatre. Abbey Theatre Digital Archive at the University of Galway. 0701_MPG_01, p.3; p. 154 – UGDA T2/9/13/755; p. 156 – UGDA T2/170-172. Image includes Jane Brennan, Vincenzo Nicoli and Kate O'Toole; p. 157 – T2/9/16/764, photo by Brenda Fitzsimons; p. 159 – image provided courtesy of Galway International Arts Festival; p. 161 – image provided courtesy of Galway International Arts Festival; p. 166 – UGDA T2/9/16/767, photo by Amelia Stein.

CHAPTER 7. p. 168 – UGDA T2/9/17/768, photo by Mark Kilroy; p. 180 – UGDA T2/9/20/783, photo by Amelia Stein; p. 181 – T2/9/17/772, photo by Ian Maginess; p. 183 – UGDA T2/9/18/773; p. 186 – UGDA T2/9/18/778, photo by Brenda Fitzsimons; p. 189 – UGDA T2/1/19/209; p. 192 – UGDA T2/1/19/209; p. 194 – UGDA T2/1/20/217

CHAPTER 8. p. 196 – UGDA T2/1/24/249; p. 205 – UGDA T2/9/23/796, photo by Ivan Kincyl; p. 206 – UGDA, T2/1/22/229; p. 210 – UGDA T2/9/23/796, photo by Ivan Kincyl; p. 212 – UGDA T2/1/23/241-243; p. 213 – UGDA T2/9/23/796, photo by Ivan Kincyl; p. 214 – UGDA T2/9/23/796/E; p. 216 – UGDA T2/1/23/241-243; p. 220 – UGDA T2/1/24/249; p. 224 – UGDA T2/9/24/801; p. 226 – UGDA T2/9/25/803

CHAPTER 9. p. 233 – UGDA T2/9/26/807 photo by Derek Spiers; p. 234 – UGDA T2/9/26/807 photo by Derek Spiers; p. 236 – UGDA T2/1/26-27/273; p. 240 – UGDA T2/9/27/813; p. 241 – UGDA T2/9/16/766 (1-2), photo by Amelia Stein; p. 243 – published on https://www.druid.ie/productions/my-brilliant-divorce-2007/; p. 245 – UGDA T2/9/28/815; p. 253 – UGDA T2/9/32/823A, photo by Keith Pattison; p. 254 – Photo by Robert Day. Features Niall Buggy, Tadhg Murphy, Denis Conway, and Karl Shiels; p. 257 – Photo by Keith Pattison; p. 259 – UGDA T2/9/33/824.

CHAPTER 10. p. 262 – UGDA T2/9/31/819, photo by Keith Pattison; p. 267 – UGDA T2/9/31/822, photo by Keith Pattison; p. 268 – T2/9/30/818 Photo by Keith Pattison; p. 271 – photo by Keith Pattison. Also included are Gary Lydon and Simone Kirby (centre) and Mick Lally and Marie Mullen (far right); p. 275 – UGDA T2/9/31/819; p. 278 – UGDA T2/9/31/822, photo by Keith Pattison. Includes Eamon Morrissey and Marie Mullen on the right; p. 279 – UGDA T2/9/31/822, photo by Keith Pattison; p. 281 – UGDA T2/9/31/822, photo by Keith Pattison, features Marie Mullen, Eamon Morrissey and Aaron Monaghan L to R; p. 282 – UGDA T2/9/31/822, photo by Keith Pattison; p. 283 – UGDA T2/9/31/822, photo by Keith Pattison; p. 284 – UGDA T2/9/31/822, photo by Keith Pattison; p. 286 – UGDA T2/9/31/822, photo by Keith Pattison; p. 287 – UGDA T2/9/31/822, photo by Keith Pattison; p. 289 – UGDA T2/9/31/822, photo by Keith Pattison; p. 291 – Published on http://archive.druid.ie/websites/2009-2017/news/druid-unveils-memorial-to-mick-lally-on-the-first-anniversary-of-his-death

CHAPTER 11. p. 297 – photo by Colm Hogan; p. 298 – photo by Colm Hogan; p. 299 – photo by Colm Hogan; p. 301 – the artist is David Rooney; p. 304 – photo by Catherine Ashmore. It features L to R Garret Lombard, Marty Rea, Rory Nolan, Marie Mullen and Aaron Monaghan; p. 305 both photos are by Catherine Ashmore; p. 307 – Photo by Joanne O'Brien; p. 308 – photo by Druid Theatre; p. 309 – photo by Manuel Harlan; p. 312 – photo by Robert Day; p. 315 – photo by Keith Pattison; p. 316 – photo by Keith Pattison; p. 317 – photo by Matthew Thompson; p. 322 – photo by Matthew Thompson; p. 324 – photo by Richie O'Sullivan; p. 325 – photo by Matthew Thompson; p. 327 – both photos are by Matthew Thompson; the bottom photo features L to R Charlotte McCurry, Clare Barrett, Rory Nolan, and Aisling O'Sullivan; p. 328 – photo by Richie O'Sullivan

CHAPTER 12. p. 335 – photo by Emilija Jefremova; p. 339 – photo by Shannon Light; p. 341 – photo by Matthew Thompson; p. 349 – photo by Simon Lazewski; p. 351 – photo by Emilija Jefremova; p. 352 published on https://x.com/DruidTheatre/status/1360683901493075973; p. 354 – photo by Emilija Jefremova; p. 355 – photo by Francis O'Connor; p. 356 – photo by Colm Hogan; p. 359 – photo by Ste Murray; p. 361 – photo by Ros Kavanagh

POST-SCRIPT: p. 364 – photo by Ros Kavanagh; p. 367 photo by Ros Kavanagh

Index

#WakingtheFeminists (#WTF) 343–4

Abbey Theatre 15, 21, 101–2, 139–41, 146, 332, 338–9, 343, 358, 360 *see also* Hynes, Garry
   co-productions with Druid 140–3
   Peacock stage 74, 113
   Waking the Nation 343
Aladineen O'Druideen 40–1
Albee, Edward
   Who's Afraid of Virginia Woolf? 30
   Tiny Alice 5
Allen, David
   Cheapside 177
Allgood, Molly 15, 285
amateur drama 111–12
Andrews, Kernan 308
Aniston, Jennifer 219
Aran Islands 83, 306 *see also* Inis Meáin; Inis Oirr
Arden, John 161–2
Aron, Geraldine 240
   Bar and Ger 45–6, 69
   Donohue Sisters 240–2, 258
   Galway Girl 69

My Brilliant Divorce 239–40, 242–4, 259, 298, 366
   Same Old Moon 114–16, 119, 240, 297–8, 366
   Stanley Parkers 240–1
Arrabal, Fernando
   Orison 17
Arrigan, Mike 33
Arts Council 24, 65–6, 68
Asterix 8
Athenry 96
Athlone All-Ireland festival 5, 23, 112
Atlantic Theater, New York 219
awards
   Athlone 5, 23
   Fringe First 73, 347
   George Devine 259
   Susan Smith Blackburn 259
   Tony xiv, 221 (nominations 220–1, 224)

Bailey, Frank 11, 14–15, 53
Barry, Sebastian 229
   Steward of Christendom 230
Bartlett, Rebecca 71–2, 99, 115, 175, 298

Baxter, Sarah 336
Beale, Simon Russell 152
Beckett, Samuel 316
    Act Without Words II 17
    Catastrophe 170
    Endgame 126, 255
    Happy Days 26–7
    Waiting for Godot 340–3, 353
Behan, Brendan 242
    The Hostage (An Giall) 153–4
Bell, Lian 343, 344
Belton, Cathy 288
Belvoir Street theatre, Sydney 146
Berlin Wall, fall of 170, 180
Berry, Cicely 152
Bird, Charlie 338
Blake, Syan 251
Bloody Sunday (1972) 182
Boal, Augusto 191
Boland, Eavan 346
Bolger, David 271, 280, 284, 303, 307, 315
Boucicault, Dion
    Colleen Bawn 316–17
    The Shaughraun 113, 151
Bourke, Brian 184–5
Bracken 34
Bradfield, Dawn 223–4
Brantley, Ben 219
Breathnach, Páraic 61, 126, 160
Brecht, Bertolt 124
    Mother Courage 116
    Threepenny Opera 62–8, 369
Brennan, Bríd 93
Brennan, Jane 115–17, 126, 139, 155, 210–11, 297–8
Brennan, Paul 126, 128, 131
Broadway xiv, 219, 223, 226–7, 298, 332
    Off-Off-Broadway 4
Büchner, Georg
    Woyczek 59
Buggy, Niall 305, 349

Burke, David xvi
Burke Brogan, Patricia
    Eclipsed 162
Butler, Anne 173–6, 207
Byrne, Catherine 151

Caldwell, Lucy
    Leaves 258–60, 366
Campion, David, and James Saunders
    Entertainment on a Marriage 96
Carolan, Stuart
    Empress of India 255–7, 259
Carr, Marina 229, 240, 255
    By the Bog of Cats 232
    The Mai 232
    On Raftery's Hill 232–9, 259–60, 366
    Portia Coughlan 232
    Ullaloo 232
Carroll, Paul Vincent
    Shadow and Substance 180–1
Casey, Bishop Eamonn 218
Céide Fields, Co. Mayo 353
Celtic Arts Centre (Galway) 11, 15
Celtic Tiger 245, 296
Chapel Lane, Galway 51–2, 172, 174, 260
Chekhov, Anton
    The Cherry Orchard 351, 353
    The Proposal 58, 158
    The Seagull 353–5
child abuse, institutional 235–7
choreography 65, 72
Christie, Gillian 341–2
Cleary, Cathal 348
Clinton, Bill and Hillary 219
Coll, John 334
Collins, David 24, 65–6
Condon, Kerry 316
Connaughton, Pat 16, 28
Conroy, Tom 160
contraception ban 14
Conway, Denis 251–3, 255

Conway, Frank 119, 166
Conway, Thomas xv, 319, 334–5
Cooke, Lily 33
Coole Park, Co. Galway 353–4, 368
Corcadora 249
Cosgrave, Liam 14
COVID-19 335, 346, 350, 359–60
Cowen, Brian 290
Coyne, Sabina *see* Higgins, Sabina
Cragie, Ingrid 166, 241
Crotty, Derbhle 244–8, 288, 310, 314, 320–3, 326–8
Crowley, John 177–8
Cúirt Festival 160
Cullen, Siobhán 346, 350
Cunneen, Paddy 225

Daldry, Stephen 207
D'Alton, Louis
  Lovers' Meeting 165–6, 299
Daly, Jane 156, 162, 170, 173–5, 181, 186–7, 209, 355
D'Arcy, Margaretta 161–2
de Burgo, Richard xiii
Dé Dannan 72
Decade of Centenaries 358
Deegan, Loughlin 194
DePaor architects 291
Department of Foreign Affairs 74
Dewar, Gus 340
divorce 239–40
Doherty, Mark
  Trad 251
Donaghue, Dick 160
Donlon, Louise 216–17, 223, 355
Donmar Warehouse, London 108, 139–40
Doolin, Lelia 256
Douglas, Kirk 314–15
Dowling, Joe 96, 145, 164, 311
Dowling, Vincent 164

Doyle, Roddy 158
  Family 41
Druid archive 296
Druid Debuts 231, 348
Druid ensemble 314–18, 338
Druid Lane Theatre 61–2, 163–4, 258–60, 291 *see also* Mick Lally Theatre
DruidGregory 335, 368
DruidMurphy 300–7, 323, 366
DruidO'Casey 359–62, 367
DruidShakespeare 318–29, 345, 370
DruidSynge 264–6, 272, 274, 276, 280–9, 319, 323, 358, 368
Dublin Theatre Festival 84, 142, 215, 255, 272
Duff, Anne-Marie 268
Duffy, Keith 311–12
Dunne, Clare 288, 298–9
Durcan, Sarah 343
Dyer, Charles
  Mother Adam 21–3

Easter Rising 202
Edinburgh Fringe Festival 68–74, 84
Educational Outreach 176, 297
Edun, Adetomiwa 350–1
Edwards, Hilton 64, 295
Els Comediants 159–60
emigration 18, 36, 100, 123, 302
Etherege, George
  Man of Mode 152
Evers, Sean 162

Farrell, Bernard
  I Do Not Like Thee Doctor Fell 113, 119
Fay, Jimmy 319
Fay, Willie 15–16
feminism 70, 78, 312–13, 343
Ferris, Kate 347

Festival of Anglo-Irish Theatre 44–5
Field Day 78, 95, 295
financial crash (2008) 296, 313, 338
Fitzmaurice, George
    There are Tragedies and Tragedies 44–5
Fitz-Simon, Christopher 164
Flaherty, Craig 335
Flying Pig theatre company 162
Fo'castle room, Coachman Hotel, Galway 30–1, 43–4, 50
Footsbarn 159
Ford, John
    'Tis Pity She's a Whore 116–18, 370
Forde (Stafford), Carolyn 146–8
Foster, Paul 32, 70
    Elizabeth I 4–6, 23, 345
    Tom Paine 23–4, 31–3
Frawley, Monica 105, 119, 150–1, 188, 192
Frazier, Adrian 295
French, Dawn 243
Friel, Brian
    The Loves of Cass McGuire 6, 8, 12–14, 209, 366
    Philadelphia, Here I Come! 225
    Translations 74–8
Friends of Druid 24–5
'From Galway to Broadway and Back Again' (2011) 297–300
FUEL 335
funding 24–6, 61–2, 66, 74, 296

Gaiety Theatre, Dublin 138, 225
Galway Arts Festival 158–61, 246, 251, 306, 348, 360
Galway Film Fleadh 160
Galway Repertory Company 11
Galway Theatre Workshop 161–2
Galway Youth Theatre 175
Gambon, Michael 357
Garvey, Ailbhe 69
gender balance 343–6
Gerald W. Lynch Theater, New York 328
Gillen, Aiden 165
Glassie, Henry 179
Gleeson, Brendan 150
Gleeson, Domhnall 271–2
Glencar, Co. Wicklow 353
Glenroe 34, 105
Gogarty, Oliver St John
    Enchanted Trousers 58
Good Friday Agreement 238
Gough, Julian
    Peig – The Musical 162
Gowen, Peter 189
Gray, Eileen 346
Great Famine 121–3, 301
Gregory, Lady Augusta 37, 285, 295, 353–4, 368
    Kathleen Ni Houlihan 323
Guildhall, Derry 78, 84
Guinness 74
Guthrie, Tyrone 315

Hallissey, Clíodhna 336, 350
Hampstead Theatre, London 306
Hampton, Christopher
    Treats 24–5
Hanafin, Mary 290
Hanley, David 223
Harris, Nancy
    The Beacon 346, 366
Harrold, James C. 172
Havel, Vaclav 170–1
    Increased Difficulty of Concentration 168, 171–2
Hawk's Well Theatre, Sligo 96, 106–7, 369
Headly, Glenne 242
Heaney, Seamus 238
Henry, Moya 31
Hickey, Tom 233–4

Higgins, Michael D. 28, 53, 158, 289, 306–7, 356
Higgins (née Coyne), Sabina 28, 157–8, 307
Hinds, Andy 116
Hinds, Ciarán 113, 117
homosexuality 240–1
Hughes, Maureen 162, 173, 207, 268, 272
hunger strikes 123
Hynes, Carmel 59–60
Hynes, Donal 61
Hynes, Feargal 355–6
Hynes, Garry xiv–xv, 3, 8, 14–19, 22–7, 31–4, 38–9, 43, 50–1, 53–4, 70, 74–5, 106–7, 140–3, 147, 210, 213–14, 277, 291, 307, 370
    and the Abbey: 149–53, 358; Artistic Director 164–5, 201–3
    choreography 72
    collaborations: Tom Murphy 120–1; Francis O'Connor 197–200
    cross-gender casting 99, 116–17, 321–3
    Druid Artistic Director 227
    Druid Consultant Artistic Director 200–1
    establishes ensemble 313–17
    honorary doctorate 333
    New York connection 4, 23, 40, 220–1
    programme notes 11–12, 368
    and the RSC 152
    teaching 334
    views: *Bailegangaire* 135–8; *Beauty Queen* 207–8; Druid 18, 331–3; Druid Lane Theatre 164; *Elizabeth I* 4; Fo'castle 30–1; Galway 163; gender balance 343–5; *Good Father* 245–8; Jerome Hynes 294–5; Keane 310; Kelly 353; Lally 34–6, 290; *Lonesome West* 224; McDonagh 205–6, 208, 215, 217–18, 310; McKenna 135, 137; marriage equality 337–8; Mullen 5–6; Murphy 129–35; O'Casey 359–61; *On Raftery's Hill* 237; *Playboy* 90, 270–1; Shakespeare 98, 317–20, 324–5; Stafford 357; Synge 263–5, 270–1, 287; Tony nominations/award 220–2, 224; Bernie Walsh 223
    writing 69–70, 99
Hynes, Jerome 59–60, 68, 74, 106–7, 125, 148–9, 197, 293–4, 334
Hynes, Oliver 18, 121

Inis Meáin 84–90, 94–5, 153, 167, 264, 353, 368
Inis Oirr 100
Irish language 38–9
Irish Times 67
Irish Women's Liberation Movement 312–13
Island Protected by a Bridge of Glass 69–72, 95, 121
Ivak, Katerina 171

Jaquarello, Roland 177
Jennings, Ollie 159–60, 162
Jesuit Hall, Galway 8, 24, 142
Johnston, Fred 160
Jones, Marie 229
    Stones in His Pockets 229
Joyce, Sara 350, 369

Kavanagh, Noeline 159–60
Keane, John B. 309
    Big Maggie 310–13, 316, 323, 345, 367
    The Field 311
    Sharon's Grave 311

Sive 310–11, 367
   Year of the Hiker 298, 311
Kehoe, Cristín 231
   Shelter 346
Kelly, Aidan 245–8
Kelly, Loretta 75
Kelly, Sonya 225–6, 231, 267–9, 346–53
   Furniture 346–50, 368, 369
   How to Keep an Alien 347
   Last Return 353, 369
   Once Upon a Bridge 350–1
   Wheelchair on My Face 347
Kennedy Center, Washington 238, 306
Kennedy Smith, Jean 238
Kennelly, Maureen 194
Kenny, Jon 224
Kenny, Tom 209
Kiernan, Pat 249
Killasser, Co. Mayo 107–8
Kilroy, Thomas 120
   The Seagull (adaptation) 353–5
Kirby, Simone 281
Kirk Douglas Theater, Los Angeles 314
Knott, Frederick
   Dial M for Murder 75–6
Kylemore Abbey, Co. Galway 354

Laffan, Kevin
   It's a Two Foot Six Inches Above the Ground World 8, 14, 22, 366
Lally, Mick xiv, 6–9, 16–18, 22, 38–9, 55, 289–90, 294
   moves to Dublin 34–6
   roles: *Beauty Queen* 219; *Cass Maguire* 209; *Deirdre* 285; *DruidSynge* 277, 282, 289; *Famine* 124; *Glass Menagerie* 29; *Happy Days* 27; *Playboy* 16–17, 43, 85, 92–3; *Skull* 213–14; *Tom Paine* 31; *Translations* 75–6; *Well of the Saints* 272; *Wood of the Whispering* 103

Lally, Peige (née Ní Chonghaile) 34, 86, 291
Lappin, Arthur 66, 96
Lardner, Collette 65
Lawson, Peter 71
Lee, Nick 275
Leenane, Co. Galway 210, 368
Leitrim 178–9
Leonard, Hugh 202
Lepage, Robert
   Dragon's Trilogy 159
Lewis, Louise 275
Lincoln Center, New York 306
Littlewood, Joan 154
Liveline 256
livestreaming 351–3
Lombard, Garrett 251, 306, 314, 349, 360
Love/Hate 255, 257
lunchtime theatre 17, 26, 178
Lynch, Sarah 255, 355
Lyric Theatre, Belfast 360

McAleese, Mary 219
McAliskey, Bernadette 185
McAnally, Ray 76
Mac an Bhaird, Shane 231
Mac Anna, Tomás 21, 63
McBride, Charlie 194
McBride, Kathleen 56, 60
McBride, Ray 56, 60, 65, 71–2, 105, 115, 126, 142, 151, 166, 189, 213, 294, 356
McCabe, Eugene
   King of the Castle 150–1
McCafferty, Frankie 189
McCafferty, Owen
   Shoot the Crow 225
Mac Conghail, Fiach 358
McCusker, Stella 189
McDonagh, Bobby 307

McDonagh, Martin 176, 204–5, 207–8, 217–19, 224, 229, 231, 265, 310, 316
   Beauty Queen of Leenane 21, 197–8, 206, 208–11, 218–22, 263, 316, 345, 366, 368
   Cripple of Inishmaan 213, 215, 298, 313–14, 316
   Leenane Trilogy 205, 211–12, 215–16, 218, 225, 227, 230, 233, 263–4
   Lonesome West 211–14, 218, 223–4, 263
   The Pillowman 213
   Skull in Connemara 205, 211, 213–14, 323
McDonogh, Thomas, and Sons 53–5, 260
McEvoy, Mary 104–5
McGahern, John
   Power of Darkness 197, 202
McGarry, Patsy 203
McGee, Noel 31
McGinley, Seán 41, 106–7, 142, 158, 166, 273
   roles: *Aladineen* 41; *Conversations* 128–9; *Empress of India* 255, 257; *Island* 71; *Much Ado* 99; *On the Outside* 126; *Playboy* 299; *Threepenny Opera* 65; *Wilde* 48–9; *Same Old Moon* 115; *Shaughraun* 151; *Wood of the Whispering* 105
McGrath, Fergal 256, 294, 355
McGreevy, Joyce 55
McGuinness, Frank 229
   Carthaginians 182–5
   Factory Girls 113–14
   Observe the Sons of Ulster 167, 230
McHugh, Meadhbh 231
   Helen and I 346
McHugh, Moya 177
McKenna, Síobhan 6–7, 12, 134–9, 307
MacLaren, Graham 358
McLaughlin, Caitríona 360

MacLiammóir, Micheál 295
McLynn, Pauline 115, 126, 184
McMaster, Anew 98
McMullin, Michael 31
McPherson, Conor 229
Macnas 160, 175
Maguire, Daisy 258
Maguire, Penelope 258
Manahan, Anna 151, 209, 221
Marie Mullen Bursary 336
Marcus, David 186
marriage equality 337–8, 347
masterclasses 334–5
Matthews, Gai 29
Matura, Mustapha
   The Playboy of the West Indies 193
Mayer, Paul Avila
   Eternal Triangle 75
Melfi, Leonard
   Birdbath 33
Mercier, Paul 158
Merriman, Brian
   Cúirt An Mheán Oíche (The Midnight Court) 185–7
Mick Lally Theatre (MLT) xiv, 291, 323–4
Minghella, Anthony
   A Little Like Drowning 155–7
Molloy, Bobby 61–2
Molloy, M.J. 100–1, 103–4, 106
   King of Friday's Men 101
   Wood of the Whispering 99–106, 119, 366
Monaghan, Aaron 251–4, 272–6, 283–4, 288, 314, 316, 323, 350, 361
Moran, Leo 162
Morrissey, Eamon 268, 276, 281–2, 288
Mullen, Marie xiv, 15–16, 18, 22–4, 28–9, 31, 38–9, 41, 47, 52–4, 147, 209–10, 249, 276–7, 288, 291, 294, 299, 314, 370
   bursary 336
   roles: *Bailegangaire* 135, 299,

306–9; Beatrice 99; *Beauty Queen* 317; *Big Maggie* 310; *Birdbath* 34; *Brigit* 308; *Cass Maguire* 369; *DruidGregory* 335; *DruidShakespeare* 325; Elizabeth I 5–6; *Famine* 125, 305; Goneril 152–3; Gráinne 70–1; Lady Macbeth 367, 369; *Lovers' Meeting* 166; Maureen (*Beauty Queen*) 153, 206, 213; Maurya (*Riders to the Sea*) 280, 367; Pegeen Mike (*Playboy*) 1–3, 91; Peggy (*Homecoming*) 131; *Riders* 370; *Same Old Moon* 115; *The Shaughraun* 151; *Threepenny Opera* 65; *Tinker's Wedding* 281; *Well of the Saints* 272, 281; Widow Quin (*Playboy*) 43, 90–2, 275–6, 283–4; Winnie 27; *Wood of the Whispering* 105
  Tony award 221
  views: *Conversations* 133; Druid 331–2; Jerome Hynes 294; McKenna 308; Murphy 308–9; *Playboy* 87–8; Stafford 357; *Tom Paine* 32–3
mumming 179, 188
Murfi, Mikel 171, 251–2, 273, 298, 369
Murphy, Cillian 226, 249, 267–8, 298, 357
Murphy, Johnny
  The Country Boy 226
Murphy, Tadhg 254
Murphy, Tom (actor) 221
Murphy, Tom (writer) 55, 110–13, 117, 120–43, 150, 203, 293, 300, 307, 316
  Bailegangaire 121, 133–9, 306–9, 317, 345, 366, 368
  Brigit 307–9
  Cherry Orchard (adaptation) 351, 353
  Conversations on a Homecoming (*The White House*) 121, 127–33, 139–40, 300, 303–4, 366
  Crucial Week in the Life of a Grocer's Assistant (*The Fooleen*) 149–51
  Famine 108, 121–6, 300, 303
  Gigli Concert 140
  The House 368
  On the Outside (with Noel O'Donoghue) 112, 121, 126
  Thief of a Christmas 140
  Whistle in the Dark 112, 140–2, 300, 303
Murray, Erica 231
Murray, Neil 358
music 64–5
My Left Foot 155

Nee, Síomha 352
Neeson, Liam 76, 221
Negga, Ruth 275
New Writing programme 297
Ní Chaoimh, Bairbre 85
Ní Chonghaile, Peige *see* Lally, Peige
Ní Neachtain, Bríd 151
Ní Nuadháin, Mairead *see* Noone, Mairead
Nolan, Rory 306, 314, 326–7, 341, 370
Noone (Ní Nuadháin), Mairead 10–11, 92, 115–17
Nowra, Louis
  Golden Age 172–3

O'Brien, Mark 360
O'Byrne, Brian F. 208, 214–15, 221, 223–4
Ó Carra, Seán 83
O'Casey, Seán
  Bedtime Story 126
  Dublin Trilogy 357, 359
  Juno and the Paycock 357, 361–2
  Plough and the Stars 202–3, 357–8, 360

Shadow of a Gunman 357
Silver Tassie 357–8
O'Connell, Jeff 162
O'Connor, Francis 315, 336
   set designs: *Beauty Queen* 197–200; *Country Boy* 226; *DruidMurphy* 303–7; *DruidO'Casey* 361; *DruidShakespeare* 322–4; *DruidSynge* 285; *Empress of India* 256–7; *Godot* 340–2; *Good Father* 247; *Leenane Trilogy* 211–12; *Playboy* 271; *Seagull* 354–5; *Shadow and Substance* 181–2
O'Donoghue, Donagh 53–5, 165, 167
O'Donoghue, Noel 111
   On the Outside (with Tom Murphy) 112, 121, 126
O'Dowd, Chris 268
O'Dowd, Ciara xv
O'Dwyer, Marion 241
Off Obie 33
O'Hara, Joan 151
Ó hEocha, Colm 333
O'Kane, Deirdre 189, 243–4
O'Kelly, Donal
   Catalpa 238
Olympia Theatre 84, 96
Ó Maicín, Caoimhín 61
O'Malley, Grace 70, 295
O'Neill, Martha 337
O'Neill, Paul 40–1, 47, 61, 71, 147
O'Punkskys, Sydney 147, 357
O'Regan, Brendan 188
O'Reilly, Christian 231, 246
   Good Father 244–9, 255, 259–60
   It Just Came Out 244
O'Rowe, Mark 229, 319
O'Sullivan, Aisling 269–70, 309, 311–12, 314, 316–17, 320, 322–3, 326–8
O'Sullivan, Eoin 236
O'Sullivan, Michael 31

O'Sullivan, Thaddeus 166
O'Toole, Kate 156, 171, 241

Paines Plough, London 249
Parker, Lynne 319
Parker, Stuart
   Pentecost 238
Parnell, David 225
Passion Machine 158
Peacock, John
   Children of the Wolf 28
Pearson, Noel 164
Pepsico Summerfare, New York 108
Perth Festival 274
Pike theatre 30
Playboy of the European Community 162
plays, submission of 176
Project Arts Centre, Dublin 33, 153
Prowse, Jane 155–6
Punchbag Theatre Company 162
Pursuit of Pleasure 47–50, 69

Quigley, Godfrey 142
Quinn, Bob
   Poitín 34, 158
Quinn, David 162

Raftery, Mary 235–6
Rea, Marty 302, 306, 314, 320, 326–7, 335, 340, 367–8, 370
recession 18, 313
Redden, Nigel 319, 328
Reeves, Gemma 275, 286
Ribalow, Meir
   Sundance 75
Richards, Lisa 177
Riordan, Arthur 157–8
Riverdance 238
Robinson, Mary 172

Roche, Billy 193
   Belfry 193
Rough Magic 158, 238, 347
Royal Court Theatre, London 142, 207, 258
Royal Shakespeare Company (RSC) 152
RTÉ 67
Ryan, Mary 115

St Nicholas Cathedral, Galway 288
Sammon, Pete 160
Sands, Bobby 123
Saunders, James, and David Campion
   Entertainment on a Marriage 96
Scannell, Ray 298–9
schools programme *see* Educational Outreach
Sealink 74
Seapoint Ballroom, Galway 123–4
set design 118–19
Shakespeare, William
   As You Like It 226
   Henry IV 319, 326
   Henry V 318–19, 325
   Macbeth 366, 367–9
   Much Ado about Nothing 97–9, 370
   Richard II 319–20
Shannon, Sharon 155
Shaw, George Bernard
   Saint Joan 6–7
Sheehy, Joan 184
Sheridan, Jim 153, 155
Sheridan, Richard Brinsley
   St Patrick's Day 157–8
Shortall, Eithne 311
Shortt, Pat 224
'Show in a Bag' scheme 347
Sihra, Melissa 237
Singleton, Brian 203
Smith, Tim 246, 355
Spallen, Abbie 231

Stafford (née Forde), Carolyn 146–8, 169
Stafford, Connall 56–7
Stafford, Maelíosa xv, 56–60, 75, 108, 142, 146–8, 166–7, 169–77, 194–5, 226, 314, 356–7, 369
   Druid Artistic Director 169
   roles: *Beauty Queen* 214–15, 223; *Bedtime Story* 126; Bergetto (*'Tis Pity*) 117; *Carthaginians* 184; *Cheapside* 177; Christy Mahon (*Playboy*) 85, 93; *Colleen Bawn* 356–7; *Island* 71; Junior (*Conversations*) 130, 132–3; Mack the Knife 65; *Whistle in the Dark* 356; *Wood of the Whispering* 105
   views: *Beauty Queen* 214–15; *Black Pig's Dyke* 188, 191; *Golden Age* 172–3; McGuinness 184; Murphy 130; New York audiences 223; Northern Ireland 185; *Shadow and Substance* 181; *Wood of the Whispering* 102–3; *Woods* 178
Stafford, Máire 56, 60, 64–5, 154–5
Stafford, Seán 56, 60, 64–5
Stembridge, Gerry 319
Strachan, Kathy 270
Sydney 108
Synge, J.M. xv, 15, 37, 81–2, 260, 263, 265, 286–7, 316
   Aran Islands 37
   Deirdre of the Sorrows 265, 284–6
   In the Glens of Rathvanna (compendium) 42
   Playboy of the Western World 1–3, 7–8, 14–17, 42–3, 82–95, 108–9, 193, 233, 264–5, 267–74, 278–9, 283–4, 286, 366, 369
   Riders to the Sea 15, 265, 280, 283, 286–7, 364, 365, 367, 369
   In the Shadow of the Glen 42, 279, 281–3, 285–7

Tinker's Wedding 42, 265, 272, 281, 283
Well of the Saints 262, 271–2, 281–3

Taibhdhearc, An 6–7, 11, 39, 57, 62, 83, 124, 154, 357
Theatre Ireland 331–2
tours 84, 96, 100, 108, 113, 190, 326–8, 350 *see also* Unusual Rural Tours
  Northern Ireland 181–5, 190, 210
Town Hall Theatre, Galway 206, 209, 249, 259–60, 309
Tricycle Theatre, London 190, 193
Troubles, the 77, 180, 188–9, 238
Tuam, Co. Galway 306
Tyrrell, Seán 185–6

University College Galway (UCG) (University of Galway) 333–5
  Drama Society (DramSoc) 1, 4, 53, 175–6, 334
Unusual Rural Tours (URTs) 96, 106–9, 125, 153, 165, 167, 180–1, 210, 224, 227

Wall, Joe 162
Walsh, Bernie 222–3
Walsh, Catherine 278–80, 282–5, 288, 309
Walsh, Ciarán 355
Walsh, Eileen 249, 288–9, 305
Walsh, Enda 171, 229, 255, 300, 369
  bedbound 249
  Disco Pigs 226, 249
  Gentrification 254–5
  Lynndie's Gotta Gun 255
  Misterman 249
  New Electric Ballroom 254–5
  Penelope 254–5, 299

Small Things 249
  Walworth Farce 249–54, 259–60, 273, 366
Walsh, Tom 148
Walter Kerr Theater, New York 220
Watkins, Brian
  Epiphany 346
Welles, Orson
  Chimes at Midnight 326
Wertenbaker, Timberlake
  Love of the Nightingale 152
West End 138, 209, 211, 215, 243, 346
west of Ireland xiii, 1, 3, 16, 26, 36–8, 81–2, 93, 98, 103, 113–14, 120, 297, 302, 368
Wexford Festival Opera 148–9
Wexford Theatre Royal 148
Wilde, Oscar 47–50
  Importance of Being Earnest 113
Williams, Mike 71, 99, 107
Williams, Niall
  The Way You Look Tonight 225
Williams, Tennessee 12, 29–30
  Glass Menagerie 18, 28, 119
  Rose Tattoo 30
Wilmot, David 189
Woods, Vincent 178–9, 192
  At the Black Pig's Dyke 179–80, 187–92, 205, 298, 367
  John Hughdy and Tom John 177
  Song of the Yellow Bittern 193–4
workshops, set and costume 339–40
Wright, Bill 342

Yeats, W. B. 37–8, 285, 295
  Kathleen Ni Houlihan 323
  Pot of Broth 39